REALITY CHECK

REALITY CHECK

WHAT YOUR MIND KNOWS, BUT ISN'T TELLING YOU

David L. Weiner

Preface by Robert D. Hare, PhD

 **Prometheus Books**

59 John Glenn Drive
Amherst, New York 14228-2197

Published 2005 by Prometheus Books

Inquiries should be addressed to
Prometheus Books
59 John Glenn Drive
Amherst, New York 14228–2197
VOICE: 716–691–0133, ext. 207
FAX: 716–564–2711
WWW.PROMETHEUSBOOKS.COM

09 08 07 06 05   5 4 3 2 1

Library of Congress Cataloging-in-Publication Data

Weiner, David L.
    Reality check : what your mind knows, but isn't telling you / by David L. Weiner ; preface by Robert D. Hare.
        p. cm.
    Includes bibliographical references and index.
    ISBN 1–59102–302–5 (pbk.: alk. paper)
    1. Thought and thinking. 2. Brain. 3. Human information processing. I. Title.

BF441.W447 2005
153—dc22

2005012201

Printed in the United States of America on acid-free paper

May we come to our senses

CONTENTS

ACKNOWLEDGMENTS

I am especially grateful to the University of Wisconsin De-partment of Psychology, in particular Charles T. Snowdon, professor and chair, for assisting me in fact checking and for finding two researchers to assist me: Melissa Rosenkranz and Matthew Majeske. Both graduate students at the university, they were invaluable in digging up facts and, probably more important, making them understandable to me. This out-standing department is consistently ranked in the top ten by *U.S. News & World Report* magazine. The department is number one in the nation in research funding received.

My thanks to Bob Hare for writing the preface to this book. Bob is an emeritus professor of psychology at the University of British Columbia and is today, among other distinctions, the world's leading authority on psychopaths. His insights into the pathology of mental disorders have been invaluable.

I am also grateful to the HealthEmotions Research Institute of the University of Wisconsin, which is led by Ned Kalin, chair of the university's department of psychiatry, and Richard Davidson, professor of psychology and psychiatry. This is prob-ably the world's leading research facility focusing on the biology of emotion and how emotions influence our health.

Attending the institute's symposiums and interfacing with some of the world's leading scientists have given me amazing insights into the biology of the mind.

My thanks to Linda Regan, my editor at Prometheus Books, who was relentless in pushing this book along. My thanks also to Chris Kramer, Mark Hall, Bruce Carle, Jacqueline Cooke, Richard Snyder, and Jill Maxick at Prometheus for their assistance, and to Jonathan Kurtz for his continuing encouragement.

My thanks also to Al Landa, who developed the illustrations for this book, and Ken Hollern, who assisted Al. And to Shirley Paolinelli, who also helped with this book's research; to Carla Salinas for her help with the bibliography; and to Suzy Chudznik for her help with the index. My thanks as well to my sons Barry and Andy, Ben Hubbard, Ann Snowdon, Ron Rattner, Frank Vallejo, Donna Czukla, Lois Martyn, Rick Asta, Elena Weckerle, Steve Herkes, Dave Olsson, Scott Caras, Heather Brown, Bonnie Borgstrom, Kristin Rivnyak, Jessica Rudis, Sarah Schutz, Tina Anatolitis, and Jim Levie for their assistance along the way.

PREFACE

Much of society's discourse is conducted at a relatively high level of abstraction. In many cases neither the speaker nor the listener has any idea about what is being said. One solution is that communication is to promote communication of difficult ideas through clear, down-to-earth prose. This is precisely what David Weiner has done in his remarkable book *Reality Check*. With uncommon common sense, he exposes the nuggets in a variety of scientific and quasi-scientific fields by cutting through the many obscurities, academic clichés, and intellectual pretensions that bedevil discourse in these fields.

I first met David Weiner at a conference on psychopathy he had cosponsored in Madison, Wisconsin, in 2003. The conference was largely responsible for the development of the new Society for the Scientific Study of Psychopathy (SSSP). It was clear from his interactions with the participants at the conference that he had an unusual grasp of the the most important topics under discussion, including etiology, genetics, developmental factors, assessment issues, and neurobiological applications and implications. His breadth of knowledge and understanding of the diverse disciplines that impinged on the study of psychopathy were impressive. Some of his questions about psychopathy set me back a bit, simply because my answers were far from satisfying (to him and to me) when couched in the jargon typical of the field. He made me think, and rethink.

David Weiner clearly is a widely read, thoughtful, and often bemused observer of human behavior. His response to much of what he sees around him is "What the hell is going on here?" He then uses keen insight, measured skepticism, and a delightful sense of humor to offer his perspective on the question, illustrating in the process that we in fact don't know nearly as much as we think we know.

His crisp, clear, down-to-earth writing style no doubt reflects the incisive and pragmatic ways in which his mind works. His analyses of some of the big issues of our time are fascinating and invariably illuminating. I am particularly impressed by his discussions of current debates in neuroscience and by his analysis of the psychology of evil. The latter topic is of particular interest to me, given my research on psychopathy. He argues that under the right circumstances even "normal" people can become "psychopathic/sadistic," the result of a battle in which the impassioned amygdala and its limbic allies win out over the more rational frontal cortex. The difference between this "situational evil" and psychopathy/sadism is that the latter reflects a systemic condition, pathology, or adaptive lifestyle that is not dependent on the right conditions. In my view, psychopaths "are what they are," and I don't know if the mechanisms that control their behavior are similar to those that prompt psychopathic and sadistic behavior in otherwise normal individuals. But the beauty of David Weiner's distillation of complex issues to understandable, basic ideas is that it generates meaningful discussion and debate, and increases the chances that eventually we will know almost as much as we think we know. However, I agree with him that we always will get a headache when contemplating the really big pictures: the size of the universe, the workings of the brain, time, the nature of mind and soul, and so forth.

This book is thought provoking and entertaining, and a terrific read. It is a worthy successor to his earlier books, *Power Freaks* and *Battling the Inner Dummy*. David Weiner's wit and clarity of thought and expression certainly will appeal to the general public. It may even have an impact on the communication styles of scientists, academics, and other deep thinkers, many of whom have difficulty in sending down piers to reality.

Robert D. Hare, PhD
Vancouver, BC
January 12, 2005

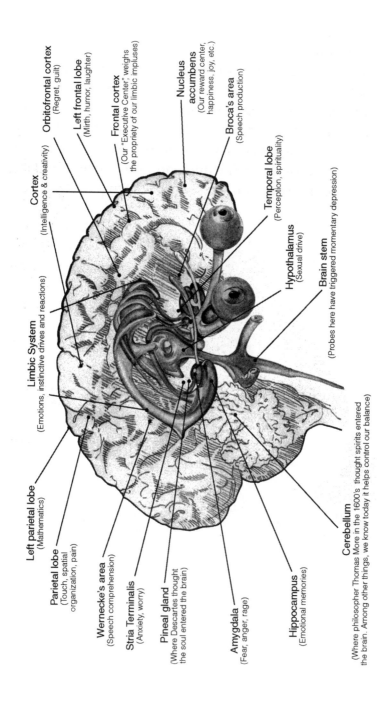

Figure 1: A cutaway of the brain showing the areas, components, and functions covered in this book. Most of the areas and components shown have other functions as well.

Left parietal lobe
(Mathematics)

Parietal lobe
(Touch, spatial organization, pain)

Wernecke's area
(Speech comprehension)

Stria Terminalis
(Anxiety, worry)

Pineal gland
(Where Descartes thought the soul entered the brain)

Amygdala
(Fear, anger, rage)

Hippocampus
(Emotional memories)

Cerebellum
(Where philosopher Thomas More in the 1600's thought spirits entered the brain. Among other things, we know today it helps control our balance)

Limbic System
(Emotions, instinctive drives and reactions)

Cortex
(Intelligence & creativity)

Orbitofrontal cortex
(Regret, guilt)

Left frontal lobe
(Mirth, humor, laughter)

Frontal cortex
(Our "Executive Center," weighs the propriety of our limbic impulses)

Nucleus accumbens
(Our reward center, happiness, joy, etc.)

Broca's area
(Speech production)

Temporal lobe
(Perception, spirituality)

Hypothalamus
(Sexual drive)

Brain stem
(Probes here have triggered momentary depression)

1.

THE MIND IS PHYSICAL AND SO ARE ITS EMOTIONS— SOULS, SPIRITS, AND ENERGY FORCES NOTWITHSTANDING

The human mind treats a new idea the same way the body treats a strange protein, it rejects it.
P. B. Medawar[1]

What is it about us?

Despite the dramatic leaps in neuroscience that prove that our mind is physical—that it is an integral part of our brain— the majority of us still believe that our ability to think and feel comes from some driving force or mysterious essence or almighty power.

At least we've moved a few steps ahead of Aristotle, who conjectured that the heart was the seat of intelligence and that the brain was basically a cooling system.

Other Greeks of his time thought that the functions we now attribute to the brain were located in the lungs. The brain's function, they believed, was to house the soul in some mystical way.[2]

If we fast-forward to the seventeenth century, almost two thousand years after Aristotle, we see that some paltry progress was made, at least by European philosophers who gave some thought to the subject of the mind.

The philosopher and poet Henry More, who lived in the 1600s, defended for most of his life the religious concept of the soul as an all-enveloping force. He called the brain "a bowl of curds incapable of carrying out the workings of the spirit."[3] He asserted that the soul comprised our intellect, but that there was also a spirit world, which molded our personalities.

Philosopher René Descartes in *Meditations*, published in 1641, was more precise. He described the rational soul as an entity that never stops thinking, either in sleep or after death. He also saw it as distinct from the body, making contact with it at the pineal gland—a small structure at the base of the brain (see fig. 1, page 14) that had long been thought of as our "third eye," or the "seat of the soul."[4] Like More, Descartes separated the spirits from the soul, which he believed resided in the ventricle chambers of the human heart. He further thought that the spirits were then pushed throughout the body and muscles by the beating heart.

The concept that the substance of the mind was different from the substance of the body was called "dualism,"[5] a term frequently dropped at sophisticated cocktail parties today.

Thomas Willis, a professor of natural philosophy at Oxford during the same period, disagreed with Descartes about the soul entering the body at the pineal gland. The reason? He couldn't find the gland in the brains of birds or fish, which he believed also had souls—an opinion that would have gotten him into trouble with today's religious fundamentalists.

He also disagreed with Descartes about where our spirit world resided, not in the heart, he contended, but in the cerebellum area of the brain. Willis believed our nerves picked up signals from the outside world and sent spirits flashing back into the brain. Interestingly, he also thought that if the brain became diseased enough, it might permanently affect the nature of the "rational soul," as he, too, called it, which would then present us "not with realistic perceptions, but with wild fantasies."[6]

This theory that the soul can literally change from damage to the brain contrasted with beliefs of some Eastern cultures in reincarnation, particularly that of Hinduism, which holds that the soul never really changes. Rather, Hindus believed, and continue to believe, under the concept of reincarnation, that the brain is merely the instrument of the soul. If the brain were damaged, it would simply no longer be capable of carrying out orders from the soul. In the next life down the line, however, the soul would presumably be ready to start all over, directing a healthy brain in a new body.

Philosopher Anne Conway, who also lived in the 1600s, assumed that humans had a choice of spirits. You could pick one or more good, bad, smart, and dumb spirits and they come into your heart and shape you.[7] In other words, she was telling us, in her way, we have choices.

We can continue with the varied beliefs about the mind and body concocted by other thinkers and philosophers since the seventeenth century, but what's the use?

As I was writing down these words, Carolyn Swanson, who cares for the plants in my home every Wednesday, came into the room. I stopped her for a moment and said, "You won't believe this." I then read out the words, tongue in cheek, about how Descartes thought that the spirits occupied the ventricle chambers of our hearts.

She chuckled as well, and said, "I don't agree with that at all, absolutely not. I believe the spirits reside in the upper part of the heart. That's where I feel them."

"In your heart? I can't believe that. You really feel them in your heart?"

"I do."

"Well, what do they feel like?"

"They feel like spirits, I believe they guide my feelings and the way I think. I believe in the spirit world."

Okay, so Descartes and the others still have a following.

Apparently even today, many of us believe the soul is our basic life force and that the spirits in their separate realm, particularly the bad ones—the demons—mold our traits. Positive spirits are either called simply "good spirits" or "eudemons," meaning good demons. In some religions, the spirits and the soul are mixed together.

A good definition of the soul, however, has eluded philosophers and others, probably because science has found no evidence of one, and no scholarly reports exist from which to refer. In his book, *Does the Soul Survive*, Rabbi Elie Kaplan Spitz says simply that the soul survives our physical plane and is an inner force that serves as a "font of who we are." He points out that the soul is hard to define because "it is not an object."[8]

That is definitely a major problem.

Clinical neuroscientist Daniel G. Amen, in *Healing the Hardware of the Soul*, declares: "The word 'soul,' as translated from Old Testament Hebrew means all of your thoughts, feelings, personality characteristics, self, desires and passions."[9] Some early Hebrews also believed that the soul was an integral part of the body that died with the body. However, most religions today, including Orthodox Judaism, and in particular its Kabbala sect, contend that the soul continues to exist after our earthly lives have ended.[10]

The point is that during all the centuries leading up to the advent of neuroscience and the study of genetics, we really had no scientific knowledge of what makes up the physical basis of who we are and how or why we thought and felt as we did. And so it was natural for teachers and philosophers—the wise men of the world, who were *expected* then and are *expected* today to have answers—to come up with amorphous concepts such as the soul and the spirit world to explain away everything. And many of us still doggedly cling to these ancient ideas, rejecting even the slightest seed of doubt.

Indeed the spirit world that many teachers, philosophers,

and religionists told us molded our characters and traits has at times extended into the realm of the occult. A vast number of people, even today, believe in divination or foretelling the future, astrology, and religious or ritual magic—and for some, even witchcraft. All this spiritual belief, whether religious or occult, has come to serve as fodder for the leading skeptics of our day, who have been unable to find any scientific basis for any of it.

I'm an agnostic, with no firm beliefs in any specific supernatural theory, but from time to time I feel a sensation that the spirit of my first ex-wife, Phyllis, a fine person, has returned from the hereafter to play some mischief. Never anything really serious, but a series of aggravating events over a day or two that harks back to some of the difficulties of our marriage. Are these events, which can be amazing in their sequence, simply coincidence? Probably. Does my thinking of them as the doings of Phyllis make me a supernaturalist? I don't think so. It is simply a part of my own "virtual reality," which we all have. Virtual realities are our individual concoctions of ideologies, convictions, opinions, attitudes, values, and beliefs that we've built up over the years and hold dearly. They may not always be rational, but they do get us through the day or in other ways guide our lives, including helping us cope with traumatic events. Our minds may confront indisputable facts that contradict the outlooks of our virtual realities, but these facts most often will not penetrate our minds, as we will see throughout the pages of this book.

Then there is another very old concept beyond souls and the spirits that continues to have a widespread following today as the basis of our minds. It's the concept of a human energy force, which theoretically surrounds us as an aura. Commonly called chi, it combines Native American culture, ancient Egyptian and Greek traditions, Hindu philosophy, and other Eastern religions. It has also been called chakra, ki, prana,

etheric energy, fohat, orgone, odic force, mana, and homeo-
pathic resonance. As behavioral expert Carol Ritberger explains
this concept:

> The human energy system is the electromagnetic field
> of energy that creates the auric glow of light around a
> person. . . . It identifies your personality traits, your
> behavioral characteristics, how you mentally function
> (how you process information and make decisions)
> . . . [it] is a holographic image of the human body.[11]

To help clarify this concept, I consulted my oldest friend,
Ron Rattner, who over the years has transformed himself, as he
describes it, "from secular Hebrew, to Born-Again Hindu [after
a traumatic divorce], to an 'Uncertain Undo,'" as he calls himself today. A skilled lawyer who ended his practice some time
after his immersion in Hinduism, he served on the board of
directors of the New Dimensions World Broadcasting Network,
an outlet for New Age and related spiritual thought and philosophy. Over the years, he has related to me how he has considered and experienced various subtle energies and states of consciousness. He told me that the human energy force incarnates
an "energy vortex, a life force that is commonly called the
soul." In other words, the concepts of the energy force and the
soul for him, as for many others, may be considered synonymous in many respects. In Hinduism, he told me, what mystics
call the Akashic Records, a "book of life," record spiritually
every word, thought, and action of our lives. Some mystics,
Ron told me, can engage these records and tell you everything
about your soul's history. Hindus call the soul Atma, and on
the Hindu Web site, it is described as follows:

> Our individual soul is the immortal and spiritual body
> of light that animates life and reincarnates again and

> again until all necessary karmas are created and
> resolved and its essential unity with God is fully real-
> ized. Our soul body was created in the image and like-
> ness of the Primal Soul, but it differs from the Primal
> Soul in that it is immature. While [God] is unevolu-
> tionary perfection, we are in the process of evolving.[12]

The theory is, according to Ron, that through each reincarnation, we can make ourselves better persons, more loving and
caring. In most New Age theories, the energy aura itself is
either a feature of the soul or representative of it, and one must
be trained to see it. The auras themselves have two main purposes: to form a protective layer around us and to act as a trans-
mitting and receiving station for implanting thoughts and
emotions in our brains—which according to these theories
emanate from a greater, universal consciousness.

The energy aura was the main thesis of James Redfield's
best-selling book *The Celestine Prophecy*, published in 1993.[13]
The book purportedly drew from ancient Peruvian manuscripts
and showed how we can learn to see the aura of the energy
fields surrounding both our bodies and plants. A work of fiction, it sold hundreds of thousands of copies. Redfield followed
it with *The Celestine Vision*, termed a "nonfiction book," which
expanded his theories.

I recall at the time reading both books as well as *Illusions*,[14]
an earlier book written by Richard Bach on the same topic. As
hard as I tried, I couldn't see any aura around me or around
anyone else, or around any plant. I still can't. Maybe I'm not
sensitive enough, or maybe I drink the wrong vodka.

The theory of the energy force in general, in any event,
continues to have a large following. It is a focus of the books
by author and lecturer Wayne Dyer and is also described in
detail in *Power vs. Force* by David R. Hawkins, who was trained
as a psychiatrist and claims the ability to measure the energy

force in each of us on a scale of 1 to 1,000. He describes the founders of three religions, Christ, Krishna, and Buddha as being at the level of 1,000; Mahatma Gandhi and Mother Teresa as being in the range of 700; and "evil," vindictive people as being in the range of 30.[15]

I don't know if he ever saw tapes of the speeches of Adolf Hitler and Benito Mussolini. The energy they generated had their audiences practically slobbering with enthusiasm. Maybe there needs to be a separate energy scale for psychopaths.

Hawkins also says the following:

> Everything in the universe constantly gives off an energy pattern of specific frequency that remains for all time and can be read by those who know how. Every word, deed and intention creates a permanent record. Every thought is known and recorded forever. There are no secrets; nothing is hidden, nor can it be. Our spirits stand naked in time for all to see— everyone's life is accountable to the universe.[16]

I don't want to be critical of Hawkins or those with similar theories, but I don't understand how they can know all of this with absolute certainty. Aside from some unmanned landing devices, we haven't even gotten as far as Mars, so how can anyone speak for the entire universe?

Carol Ritberger, as noted earlier, mentions holographic images, which comprise yet another set of beliefs about external influences on the mind. Karl Pribram, a leading cognitive scientist at Stanford University, gives this theory some weight, though in a different way. He believes that the brain consists of holographic illusions. A hologram is a three-dimensional picture that in everyday life can be projected with the aid of lasers. It looks real enough, but when you put your hand through it, nothing is there.

According to the concept of Pribram's holographic brain model, a theory that has been supported by other reputable scientists, the possibility exists that things in our objective reality—the world of coffee cups, flower pots, elm trees, our parents and friends—may not exist in the way we believe they exist. They could all be illusions, ones we can feel as emotions and as hardened objects, but which exist only in our minds as realities created by internal holograms. Pribram and other respected scientists, including University of London physicist David Bohm, also theorize that the universe itself is holographic and that our everyday world as three-dimensional might be an illusion.[17] The concept was featured on the cover of the September 2003 issue of *Scientific American*. Who knows? However, as we'll see in the next chapters, there are probably better explanations for the processes of our brains.

A mountain of religious and secular literature deals with the concepts of the soul, the spiritual forces within us, and the human energy force as influences on how we think and feel. The theories go on and on, and all have their believers, many of whom are fanatical. And so in the interests of establishing a benchmark for what people today actually believe about the mind, I worked with the polling firm Synovate (a unit of a publicly held marketing research firm), to poll one thousand people in the United States, in order to learn what they, in fact, believe. We asked two questions: (1) How often do you think about the human mind and what makes up the essence of the human mind? (2) What do you believe makes up the essence of the human mind? We provided them with choices on this second question, with a chance to add their own answers, as noted below.

Synovate advised, because of the nature of the questions, that asking them by telephone wouldn't give people enough time to ponder them. So they suggested another unit of their company, Enation, to do the polling by e-mail. The one thousand persons responding had four days to report their answers, which have a margin of error of ± 2.6 percent.

The following are the results for question one: *How often do you think about the human mind and what makes up the essence of the human mind?*

- 16.6 percent said frequently.
- 32.3 percent said somewhat often.
- 38.3 percent said not very often.
- 12.8 percent said rarely or almost never.

The following are the results for question two: *What do you believe makes up the essence of the human mind?*

- 40.2 percent said components of the brain control our intellect, while the heart or spirits control our emotions.
- 19.3 percent said components of the brain alone control both our intellect and our emotions.
- 10.2 percent said a single soul force that enters our body at conception or birth.
- 5.2 percent said a combination of spirits that enter our body at conception or birth.
- 2.0 percent said an energy force that surrounds our bodies in an invisible aura.
- 1.1 percent said God's creation.
- 0.5 percent said how a person was raised/life experience.
- 0.3 percent said a combination of genetics/nurture/upbringing.
- 19.7 percent said they weren't sure.

Oddly enough, there were very little differences in gender, education, or other demographics among those who answered only "components of the brain."

With the majority of the general public reporting that our emotions are housed beyond the brain, despite all the studies and the reporting done in the past twenty years to the contrary, many of us apparently find it extremely difficult to absorb the fact that our minds are strictly biological. Science writer Sandra Blakeslee put it succinctly in the November 11, 2003, issue of the *New York Times*:

> They [neuroscientists] can see trees, but no forest. They do think they have solved one longstanding mystery, though . . . the mind is in no way separate from the brain. In the brain they have found a physical basis for all our thoughts, aspirations, language . . . and sense of consciousness, moral beliefs and everything else that makes us human. All of this arises from interactions among billions of ordinary cells. Neuroscience finds no duality, no finger of God animating the human mind.[18]

Neuroscientist Vernon B. Mountcastle of John Hopkins University writes that "what makes man human is his brain. His humanity includes those aspects of behavior traditionally classed as mental. . . . The vast majority [of neuroscientists] believe that no nonphysical agent in the universe controls or is controlled by brains."[19]

Is there such a thing as a soul? Science hasn't found it. Are there spirits or an energy force? Science hasn't found them, either. Everything that science has found points to the fact that we are all biological, right down to our cravings for french fries and romantic love—which some neuroresearchers have classified as bondings created by our brain's "biosocial romantic attachment mechanism," a collection of brain components that foster romantic love.

I'm not sure this would be great conversation on a first date.

I have read the books of the nation's leading skeptics, who contend that there is no soul or spirit force or afterlife. And their arguments are convincing. I cannot argue with anything they believe.

On the other hand, nobody has returned to life after spending six months in a grave or mausoleum to say, "Well, you won't believe it. That white light they talk about when you are nearing death? Well, actually, at the actual point of death, it turns into a green light. Then, when we actually die, the first thing that happens is that we turn into a drop of water that rushes past the planet Pluto. Then after that, things get hazy. But here I am again."

Nobody has come back to tell us stories like this—or that there is a heaven, or a hell, or any other location that our spirits, or soul, or energy force are transferred or reincarnated to, temporarily or forever. So if you'll excuse my chutzpah, it would appear *that no one knows anything about any of this for certain* and that anything is possible, including soul forces, spirits, energy forces, an afterlife, and everything else, although the odds that they exist are definitely not good.

In the meantime, the zealots among us, or as my friend Ron Rattner calls them, "Chronic Believers," who subscribe passionately to one of these theories or another, need not worry. The study of the functions of the brain, including our cognitive thought processes, emotions, and impulses, is a slow, arduous process, giving those zealots a long future to drive us crazy with their arrogance and evangelism. It also provides the militant fanatics plenty of time to try to kill off the more normal among us, who are content with whatever we believe and are just trying to get through the week.

To give you one example of the arduous process of uncovering the biology of the mental side of the brain, I recall sitting in a seminar sponsored by the HealthEmotions Institute of the University of Wisconsin, one of the top five entities of its type in the world, and watching a neuroscientist present his findings on the "startle effect." This effect is the feeling we get when we are walking down a dark alley and someone jumps out and yells "boo." On a large screen in the auditorium he showed a diagram of a rodent brain, which has a primal emotional system very similar to that within the human brain. On the right side was a relatively short line, which he had highlighted. I watched with intense focus, as he traced the line on the screen, how it produced instantaneous adrenalin responses in the body when it was triggered from a fright. What really amazed me, however, was the fact, which he mentioned in passing, that this little bit of research took seventeen years.

Seventeen years? How long will it take to trace greed or envy? I can't wait that long.

What the research on the startle effect reflects is how difficult the study of the brain as a whole really is. And with only 16 percent of us thinking about our own minds with any frequency, as the survey indicates, what relatively little being learned must be difficult for neuroscience to communicate to the public at large.

One might assume that learning that the mind is biological—that spirits and the soul are not entering the brain via the pineal gland or any other brain component—should sow some seeds of doubt in our thoughts and our conceptions. Most of us, however, are content not to let facts such as these, as they are uncovered, get in the way of our preconceived notions.

In this chapter and in the pages ahead, we present reality as it is being uncovered for us by science from a purely rational point of view—in short, a reality check. In giving ourselves a reality check, we can choose to continue with our virtual realities as they exist or alter them to take into consideration more of what science has discovered about our minds, our brains, the universe, the concept of time, genetics, and our need for status and religion. The viewpoints of the mind, as we shall see, are in fact capable of change, but the process for most of us can be extremely difficult. Further, if we consider the mysteries and uncertainties of life in general that continue to exist, despite the efforts of science, whatever mistaken outlooks and notions our virtual realities consist of today may not always pose a problem—that is, as long as they do not contribute to our abusing others. Unfortunately, too many of them do. In the meantime we might hope that neuroscientists will find faster techniques than those used for uncovering the startle effect to piece together the vast unknowns of our mental mechanisms. This is perhaps the most important quest of all today, not only for our health, but because what we learn may one day allow us, all the people of the world, to live together in a more harmonious way.

Or put another way, we might yet prove the science fiction writers wrong. Thousands of years in the future, we may have learned to tame our minds and brains to the point that we're not zapping other people to death with strange weapons—that is, if we have any people left.

It will probably be a race against time.

2.

OUR MINDS, OUR INTELLIGENCE, OUR CREATIVITY, OUR FEELINGS, AND OUR ATHLETIC PROWESS ARE ALL CREATED FROM ZEROS AND ONES

The trouble with the world is that the stupid are cocksure and the [truly] intelligent are full of doubt.
Bertrand Russell[1]

Even if we fell asleep during our computer science classes, or in a seminar about computers, or we read our last book about computers ten or twenty years ago, most of us have heard of the term "binary system." It is a form of mathematical calculation that can be used to add, subtract, multiply, divide, employ the decimal system, and so forth. It is similar to the abacus, which, five thousand years old, contained twelve columns of beads in a wooden frame, and is still used as a calculator in many regions of the world.

The binary system is not complicated at its very essence. It consists of two numbers, 0 and 1. Even I can understand this: 0 and 1. It is the basis for the operating system of computers, and it also appears to be the basis of the operating system of the brain.

When we turn on our television sets, the images we see crossing the screen are, in actuality, made up of combinations of zeros and ones, arranged and coded in such a way as to produce characters and images. Our DVDs that create moving, four-color images with full-spectrum Dolby-like sound are comprised of zeros and ones that are microscopic, deeply embedded, and compressed. These zeros and ones are read by a diminutive laser beam as the disk rapidly spins to recreate the images and sounds they represent. Digitizing is basically the translation of all information into zeros and ones.

Only a few years ago, scientists were telling us that the DVD was impossible. There was no way, they said, that we could put a two-hour movie in full color, with full sound, encoded in zeros and ones on such a small disk.

But we have. By comparing our brains and our minds in a very narrow sense to the digital images and sounds we see on our televisions and computers, we can more easily gain an insight into what makes our own brains work, at their very basic levels.

In computers as well as in digital television sets, the zeros and ones from DVDs are ultimately fed into a microprocessor, such as the Pentium and other chips, which now hold millions of transistors. A single chip, the size of a fingernail, may now hold as many as 5,500,000 or more transistors.

The transistor is the key to it all. Years ago, transistors were composed of vacuum tubes, the size of small electric light-bulbs—those of us from an older generation remember their powering our radios and early television sets. We could feel their heat, which was one of their biggest problems, since they would burn out easily.

But what they had the capability of doing was *turning on or off instantly*.

And that's what today's microscopic transistors do, turn on or off instantly. The result is the perfect platform for the binary system. A transistor that is fed the code of one (less than five volts of electricity) is turned on. A transistor that is fed the code of zero (frequently five volts of electricity is the code) is turned off.[2]

At the very basis of it all, that is it.

When you type the letter "P," on your computer, it is represented in the software of your word processing system as the binary code 01001111. You see? The letter is made up entirely of zeros and ones, called "bits" in computerese. Eight of these bits make a "byte." (If you already know this stuff, skip to page 32. If you don't and are not technically inclined, read slowly and take deep breaths. This is the toughest chapter in the book, but it is an essential one.)

When you view a color image on your computer screen, what you are actually seeing is the result of tens of thousands of zeros and ones that are coded to create the colors and shading that you perceive. As amateur computer camera enthusiasts have learned to understand, this coding for color images is reduced to individual pixels—tiny units of space representing a shade of a color—which when seen from a given distance determine how sharp the images are. Look at the image on your computer screen with a magnifying glass, or use the zoom-in feature on a four-color computer image, and you can make out the individual pixels.

The pixels, again, are coded through zeros and ones.

The more pixels that can be jammed into the image, the higher the resolution, and thus the more costly the camera. High-definition television crowds even more pixels into a given space. All of this is an extremely complicated process, and if I attempted to describe it in any greater detail, I would lose myself, and perhaps you.

The main point we need to keep in mind, at this moment, is that digitizing, which can create lifelike images and sound, as well as the memory of images and sound, in addition to data in general, is at its very basis composed of zeros and ones.

The whole thing seems incredible to me, but that's the way it is.

The neurons of the brain, at their very essence, act very

much as a transistor does. We have about 100 billion neurons in our brain, although the exact number is apparently a source of some controversy among scientists. I have seen the number as high as 300 billion, and as low as 50 billion. Further, the brain has what are called glia cells, the structures responsible for making sure that neurons get nutrients, removing their waste matter, and performing other housekeeping duties. It is estimated that there are more than ten times as many glia cells in the brain as there are neuron cells.[3]

Almost all the neuroscientists whose works I've read or with whom I've talked agree that although we've advanced tremendously in our knowledge of the brain, we appear to be still at the beginnings of its research. Neuroscientist Larry W. Swanson describes this most succinctly in his book *Brain Architecture*:

> Most of us don't think about our brain—let alone how it works—until something goes wrong with it. Then we wonder why this or that distressing symptom happened and whether we can do anything about it. Stroke, depression, retardation, epilepsy, dementia, addiction, schizophrenia—the list of heart-wrenching afflictions is long indeed and doesn't even include a host of other less severe, yet frustrating real problems like anxiety, learning and memory disorders, attention deficits, and on and on. For answers we often turn to the medical experts—to neurologists and psychiatrists who usually prescribe drugs or surgery that may relieve symptoms in a more or less effective way, at least for a while. *But ask 10 of the world's leading neurologists how the brain works—how it thinks, feels, perceives and acts as a unified whole—and you will get 10 very different answers, unless they are narrowly framed around the biophysics and chemistry of nerve impulse conduction and synapsis transmission.* [Italics mine][4]

In other words, brain scientists are advancing more rapidly in discerning the smaller pictures of the brain, the synaptic operating system for one (which includes the binary system), than they are in capturing the big picture, how the parts and pieces all work together.

A neuron, like a transistor, is, for the most part, either turned on or off. The terms used are "excitatory," when a neuron is fired and turned on, and "inhibitory," when the neuron is influenced not to turn on and remains off, in a resting state. It is the same binary system as that of a computer, which is probably why the brain has been referred to as a computer. But there remains a lot of controversy about that. Stephen Pinker, professor of psychology at Harvard, in *How the Mind Works*, spends more than 110 pages asserting that the brain acts very much like a computer—that it is a computational device.[5] In contrast, neuroscientist and Nobel Prize winner Gerald M. Edelman, in his recently published book *Wider Than the Sky*, spends most of the book refuting that theory, stating, in essence, that the brain is far more than a computer.[6] So does Jerry Fodor of Rutgers University, in *The Mind Doesn't Work That Way: The Scope and Limits of Computational Psychology.*[7]

After plowing through their books, as well as dozens of other recent books about the brain, it would appear to me that both ideas are right, and here is why:

Figure 2 on page 34 illustrates what a classical transistor looks like today, as compared to a neuron.

As you can see, there is one line of low-voltage electricity going into a transistor, called a "collector." There is one line going out, called an "emitter." Then there is a third line going into the transistor referred to as a "base." This line carries a very small level of electricity, as we've described, the five volts or less that control a gate in the transistor that turns it on or off.

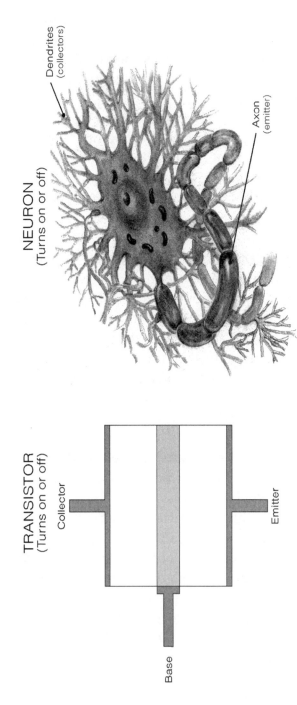

Figure 2: The schematic on the left of a classical transistor has one line of low-voltage electricity going in called a "collector." There is one line going out, called an "emitter." Then there is a third line going in called a "base." This line carries a very small level of electricity, usually five volts or less, that controls a gate in the transistor that turns it on or off.

The neuron's "collector" is composed of *thousands of thousands* of dendrites, which collect neurotransmitters over synaptic gaps that create an electrical force, the strength of which determines whether the neuron will be turned on or off. If turned on, the axon, or the "emitter," through its branches, will carry signals out to the dendrites of thousands of other neurons.

Now we're going to get into how a neuron is turned on or off, and this is one of the most amazing pieces of information you're ever going to come across, especially if you consider that this is happening in your head this instant. This process is the digitized reality of what goes on in our brains as a whole and our minds in particular—and it took me two months of research to figure it out. Of course, every time I play a DVD, I have to look at the manual, so maybe someone else could have figured this out much faster.

First of all, among the tens of billions of neurons that exist in our brains, no two look alike, making it obvious that they didn't evolve on a factory production line. Further, there are more than two hundred different types of neurons, which vary in size, shape, and function.

And even though the brain uses electricity in very low-voltage quantities, much lower than a microprocessor, *no neurons actually connect with each other via a direct line*, although they and their fiber connections are really tightly packed in together. Among the billions of neuronal cells in one cubic inch of the brain are also ten thousand miles of connecting fibers.[8]

That's ten thousand miles in one cubic inch. Visualize beginning a hike in New York City with your one cubic inch of brain, then walking all the way to Los Angeles and back, allowing the fibers to unwind, and you'd still have some left over. Who'd have thought of this?

As we'll demonstrate, our brains appear to be handicapped when it comes to absorbing facts like these—that consist of large, unreal numbers—and putting them into perspective.

It is probably useful to keep in mind, as we review these facts about the brain, that we as humans had nothing to do with its design. We emerged from the womb, and there within our skulls was our brain, ready to grow and absorb knowledge, language, experience, and training to become who and what we are. In an analogy with a computer, the brain's neuron cells comprise the hardware, and how those cells are connected apparently comprises its software. Together they provide the potential ability, for example, to speak English or French.

The connective device of a neuron is called a synapse: a space, actually, rather than a direct connection, between two neuron cells that measures about one millionth of a centimeter.

While a transistor uses only electricity to be on or off, the neuron uses both electricity and chemicals. The electricity is generated by brain chemicals, particularly sodium and potassium, which work almost like an ordinary flashlight battery, helping to create at the synapses of the cell what is called an *action potential*—an electrical charge.

It is the complexity of the connection at the synapse that I find so mind boggling. While some of the textbooks describing neural science and synaptic behavior are well over one thousand pages, I will attempt to boil down the salient facts into a few paragraphs, to save you the disorder I ended up with, glazed-eye syndrome.

First of all, you might remember from a high school or college science class or a book or article about the brain that there are three basic parts to a neuron: the *cell body*, an *axon*, and *dendrites*. The cell body itself is much like other cells in our bodies, surrounded by a membrane, which contains a nucleus, DNA, and other standard cell parts. The axon, the second major structural apparatus of a neuron, is a lone fiber that emanates from the neuron but which branches out into many buds and creates synaptic connections (close but not touching) on the dendrites of surrounding neurons. Dendrites are a collection of nerve fibers reaching out from the cell body, which mimic the collector function of a transistor. The dendrites receive signals from the axons of a host of other neurons.

If you feel yourself dozing off at this point, keep in mind

that this is how your mind works, without which you wouldn't be able to comprehend the Cubs, the Knicks, an opera, paintings, literature of good or poor quality, or the sight of your family. It would appear to me that as humans we should make every effort to understand what is going on in the three-pound organ we carry within our skulls. The brain, by the way, can be carried in the cup of your hand, burns oxygen and glucose at ten times the rate of all other body tissues at rest,[9] and has a consistency of a raw egg, which is why it's always a good idea to do everything possible to keep one's skull intact.

One other interesting point to note, as made by Susan A. Greenfield in *The Human Brain*, is that the main fuel for the brain from the food we eat are the carbohydrates.[10] This may not be good news for the followers of the Atkins diet.

Now here is something else that is fascinating. The average computer transistor, as we've described, has the one very low microscopic voltage base line going into it that turns it on or turns it off. The neuron at a synapse doesn't connect directly, as we've also seen, but uses chemicals called neurotransmitters that it releases, which travel across the synaptic cleft or gap—remember, the gap is only one millionth of a centimeter—and only *influence* whether or not that next neuron will "fire" or be turned on.

So what you basically have is electricity in a neuron that travels to the synapse, releases a chemical, and then turns into electricity again in the next neuron. So the brain action is electricity-chemicals-electricity-chemicals, and so on.

The design is stunning. Approximately one hundred neurotransmitters have been identified in the brain (up from fifty-two, which was the number given to me when I wrote my last book in the year 2002), and they all have one purpose: either to inhibit the neuron that they are traveling to from firing and keeping it "off" or stimulating it to fire and turning it "on."

Most neurons at a synapse release only one type of neurotransmitter. The main ones are *glutamate*, which is intended to stimulate or excite the firing of the neuron it is traveling to, and *GABA*, which is intended to inhibit the firing. It is interesting to note that when the inhibitor transmitters aren't working properly, our brain cells fire on a nonstop basis, literally driving us crazy and wearing themselves out before their time. So let's give these inhibitors some respect.

Then there are many neurons that contain storage sacs for more than one neurotransmitter. Thus several neurotransmitters may travel across the gap from a single "presynaptic" neuron to influence the action potential of the receiving neuron, or what is called the "postsynaptic" neuron. If the action potential or the charge of electricity generated by all the inhibitory and excitatory neurotransmitters that have crossed the gap, or better gaps, reaches a given level, that neuron is fired. If not, it remains relaxed.

In some cases where more than one type of transmitter is released from a single neuron, some may be excitatory, the others inhibitory. It's called cotransmission. Talk about complicated and confusing.[11]

Hello, hello, wake up—all this is going on in your mind this instant.

One other fascinating thing about this design is that the dendrites of the receiving neurons have receptors, ports of call, which are designed precisely to accommodate each specific neurotransmitter. If a transmitter hits the wrong receptor, it bounces away without influence.

But here is the part that gets me. It may take as many as one thousand different connections to the postsynaptic neuron, consisting in some cases of one hundred or more different chemical neurotransmitters like serotonin, which is primarily an inhibitor, before the neuron reaches a given action potential, or charge, and fires, or does not reach the required charge level and remains relaxed. And this all has to be orchestrated so that all the neurotransmitters crossing all the millions or billions of synaptic gaps involved in the mental or physical process we are undergoing do so simultaneously.

This is akin to our getting one thousand e-mails either encouraging or discouraging us to stand up from our chairs. If the preponderance of the e-mails are encouraging, we would be triggered to stand up. If the preponderance are discouraging, we would remain seated in a relaxed state. And the decision has to be made in one one-thousandth of a second. All the action in the brain takes place in that almost instantaneous time frame, after which the neurons again, almost instantaneously, return to their normal resting state, ready to be motivated once again to fire or not.

And believe me, I am just skimming the surface here. For example, serotonin is a slower-acting neurotransmitter, whose generating neuron cells are located primarily in the brain stem, but which have long axons that connect to other appropriate neurons. Once this neurotransmitter is released across the synapse, it usually provides an inhibitory effect.

Neuroscientist Joseph LeDoux, in *The Synaptic Self*, reports interestingly on one aspect of what serotonin does:

> Prozac, for example, prevents the removal of serotonin from the synaptic space. Normally, as part of the process by which transmitter action is regulated, neurotransmitters are sucked back into the terminals that release them. By preventing the removal of serotonin, allowing more to stay around longer, Prozac amplifies its effect. One theory holds that there is a deficiency of serotonin in depressed or anxious brains, which Prozac helps correct.[12]

LeDoux also describes the brain, with its billions of neurons and trillions of connections, as "chemicals that are oozing and sparks flying constantly, during wakefulness and during sleep, during thoughtfulness and during boredom."[13]

This is great news for those of us who may be frequently accused, particularly by unhappy, hyperactive significant others, of being deadly dull. We can now retort that, despite how we appear, our brains are oozing and sparking in great fits of energy. So mind your own business.

Synaptic connections appear to be the key to the operating system of the brain, this oozing and sparking, both for sensory functions—what we see, feel, think, hear, smell, and so on—and for motor functions, all the tens of thousands of physical movements of which the human body is capable.

We stated that the average neuron may have as many as 1,000 connections, but some are even more complicated. A spinal neuron controlling motor functions (communication to our muscles) in the spinal column may have as many as 10,000 connections. The interesting thing is that 2,000 of these connections are made right on the body of the cell, instead of on the dendrites. The remainder are on the dendrites. In other words, the cell bodies themselves are capable of having synaptic connections, in addition to their dendrites. Further, an axon bud of a given neuron might twist around and form a connection on its own cell body, helping to excite or inhibit itself.

Forgive me if I think this sounds salacious.

But there is one sentence in the massive tome *Principles of Neural Science* that really threw me: "The dendritic tree of a Purkinje cell in the cerebellum is much larger and bushier, as well it might be—it receives approximately 150,000 contacts."[14]

I was looking for a "Gee Whiz," or some other editorial comment, but there was none. This poor cell has to measure the action potential of those 150,000 connections in the same one one-thousandth of a second as any ordinary neuron cell would, before it knows whether it should fire or not. It would be as if every one of the 150,000 adults over the age of twenty, in Madison, Wisconsin, would need to vote simultaneously on whether to stand up or sit down.

In the brain, this does happen instantaneously.

Neurotransmitters play this enormous role. As an aside, at a seminar for neuroscientists, I asked one of the leading neuroscientists in the world, we'll call him Ed Byrnes (a man who also manages a staff of more than one thousand psychiatrists for a system of research hospitals), while we were out having drinks, what the difference is between a neurotransmitter and a hormone.

He said to me: "Do you know what makes a hormone?"

"No, Ed," I replied.

"When you don't pay her."

He then began to laugh so hard that he almost fell off the bar stool, before I reached out to catch him.

The wonderful thing about the best scientists in the world like Ed is that they understand how much they don't know and are humbled by it. This also tends to give them a great sense of humor—whether you appreciate the joke or not.

So now that I have learned from other sources what the difference is, let me tell you: A neurotransmitter has been defined as a chemical that travels the synapses and is capable of binding to a receptor, the port of call for that transmitter on a corresponding synapse in the brain. Hormones are *chemicals that can travel rapidly through the blood stream.*

I was relieved to learn this. But then I became confused again when I heard that adrenalin, as one example, can be both a neurotransmitter and a hormone.[15] When we walk through the woods and see a snake that looks threatening, adrenalin is released as a neurotransmitter by the neurons that have storage sacs containing it, and at the same time it is released as a hormone in our blood stream. In no time at all we are on extreme alert and probably frightened stiff. When we see the snake slither off, we are relieved, but the adrenalin remains in our bloodstream and we can feel the "high" from its effects for some time. Oddly enough, adrenalin is also released during laughter,[16] which helps create the high that Ed Byrnes felt when he almost fell off the bar stool telling me that corny joke about the hormone.

Neurons, with all their magic, need to work together to create all the wondrous things they do in our experience of life. In other words, it takes a village, if you'll excuse the expression. They first link together in neural circuits, which then form a hierarchy of circuits in the brain. The single neuron firing an inhibitor or exciter to the next cell over is also part of a circuit of neurons that can communicate to another circuit. These circuits build in a hierarchy until they form a neural system, which controls things like seeing, hearing, moving across the room, or detecting danger.

Again, it appears that the strongest similarity between the brain and a computer is the fact that they both operate on the binary system: the transistor is either in an on or off state, and the neuron is either fired or is not. There is no hard disk in the brain to store digital information. While we can store thousands, if not millions, of pages in the memory systems of the average personal computer, the average brain has nowhere near that long-term memory capacity. It appears to select without reason on our part what it wants to remember long term and forgets what it wants to forget.

Further, the brain comes to us without any software selections. There is nothing we can purchase and install. The brain's software, it would appear, is not immediately working and accessible. For example, the brain fresh out of the womb is not prepared to speak a language. But there is a neural system for language in the brain, called the Broca area, ready to absorb and learn the language being spoken in our household, shortly after birth. If we are born into a household that speaks English, we learn to speak English. If we are born into a household that speaks Lithuanian, we learn to speak Lithuanian. This isn't exactly news, but we tend to forget how automatic it is.

As we begin to learn skills and absorb knowledge, we actually grow more connections, which, in ways that neuroscience doesn't really understand, makes the neural circuitry stronger. This would be easier to comprehend if the learning process involved growing more neurons and miniaturizing them in such a way that they filled the same amount of skull space. In computers and other electronic devices containing microchips, the key to the advances we've made is in the increasing number of transistors we are able to place on those chips, which has resulted in such things as a cell phone that shoots videos.

Neuroscientists have found the changes in the brain that can take place are primarily in the gene expressions of the neuron. What happens, in essence, is that the genetic material of the neuron cell can cause it to grow more synapses. This increases the number of its potential connections, which, in turn, can lead to stronger influences on memory, knowledge, and skills.

We can hypothesize that what the brain is doing as it grows new connections in reaction to our learning or exercising a new skill, for example, is strengthening the pathways of the neural circuitry involved in that skill. While a computer uses one basic pathway to send a voice audio to its speakers, the brain might use twenty to forty or even more pathways for a thought to be converted to human speech. That's probably one reason why neuroscientist Gerald Edelman calls the brain an "ecological jungle."[17] One might conjecture that the use of these multiple pathways may be one reason why amateur athletes and young scholars might be inconsistent in how they demonstrate their skills. Perhaps as they mature, the newer neuronal connections narrow and strengthen those pathways, which influence the neuronal circuits involved to fire in a more consistent pattern. They function better, more like a programmed series of transistors, as we continue to exercise a specific skill.

Or, we might presume, anything that we know by rote is a result of strengthened connections, which produce the same result every time. We read a sentence in English, if that is our language, and we understand it immediately, because for years we worked hard to master the reading and writing of English. Thus the major neural circuits involved in language skills fire each time in much the same pattern. As we start to learn a new language, German, for example, we begin the same exercise anew, and the growing of connections that make this language immediately familiar to us depends on the intensity of our learning and on our neuronal propensities for absorbing a new language.

If we then suspend speaking or reading German for an extended length of time, we can assume that we'll lose connections and become "rusty" with the language.

But on a grander scale, this system allows expansion of our general skills, knowledge, and talent. We are not necessarily stuck with who we are, if we are not satisfied with what we have achieved or who we have become. As Gerald Edelman points out in his paper "A Picture of the Brain," in the compendium *The Brain*:

> At the finest scale, no two brains are identical, not even those of identical twins. Furthermore, at any two moments, connections in the same brain are not likely to remain exactly the same. Some cells will have retracted their processes, others will have extended new ones, and certain other cells will have died. This observation applies to patterns at the finest scale, consisting of individual neurons and their synapses.[18]

While this is good news for those of us who want continually to improve ourselves, the problem is that because each of us has neuronal connections that are different, we do not always know what our ultimate potential is. Some of us might take five hundred golf swings a day on a practice range to improve our game and, over time, become a scratch golfer. Others of us might make a little improvement with the same exercise, while others of us might see no improvement at all.

Most of us can remember, from when we were students, classmates who skimmed their reference books and aced their exams, while the rest of us struggled mightily with our comprehension and retainment. Worse, we can remember the arrogance and pride of those super students, who never realized how lucky they were. The specific neuronal circuits and systems in their brains which were involved in that process were apparently genetically predisposed to growing more connections more rapidly than ours, even though we made a greater effort. We call such skills "aptitudes," and each of us obviously has different neuronal potentials in different areas, the testing for which might provide only small clues to our full potential.

Another important characteristic of this system is that if we don't continually exercise our brains in the areas that are important to us, we can lose connections. Instead of improving in knowledge or skills, or even holding our own, we can regress. Most of us realize this innately. If we haven't played bridge for eight or ten years, we might have trouble even remembering the rules of the game. We all know that if we ignore skills such as these, both physical and mental, we may grow rusty. The connections regress for some of us more than others.

The bad news about this system is that there is no built-in filter for sifting out learning and life experiences that may not be beneficial. And so strong connections might be created that produce dysfunctional behaviors and mental disorders. Thus, as reported in greater detail in chapter 5, we may become victimized by distorted realities that are not easily changed, since those of us suffering from them may not recognize them as distortions. If we come to realize that these distortions exist in certain of our outlooks, we may be able to mitigate them. If we don't recognize them, the circuitry creating them might actually grow stronger, making those of us who have to live with these people the victims. If it's us, we'll have a far more difficult time breaking free of these thoughts. And so the brain's synaptic connections, and the images and thinking they produce, may not always work in our best interests.

We have always known in life that we experience ups and downs. Through our studies of the synapses, we are beginning to understand the very basic neural physicality of our skills, aptitudes, and knowledge.

3.

HERE'S WHAT IT TAKES TO HIT A TENNIS BALL OR DEAL WITH OTHER MOVING OBJECTS, AND WHY IT'S SO DIFFICULT TO BE CONSISTENT UNDER PRESSURE

'Tis an ill wind that blows no minds.
Malaclypse the Younger[1]

Since tennis is my recreational game of choice, I was fascinated by a few paragraphs I ran across in *Principles of Neural Science*, which theorized about what goes on in the brain when one is about to hit a tennis ball. Though some of the most important functions of the brain, such as what creates and synthesizes our intelligence, remain largely unknown, a great deal is known about our visual system. We also have some idea of where the physical and emotional—yes, emotional—activities involved in hitting a tennis ball or dealing with other moving objects appear to be processed in the brain.

And so we can assume there is some validity in the following description from *Principles of Neural Science* of the process of hitting a tennis ball. This also might be applied to simpler tasks such as reaching for a pen that dropped on the floor, dancing, skipping over a puddle, swatting a fly, driving a car through traffic, or working to avoid being sideswiped by another shopping cart in a crowded supermarket:

Visual information about the motion of the approaching [tennis] ball is processed in the visual system, which identifies the flying object ["Okay, that's a tennis ball, not a volleyball."] and computes its direction and velocity. [Sensory] information about the position of [our] arms, legs and trunk in space are also computed by the brain to plan the appropriate positioning of the body for interception of the ball.

All of this sensory information ultimately reaches multisensory processing regions . . . where the information is combined to elicit the memory of earlier attempts to hit a tennis ball [attempts, I would add, of similar velocity, height, and spin versus your position on the court]. In addition, the . . . information for the planned behavior recruits activity in the amygdala, a structure concerned with emotion and social behavior. The amygdala in turn activates the autonomic [automatic, occurring involuntarily] nervous system to prepare the body for action. [More or less, what we do instinctively without thinking about it.] . . . The multisensory association areas make connections with higher-order motor centers that compute a program [something like a World War II submarine captain computing the direction for a torpedo] for moving the racket into position.

This program is then passed on to the primary motor cortex for execution. . . . Once the behavior is initiated the job of the brain is not over. As the arm is raised and the ball approaches, many minor adjustments of the initial motor program are made, based on more recent sensory information about the exact trajectory of the approaching ball before the arm moves the racket against the ball. Of course, as the behavior is being executed, the brain is also engaged in maintaining the player's heart rate, respiration and

other autonomic functions that are typically outside
the awareness of the player.[2]

The next time I whiff on a ball, I'm going to show this
information to my tennis partners, who have the empathy
levels of fruit flies. The point is, how many of us have ever
given a moment's thought to the specific activities going on in
our brains while we are in the midst of doing anything physical, or even mental, such as reading a book? But as neuroscientists have demonstrated, at any given moment of our lives,
the tens of billions of neuron cells in our brains are oozing,
sparking, and allowing us to do physically what we do without
a thought.

There is also an emotional component to properly hitting a
ball in any sport, be it tennis, golf, baseball, soccer, volleyball,
or what have you. Our emotions well up in competitive situations when we feel pressured to succeed. The amygdala—the
brain organ that mediates for fear—is activated as part of the
process (as described in the above quote from *Principles of
Neural Science)*. Most of us have an innate understanding of
this. We see basketball players at free throw lines, and baseball
players coming up to bat, looking up to a god, crossing themselves, or going through a bevy of superstitious physical movements; they gesture aiming to get the attention of the god they
believe in or the spirit world they believe surrounds them to
make their efforts successful.

In effect, what these gestures do, more important than
appealing to a god or spirit world, is work to calm the amygdala so that it will impede the release of chemicals, such as cor-
tisol, which raise our stress levels. The calming gestures and
thoughts may also trigger serotonin to be transmitted across
the synapses, inhibiting firing activities in specific neural circuits. This can calm our anxieties. If this process works for us,
our physical motions will not be impinged upon by what we

commonly call "a case of the nerves," "stage fright," or, in golf, the "yips."

Most of us understand innately that some components of our mind do not always act in our best interests. This problem makes for great drama and evening sitcoms. We lose our tempers and lash out in inappropriate situations. We are asked to give a presentation to an important audience and find that we can't sleep for a week. Though we might have won three important tennis or golf matches in a row, we go to pieces when facing a championship match. And so we realize, without needing to understand how the amygdala works, that we need to find our own coping mechanisms for overcoming thoughts, emotions, and impulses that are inappropriate to the situation. These negative thoughts and feelings are not supportive of what the rational side of the brain—our cortex—is directing us to do. This is where Zen techniques come in. They may help us overcome these negative thoughts and feelings through yoga and meditation. For others it may be prayer, counting to ten several times, thinking of old movies, or a host of other remedies. One or more of these mechanisms may work for some of us; while for others, none of them may work. When we see well-known motivators, counselors, and therapists on television or in person telling us we can overcome impulses that drive irrational behavior by doing this or that, we suck it in with great expectations. Later we wonder why it worked for so many others, who gave testimony to the fact, but not for us. If, on the other hand, we remember that each of us, the more than six billion persons on this planet, is uniquely different, that each of us has a unique brain, then we would know the necessity for each of us to seek out and find his or her own methods for coping and succeeding. It might be the very thing that famous counselors such as Deepak Chopra or Tony Robbins or Billy Graham tell us, or it might be that we have to keep searching until we find answers that are more precisely tailored to us.

For me, learning recently that it is my brain's amygdala that creates irrational fears and stress, particularly in a tennis game of doubles, when I am about to hit a second serve in a critical situation, I scream inwardly at my amygdala: "Would you just shut up and leave me alone?" Humans, as well as other higher animals, actually have two amygdalas, one in each of our brain's hemispheres. I don't know which is more or less responsible for the tightness I feel in those competitive, critical moments, so when I am screaming inwardly, I direct the tirade at both of them. Sometimes this works, sometimes it doesn't. When it doesn't, I just plop the ball across the net to avoid fear of failure, even though I know that my doubles opponents will blaze the return back at me.

The point is that though some of us have areas of the brain cortex that may be able to compute wonderful programs to hit tennis balls or golf balls, or to dance across a stage, our amygdala, and other emotional circuitry, may actually work to sabotage us.

On an airplane flight recently, I found myself sitting next to a baseball scout around my age, who told me he was about to retire. Here is the gist of our conversation, as I recall it:

"How long have you been doing this?" I asked.

"Oh, close to forty years."

"Where do you scout these players?"

"Mostly at high school games, fewer college games, because there are a lot more high schools."

"How many players have you scouted?"

"I've often been asked that. I guess anywhere between ten and fifteen thousand."

"And how many of those players have had a successful career in the major leagues?"

"Really successful, I would say about ten."

"Why so few?"

"Well, first of all, to play at the top professional levels, you have to have the basic genetics. Any good coach will tell you that. Certain things can't be taught. These kids have to have the basic mechanics to start with. If they're a pitcher, they need to be able to throw the ball at least 90 miles per hour and get it over the corners of the plate; they need to master the curve ball and other pitches. If they're a batter, they have to be able to hit a fastball being thrown at them at 90 miles per hour or faster, as well as balls with all kinds of spins being thrown at varying velocities, the change-ups. They have to be smart, too, to be able to predict more often than not where and how the next pitch is going to be thrown so that they can prepare themselves. They have a fraction of a second to decide what to do."

"And that's it?"

"No, that's just for starters. We find a lot of kids who have the mechanics. The next most important thing is consistency. Can they pitch or bat at high levels consistently? And connected with that in some way is: can they handle competitive pressure? With three balls and two strikes in a pressure situation, will the pitcher or the batter choke up, lose his confidence, and lose his mechanics? We lose most of what appear to be promising players because of consistency or pressure problems, or both. As I said, I think they're intertwined in some way, the mental side, that is. There is the famous quote from the old-time manager of the New York Yankees, Casey Stengel, who said, 'Anyone can hit a home run in batting practice.'"

"What did he mean?" I asked.

He meant that in practice, when there is no pressure, it's a lot easier to hit a home run. Even lousy hitters can hit a home run during batting practice. It's during the pressures of the game that the difficulties increase.

"What about chemistry? I hear a lot about that. Coaches want their players to get along; they're not happy to have egomaniacs on the team."

"That's important, of course. But strangely enough, that can cut two ways. Some players with large egos may have higher confidence levels and feel less fear. They want to be placed in pressure situations so that, if they succeed, they are viewed as heros. Others protect their large egos by attempting to avoid pressure situations. On basketball teams, these are the men or women who will do almost anything to avoid taking the last shot."

"How many prospects have you passed on, who you didn't think had the attributes you've just described?"

"Too many. And many times it's a mistake. The kid you see who has the mechanics but shakes like a leaf in a pressure situation and who you write off may go through some kind of epiphany, I don't know what, religious, or something else, and all of a sudden, he becomes some confident dude and mows everyone down and makes me look like a fool. That's why scouts like me give these kids a lot of looks, for as long as we can, before we make a recommendation to our bosses."

This conversation took place a few months before I found that piece in *Principles of Neural Science* that describes what actually takes place in the brain of an athlete. I could have given it to him, but would it have helped? I can't imagine his adding to his vernacular of encouraging phrases to a pitcher, for example: "Kid, you have two jobs to do. First you have to practice your mechanics, and you have to do it thousands of times. This way, your brain's synaptic connections involved in your throwing motions will grow more numerous and strengthen, so that those motions will become almost automatic. You won't believe what your brain goes through just to get your hand to throw a ball in the direction it's supposed to go. Second, you need to work on your amygdala to keep you calm in pressure situations, so that your motion isn't affected by that little weasel. That's what you have to do." I don't think this kind of explanation would fly, but who knows, maybe someday it will.

I found an Internet site of statistics compiled by the Minnesota Department of Employment and Economic Development that stated, as of the year 2000, there were 17,700 professional athletes in this country, with a projection of 21,700 by 2010. Jobs in this category are lost at the rate of 4,000 per year, which means that only 4,000 become available.[3] So among athletes who aspire to professional levels, the odds are long; about three one-thousandths of 1 percent of the US population will become a professional athlete between the ages of eighteen and forty-five.

Long odds also apply to the best musicians, singers, dancers, artists, as well as for the top physicists, lawyers, business managers, doctors, and practically every occupation in which high mental or physical dexterity, or both, are required.

Will it ever be possible to physically manipulate the neural circuitry of the brain to help us along in the process of becoming more competent in the skills of our choice? Perhaps so, but we have a long way to go.

Emilio Bizzi, professor in the Brain Sciences and Human Behavior Department at the Massachusetts Institute of Technology, says the following in his paper "The Acquisition of Motor Behavior":

> The human body is capable of an extraordinary range of movements. Years of practice shape the complex skills of professional dancers, pianists and tennis players. But to neuroscientists, even the simplest, everyday movements—reaching for a cup, buttoning a jacket, descending a flight of stairs—present a challenge to scientific explanation. We still do not fully understand how the brain controls these actions, nor can the most sophisticated robotics create a machine capable of matching the everyday competence of the central nervous system of the bird, the frog, or the cat, much less that of a human being.[4]

Maybe we should content ourselves with sending the earlier excerpt about what the brain appears to go through just to hit a tennis ball to the egomaniacs in athletics and other professions, who think they are in control of everything and know everything there is to know about practically everything. Maybe the information would create a reality check for bringing them down a peg or two.

On the other hand, their knowing that they have succeeded so magnificently despite all odds may make their egos swell more, and if they are on a team we're fans of, or they happen to be our own lawyer, or in other ways on our side, maybe it's better that they don't feel humble. Let them be egomaniacs, if it allows them to perform consistently under pressure, as long as it's on behalf of our cause and we don't have to have dinner with them.

Is this hypocritical? Let's not think about it right now.

4.

WHERE IN OUR BRAIN OUR CONSCIOUSNESS RESIDES AND HOW WE ADD TWO AND TWO REMAINS A MYSTERY

Before my teacher came to me, I did not know that I am. I lived in a world that was a no-world. I cannot hope to describe adequately that unconscious, yet conscious time of nothingness. . . . Since I had no power of thought, I did not compare one mental state to another.
Helen Keller, 1908[1]

It is probably one of the great tragedies of our time that so few people think about their minds—what makes them act as they do. If they did, maybe more of us collectively could do more about the irrational terror and chaos that plague our lives and the world at large. We would understand with clarity that our minds are part of our biology, that they are barely understood, and we should be humbled by that knowledge. Our poll in the first chapter, however, indicates that less than 20 percent of our population give the mind any thought. This oversight must certainly be worldwide, where more than one-fifth of the world's population live below the poverty line, so their focus would be on sheer survival, not on how neurons interact in their brains.

Unlike the time of the seventeenth-century philosophers, today we have access to enormous amounts of research about the brain. Some of this is publicized in television documentaries and by science writers, as well as in hundreds of books about the brain. It is apparent, however, that too few of us are drawn to the subject matter, and so the vast majority of people don't know what we don't know about the brain and the mind.

I find most it humbling that we don't know where our consciousness resides. In his book, *Consciousness Explained,* cognitive scientist Daniel Dennett points out that science has found no "Cartesian Theater." He is referring to philosopher René Descartes's concept that imagines a central point in the brain where our passions, reasoning, and consciousness all come together to create the feeling of what is happening at every conscious instant of our lives.[2] While science has made progress in learning about our sensory systems—how we see, hear, speak, taste, smell, touch—and much about our primary emotional systems, fear, anxiety, and sex drive, for example, *no one knows as yet where it all comes together to produce consciousness.*

Neuroscientist Antonio Damasio, in *The Feeling of What Happens: Body and Motion in the Making of Consciousness,* uses the metaphor of "movie-in-the-brain" and alludes to the problem of who is the owner of the movie and who is the observer "for the movie within the movie."[3] This poses the question that we may not "own" our consciousness, which in fact remains a mystery. We may be only an observer of it as it goes its own merry way, a discourse found in many of the books of the Indian philosopher J. Krishnamurti, which were written to help us transcend our minds—to simply be the observer of our mind's craziness and not act upon it. While advances have been made in discovering how memory works, in what area of the brain we remember language, for example, and how repetitive action can grow synaptic connections, science is not yet at first base in understanding how our consciousness or our memory system in general works. We also don't know the mechanics of how we think, create art, and communicate. This is a lot not to know.

As Stephen Pinker asserts in *How the Mind Works*, "The two deepest questions about the mind are 'What makes intelligence possible?' and 'What makes consciousness possible?'" He claims that cognitive scientists have taken steps to make intelligence at least "intelligible," but consciousness, "is still a riddle wrapped in a mystery inside an enigma."[4]

Dennett in *Consciousness Explained* contends:

> We do not yet have the final answers to any of the questions of cosmology and particle physics, molecular genetics and evolutionary theory, but we do know how to think about them. . . . With consciousness, however, we are still in a terrible muddle. Consciousness stands alone today as a topic that often leaves even the most sophisticated thinkers tongue-tied and confused.[5]

Dennett then goes on for another 433 pages attempting to explain it, primarily exploring the computational nature of the brain, but admitting that his premises are only theoretical.

Neuroscientists Mark Bear and Leon Cooper, after describing what science has discovered about the role of synapses in learning, memory storage, and information transfer, state in their article "From Molecules to Mental States":

> But we are not yet ready to uncork the bottles of champagne; for how all of this neural machinery is put together to produce our self-awareness, our consciousness is not understood. This problem seems so baffling that first we must convince ourselves that a solution is possible. Think about it in this way: Is it possible for us to construct from ordinary materials such as synapses, neurons and systems of neurons, a machine that is conscious?[6]

As I was writing these words, a panel discussion on consciousness at the UCLA campus was beginning on C-Span featuring four science authors, including Jeffery Schwartz, who is the author of *The Mind and the Brain* and also a practicing Buddhist. Holding a plastic brain in his hand, he was making the point that there is no evidence that consciousness exists in the brain. He said: "There is no way of explaining how this material stuff causes consciousness to arise."

But as we shall see, our consciousness may be altered by brain damage and disorders, and so it must be biologically encased in our brain—that is, unless one is fixated on a point of view that since consciousness is a mystery, a terrible muddle, that it may be, as Descartes contended, imported from the world of souls and spirits via the pineal gland.

One of my researchers for this book, Matthew Majeskie, a postgraduate student at the University of Wisconsin–Madison, sent me a note. I had asked him for materials relating to the physicality of consciousness, and he replied:

> In thinking about this, I am thinking about a quote made by John Horgan, former editor of *Scientific American*, writer and general contrarian. He once wrote that neuroscientists are like childlike prodigies who love to take things apart (e.g., a radio), but invariably are left with innumerable pieces (e.g., radio parts sprawled across the floor). Horgan and others have talked about this as the "Humpty-Dumpty Dilemma," one of the struggles of modern-day neuroscientists. That is, there are a lot of brilliant people working very hard when it comes to deconstructing the brain, but struggle mightily when it comes to putting it back together to make sense of a larger behavior.

This is probably why the theories of consciousness were left for so many years to philosophers and have only recently been taken up by neuroscientists; moreover, neuroscience is a relatively new field. What neuroscientists appear to be focusing on currently is finding what are called "neural correlates," the processes in the brain that appear to create consciousness. They do this through imaging techniques that make it possible to observe which areas of the brain are at work during various types of mental activities. In a special issue of *Scientific American* about the brain, Gerhard Roth writes: "Consciousness may be one of the greatest unsolved puzzles of neuroscience, but by learning more about the processes involved, researchers are at least gradually identifying the pieces."[7]

But where does this leave us?

Neuroscience is gradually demolishing the concept of the soul and the spirit world. As discussed earlier, neuroscientists can find no evidence that these nonmaterial entities influence the synaptic connections in our brain. Is the oozing and sparking of the synaptic connections that make us who we are in the soul, if it exists, and does it leave the body after death as the last function of the pineal gland or some other brain organ?

We know from studies of brain damage that synaptic connections and the neural circuitry they form do indeed control who we are. This is made evident in books such as *The Man Who Mistook His Wife for a Hat*, by neurologist Oliver Sacks. Sacks recounts the case histories of patients lost in the world of neurological disorders: people afflicted with enormous perceptual and intellectual distortions; patients who have lost their memories and with them the greater part of the pasts and are no longer able to recognize people (Sacks describes a man, who after a severe automobile accident, couldn't recognize himself in a mirror)[8] or common objects; people who are stricken with violent tics and grimaces or who shout involuntary obscenities, such as those with Tourette syndrome; or people whose own limbs become alien to them.

The neurological and severe mental disorders with which

we may be afflicted are generated from abnormalities in our synaptic connections that produce distortions of consciousness. Dozens of medications available today are aimed at mediating the mechanisms of synaptic connection. So we know that's where the problems reside. Even theologians attending the Vatican-sponsored conference on "Neuroscience and Divine Action," as reported by Joseph LeDoux in *Synaptic Self,* believed less in the nonmaterial concept of the soul, "but believed in a soul that is pretty much one and the same as the neurally mediated mind, a part of the physical world."[9] The conference ended inconclusively, however, according to LeDoux. Despite taking a wider view, the theologians couldn't make all the pieces fit together. Actually, no one has.

For those of us whose proclivities run to the more rational, we are still left adrift at sea. As we saw in chapter 1, we haven't been able to prove that the soul and the spirit world *doesn't* exist, but we still know that great doubt has been cast over their existence. We can't hang our hat on them as easily as the seventeenth-century philosophers who didn't know about the work of our synapses. This leaves us with our own consciousness to make sense of the world. But having gotten this far in our quest to understand where our consciousness exists as a biological unit in our brains, we are still, unfortunately, in the Humpty-Dumpty stage. Further, while we have learned that our memory is stored among the neural circuits that are created by formations of the synapses, we don't know very much about how we use that memory to generate our intellectual capacity and our sense of reason. We learn by rote how to add 10 plus 10, but we don't know how we synthesize that memory in our consciousness to think about the result, or to write it down, or to speak it. If we have aphasia, a speech disorder, for instance, we may be able to think about the result but not speak it.

The upshot is that we don't know what happens in our brains when we add 10 plus 10, let alone when we do complicated mathematical equations. In other words, we don't know how we think—what the physical mechanism of it is. We could thus formulate the proposition: *If we don't know how we think, then what do we know for sure?*

Is it possible that the brain—with its mental mechanics that were not designed by any of our engineers and which we have relatively little knowledge of—is capable of deceiving us into thinking we are more than we are? This is difficult to ponder because the mind as it resides in the brain, as previously noted, appears intent on keeping us in our little virtual realities that provide us with explanations in a world that is, in actuality, enigmatic. If we hear questions such as "What is the meaning of life?" the less spiritual among us will usually drift away, because, as we will see later, questions like these are rationally unanswerable and, moreover, can end up deflating our sense of status. And we don't like losing status.

One thing we know for certain is that the architecture of the brain involves thousands of parallel neural circuits that control what we think, feel, and do at any given instant; they in some way work together at any given moment to create our consciousness, as well as to control our unconscious functions, in addition to regulating our heart beat, for example.

Steven Johnson, in *Mind Wide Open*, analogized the brain's architecture as "more like an orchestra than a soloist, with dozens of players contributing to the overall mix. You can hear the symphony as a unified wash of sound, but you can also distinguish the trombones from the timpani, the violins from the cellos."[10]

It would appear, however, that there are far more than "dozens of players" contributing to the overall mix. If we're a psychologist on a small cruise boat in a raging storm, simultaneously attempting to keep our balance and keeping our fears in check, while giving a speech to a group of our peers, there may be hundreds if not thousands of players in our brain contributing to Johnson's metaphorical "overall mix." Somehow, all these individual transmissions in our consciousness work together to keep us steady in the storm, while reciting our speech and interacting with our audience.

I kept this chapter short to reflect and emphasize that one of the most important things that we should know—where our consciousness resides and how it works, and how we think—we probably know next to nothing about.

It would appear that when all is said and done, on this high plane of conjecture, we are all equal in our ignorance, scientists included, though many know that they don't know. It's time to get off our high horses.

5.

OUR PRIMAL EMOTIONAL DRIVES AND REACTIONS ARE BASICALLY AUTOMATIC AND FREQUENTLY FLAWED

The advantage of the emotions is that they lead us astray.
Oscar Wilde[1]

Why do we know as much as we do about our primal or primary emotions, such as fear, anxiety, aggressiveness, and sexual urges and feelings, and so little about our consciousness and intelligence?

In a word: rats.

As the second of my researchers, Melissa Rosenkranz, another graduate student at the University of Wisconsin–Madison, who specializes in neuroscience, put it in a note:

> The structure of neuron cells and the nature of synaptic communication/connection is the same in all animals, even in insects. Rats are one mammal which have a brain organization that is relatively close to humans, or close enough from which to gather useful information. Rats in our society are a much less valued creature than other animals we could use for research. They breed frequently and are plentiful and cheap.

In other words, everything we described in chapter 2 about neurons and synapses applies not only to humans and animals, including rats, but to insects. The difference is in how those neural circuits are organized. In dogs, for example, there are far more neural circuits applied to their senses of smell and hearing than in humans, so their senses in these areas are more acute. Humans, on the other hand, have much more circuitry devoted to sight than do dogs. We can see better, and we can also get glasses from an optometrist to improve impaired sight, because, unlike dogs, we can use an eye chart. The bee has 90,000 neurons, with circuitry that allows it to work amiably with compatriots on a virtual assembly line to produce honey.

All species of animal have neural circuitry that allows them to flourish in their manner of living and survival. But that circuitry all evolves from the identical neurons and synaptic mechanisms, including the same neurotransmitters found in humans.

For brain research among humans, we are basically limited to brain imaging and the study of the consequences of various forms of brain disease and damage, as well as their treatment. As Francis Crick, codiscoverer of the structure of the DNA molecule, and other scientists have pointed out, they aren't allowed ethically to tinker seriously with living human brains.[2] And you can't ask a dead brain anything.

Humans also share with higher animals the brain's limbic system, an area just below the cerebral cortex that controls many of our bodily functions and also mediates central features of our basic emotional mechanisms. Primatologists such as Jane Goodall, Dian Fossey, Birute Galdikas, Frans De Waal, and Charles Snowdon have spent years studying higher animals in the wild, including chimpanzees, gorillas, baboons, and, in Snowdon's case, marmosets and tamarins—small South American monkeys, which, Snowdon observes, "appear to have better family values in general than humans do: fidelity, low levels of conflict, parents rewarding offspring for helping with infant care, no teen pregnancies."[3]

Before I wrote *Battling the Inner Dummy: The Craziness of Apparently Normal People*, I could perceive the humanness in these higher animals, but I couldn't make a strong connection between them and us. Learning from the above-named scientists how we share many aspects of the limbic system with these higher animals put it all in place. We are different from the chimp, the animal closest to humans genetically, primarily because we have a much larger cerebral cortex, which allows us to think in more complex ways. Theoretically, through the cultivation of civilizations, this should have diminished the aggressive instincts we share with chimps; after all, we have the capacity to observe and reflect on these destructive tendencies as if they were part of a second human within ourselves. Indian philosopher J. Krishnamurti, mentioned in the previous chapter, might have been alluding to our inner primal drives as the "observed" and our cortex as the "observer."[4] Many of us, however, don't get this. We think of ourselves as one. We may have an impulse to backstab someone at work who is in the way of our getting ahead, and some of us will do it, because, we'll say, "this is who I am." The point is that this doesn't have to be who we are, but only a part of us that needs to be observed, disciplined, and repressed when necessary.

Among other things, the limbic system mediates our primal systems for status and aggression, territorialism, attachment to others, sex, and survival. Neuroscientists use the term "mediate" when describing the functions of this system because other brain components are usually involved in generating emotional drives and the feelings they produce.

Survival embraces our general well-being, including our fight or flight mechanism, which pressures us to do one or the other when we are seriously threatened. If you were an animal in the jungle, or an early human living in caves, these are the very basic systems you would need to survive long enough to reproduce, which, according to Richard Dawkins, author of *The Selfish Gene*, is really all nature has in mind for us.[5]

If you have a large number of siblings, or are a student of politics, or are working in a harsh corporate environment, you understand innately what "the status system" is. The stronger among us fight to be in charge, to be dominant. The status imperative for the earliest humans had to be of paramount importance because it maintained order within the tribes. It still does in animal clans. In these primitive environments, alphas rise to the top through battle, eye stares, or other aggressive rituals; and there is hierarchal ranking down to the omegas. Among many monkeys, Charles Snowdon reports that "status tension," the struggle for gaining a higher position within a clan, exists on a daily basis among all individuals, except for the alphas, who are certain of their dominant rank, and omegas, the lowest of the lows, who appear to know their place and have no fight left.[6]

We humans also innately understand the territorial system. Among many of the higher animals, we see them staking out their territories. Wolf packs are known for urinating on their borders, and alien wolf packs that penetrate those borders will be subject to vicious attack. (Yet, wolves, marmosets, and other cooperative species show little aggression within their families.) We see this system in ourselves. We are innately impelled to protect our territory and possessions from outsiders, sometimes passionately. A friend of mine had a beautiful willow tree located near the borderline of his property. Every time the leaves and branches of the tree spread over the property line, no matter how delightful the sight, his neighbor would climb a ladder and cut down the intruding branches. They weren't his branches, but his territorial system led him to think that they were intruders. Craziness. This behavior emanates from these compelling drives that continue to intrude in our lives, when we let them, which lead to irrational outlooks and actions. In general, many of these limbic drives were more useful among our primitive ancestors.

We also innately understand the attachment system, or social bonding, which experts in the field break down into five compartments: romantic, family, kin, friends, and strangers. Our attachment mechanisms are well studied. The romantic attachment, or the biosocial romantic attachment mechanism, is an evolutionary system of neural circuitry in our brains, male or female, that impels us to seek out mates who, theoretically, under the pressures of natural selection, will produce the strongest possible babies.

That's what it does, even if we are just out on the town having a drink and indulging in interesting conversation, with the thought of babies the furthest thing from our minds. Then, suddenly, we look across the crowded room and see someone who this romantic system thinks will produce a strong baby—but to motivate us, it may impel us to think this is the love of our life. In reality, this stranger may be psychopathic, someone who would cause us nothing but misery after the initial sexual episodes. While this biological system of attraction might have served its purpose when we were living in the caves and on the savannas, when coupling with a psychopath and being unhappy was not a matter of great concern to the group as a whole, or when women may have been sold into marriage by their families, it frequently hasn't adapted well to the needs of today. This can be illustrated by the 50 percent divorce rate and the millions of unhappy relationship breakups.

Family attachment is obvious to most of us. The more normal of us feel immediate love for our offspring, and we feel familial love for our parents, siblings, and other relatives. Familial love, however, can be eroded by persistent family conflicts. As a result, feelings of affection toward family members may last a lifetime or only a few years or even less. Feelings toward friends can be just as strong, but they may be equally or more vulnerable. And finally, some of us are better at meeting, mingling, and bonding with strangers than others.

The sex drive is obvious for most of our readers and needs no further explanation. We also understand to some degree the components of our survival mechanism, which includes the feelings of fright, anxiety, and terror at the prospect of being hurt or killed as well as the drives to eat and drink to stay healthy.

All these drives and the feelings that emanate from their outcomes can be tracked on psychological scales. My favorite psychological scale is 1 to 10, because it is straightforward. There are other psychological scales composed of complex mathematics called "constructs" that are much more difficult and beyond the scope of this book.

For example, the neighbor who cut down the branches of the beautiful tree extending on his property can probably be labeled at least a 7 on the territorial scale. If he were a 10, he would probably exact cruel punishment on the neighbor who owned the tree, perhaps even growling, cursing, or threatening him with a baseball bat.

A woman who is a number 10 on the sexual scale would be a sex addict who could never get enough. A woman who is a number 2 would be asexual and couldn't care less if she did it or not.

The more normal of us fall in the middle of the scales of most drives and emotional reactions. We may feel a strong drive to have sex with a friend's wife, but we've learned how to control and mask the impulse and thus project an air of nonchalance. We may feel intense envy when we see that a neighbor has purchased a car that is a good two notches in status over ours, but we are able to go on with life with the old car, even though the envy might rankle us every time that neighbor's car rolls past our home. If the scale of that envy, however, is high, and our impulse control at any given moment is low, we'll be visiting an auto dealer in no time and spending money on a new car that we can probably ill afford.

Our drives or motivations for status, territory, attachment, sex, and survival carry with them what Stanford professor of pyschology Albert Bandura has called *outcome expectancies*.[7] Depending on our rank on the appropriate psychological scales, some of us feel stronger expectancy feelings in given areas of our lives than in others.

Most of us know that when we meet our expectations, or "outcome expectancies," as Bandura describes them, we feel *rewarded* with positive emotions. We'll feel happiness, elation, gladness, triumph, delight, joy, and jubilation. If our expectations are not met, we may feel *punished* with sadness, anguish, depression, irritation, disappointment, and frustration. We may experience these even if the matter is relatively trivial, such as our favorite football team losing an important game.

What most of us don't understand is that this reward and punishment system is built into our brain's basic emotional circuitry, of which the limbic system is a significant part, *and it is practically automatic.*

We drive into our apartment garage one day prepared to park in our reserved parking space. Our "expectancy" is that this space will be ready for us. We see another car has taken our space. The expectancy is thus unmet, and we may be punished with feelings of anger, frustration, and vindictiveness. Or someone steps in front of us at a checkout counter line in a supermarket. Our expectancy is that the space in front of us is ours. Again we may be punished with the same emotions.

Are our reactive emotions to a met or unmet outcome expectation really that automatic?

They apparently are. Our reward/punishment system, which Freud called the "pleasure-unpleasure principle," has since been abridged in a separate body of academic work to the "pleasure principle."[8] If we imagine ourselves as a deity or the intrinsic force behind natural selection in charge of designing this primitive section of the brain, for the sheer survival of our early primitives, with little or no communication skills, we would have probably done the same.

Now imagine yourself as a leader of a tribe of Neanderthal cave dwellers some fifty thousand years ago, when our language skills were brusque and tools were crude. Life was harsh. Children of fifteen were considered adults, and the early thirties was considered old age. If you were successful in leading a great hunt or in gaining the territory of a rival down the river, the pleasure system *rewarded* you by triggering neural circuits that released joy and happiness. You likely hopped about with elation in response to your victory. You loved the feeling so much, you wanted to conquer again. If you failed in the hunt or in leading the fight against another tribe, you would likely experience the punishing feelings of depression, gloom, despondency, frustration, anxiety, and so on. You would likely sit there that evening, sulking around the fire (Neanderthals knew how to make one), while others in the tribe might try to comfort you. Then that night you gained a fresh sexual conquest, and you'd become joyful and elated again. The next day a rabbit you were chasing got away, and so once again, you'd become frustrated and depressed.

Was this the start of our ups and downs?

While this emotional system of reward and punishment was critical to our survival as primitives, the neural circuitry that harbors it remains with us today. Some of us, however, have become more adept than others at repressing and masking the feelings that they trigger, particularly the best poker players. It is probably the limbic area of the brain and related circuitry that we can blame for mediating our daily ups and downs. It is either satisfied, not satisfied, or in a state of rest.

In her book, *Therapist's Guide to Clinical Intervention*, Sharon L. Johnson creates a "List of Feeling Words," divided between "pleasant feelings" and "difficult/unpleasant feelings."[9]

I counted 116 "pleasant feelings," such as peaceful, thankful, thrilled, gay, confident, delighted, content, joyous, hopeful, happy, satisfied, fulfilled, chipper, upbeat, optimistic, lighthearted, and cheerful.

I counted 139 "difficult/unpleasant feelings," including ashamed, powerless, fearful, crushed, desperate, confused, embarrassed, miserable, sulky, infuriated, enraged, insensitive, lonely, remorseful, suspicious, menaced, rejected, and tense.

In addition, I added about 60 more unpleasant feelings from a perusal of a pocket dictionary, including jealous, suicidal, antagonistic, regretful, hopeless, outraged, violated, shocked, manipulated, reproached, chastised, forsaken, slighted, abandoned, disgraced, unraveled, intimidated, envious, embittered, dirtied, slighted, scornful, and stressed, which put the total at approximately 200.

The brain's range of feelings apparently includes far more to punish than to reward us, which probably means that whoever or whatever designed our brains was presumably a strong disciplinarian.

To get back to the question, do these rewarding and punishing feelings hit us automatically, or "autonomically," to use the scientific word? It usually is automatic, but because the brain is ever changing—it is not the same any two minutes at a time according to neuroscientist Gerald Edelman[10]—there may be modifying circumstances. If we are waiting for an overdue city bus on a rainy, cold night, when we just received some depressing news at the office, and we have to get home quickly to pick up the kids, we will probably feel more anger and other negative feelings than we would on a balmy summer night when we are under less pressure.

Our emotional reactions at any given time also help establish our moods. If we get extremely good news, it puts us in a good mood, for a period of time that correlates with the weight of the news received or until we receive bad news, which can put us in a bad mood. (The weight of the news may vary from person to person, since what may seem catastrophic to one person may seem less serious to another.) Moods are basically the sustaining of a given emotion over a period of time. Most of us have mood swings. For the more emotionally stable among us, those swings might be hardly discernable; at the other end of the scale they may be extreme. The latter may be happy one moment, sullen the next. On the extreme end of this scale is bipolar disorder, in which the mood swings between depression and elation or mania can be enormous. The majority of us are apparently somewhere in the middle.

Our reactions to given situations also vary in intensity according to the intensity of our outcome expectations. An excellent illustration would be envisioning two teams competing with one another in a baseball game.

At the end of a regular season game, the winners stay on the field, and their positive emotions are radiating. They are happy, elated, and smiling, congratulating one another. Then they walk with shoulders high off the field to the dressing room. The losing team, immediately after the last out, walks sullenly to the locker room, looking unhappy. If it's the World Series, the expectancies are much higher, more intense, and so are the rewarding and punishing feelings. The winning team is now on the field, some of the members crying with happiness, hugging each other, totally jubilant. They finally go to their locker room, where they pour champagne over each other, then come back on the field for encores before their adoring fans, who mirror many of the same rewarding feelings. In the losers' locker room, we see scenes of total dejection, heads hung in despair, tears streaming down faces. They are experiencing extremely depressed feelings that in some may linger for months or even years. They are being punished by the "unplea-sure" neural circuitry that kicks in when an outcome expecta-tion isn't met. In general, the greater the consequences of our outcome expectancies, the greater the intensities of our posi-tive or negative emotions.

The neural circuitry for only some of our emotional feelings is understood. As noted, the limbic system's amygdala is known to regulate our fear, anger, and rage. The stria terminalis mediates our feelings of anxiety. The hypothalamus is involved in the regulation of our sexual drive and sexual behavior. Many neuroscientists believe that love, hate, and our drive for social bonding is regulated by the limbic system as a whole—"broadly distributed," is a favorite scientific term. However, rel-atively little is known about the neurobiology of the circuitry that regulates the hundreds of specific rewarding, painful, and other feelings that we experience every day.

Neurologist Antonio Damasio, in *Looking for Spinoza: Joy, Sorrow and the Feeling Brain*, describes how one of his colleagues was treating a patient who had Parkinson's by implanting elec-trodes in her brain stem.[11] She had no history of depression, mood swings, or of any psychiatric disorder. She was awake and chatting amiably during the treatment. While one electrode relieved her symptoms, another created something unexpected:

> The patient stopped her ongoing conversation quite abruptly, cast her eyes down and to her right side, then leaned slightly to the right and her emotional expression became one of sadness. After a few sec-onds, she suddenly began to cry. Tears flowed and her entire demeanor was one of profound misery. Soon she was sobbing. As this display continued she began talking about how deeply sad she felt, how she had no energies left to go on living in this manner, how hopeless and exhausted she was. Asked about what was happening, her words were quite telling:

> *I'm falling down in my head. I no longer wish to live,*
> *to see anything, hear anything, feel anything. I'm fed up*
> *with life. I've had enough. . . . I don't want to live any-*
> *more, I'm disgusted with life. Everything is useless. . . . I*
> *feel worthless. . . .*
>
> The physician in charge of the treatment realized
> that this unusual event was due to the [electrical] cur-
> rent and aborted the procedure. About ninety seconds
> after the current was interrupted the patient's
> behavior returned to normal. The sobbing stopped as
> abruptly as it begun. The sadness vanished from the
> patient's face. The verbal reports of sadness also termi-
> nated. Very rapidly, she smiled, appeared relaxed, and
> for the next five minutes was quite playful, even joc-
> ular. What was that all about? she asked. She had felt
> awful but did not know why.[12]

Damasio conjectured that the electrode's current had flowed
into one of the brain stem's nuclei, "an ensemble," he noted, that
produces the emotion sadness. The behavior of the patient mir-
rored that of someone with a classic case of clinical depression.[13]

In another case, Damasio describes how electrical stimulation in the left frontal lobe of the patient "consistently and
exclusively evoked laughter. The laughter was quite genuine, so
much so that the observers described it as contagious. It came
entirely out of the blue—the patient was not being shown or
told anything funny." When the treatment stopped, the excessive laughter stopped. The patch of brain affected measured
only two centimeters by two centimeters.[14]

Steven Johnson, in *Mind Wide Open,* describes a similar inci-
dent:

> Doctors at the University of California Medical School
> . . . recently located a small region near the front of
> the left brain that appears to trigger the feeling of

mirth; while treating a sixteen-year-old epileptic patient, they applied a tiny jolt of electric current to the area, which caused the patient to find humor in whatever she happened to be looking at. This wasn't merely a physical reflex of laughter; things genuinely seemed funny to her when the region was stimulated. "You guys are just so funny—standing around," she told the startled doctors.[15]

I found these descriptions fascinating—including another one, which turned a patient ardently religious—because they reflect that our emotional feelings are *physical*, that they are part of our brain's biology, and that they ostensibly have a propensity for being turned on and off as easily as a light switch.

Joseph LeDoux, in *The Emotional Brain*, brilliantly describes the nature of our "emotional memories."[16] They differ from our normal memories in that they result from traumas of all sorts—an accident, a terrifying experience, death of a loved one, abusive parents, bullying in the schoolyard, rejection, a serious argument or fight. They are frightening at the time, but, even worse, these memories can become enduring and distort our outlooks thereafter. They appear to react more strongly to negative than to positive events. Emotional memories are locked in separate neural circuitry in the brain, mediated primarily by two of the limbic organs, the hippocampus and the amygdala. The late Ronald Reagan, in his heyday as an actor in Hollywood, took a plane to Catalina Island, just off the coast of Los Angeles. The plane ride was so rough, it created such terror in Reagan's mind, that he didn't fly again for thirty years. It created an emotional memory that twisted his disposition about air travel. Even if later he forgot most of the details of the harrowing flight, the memory still remained and continued to affect his attitudes about flying and possibly other things related to heights and being confined. If we are aware of these memories and want to rid ourselves of them, we may be able to do so through cognitive therapy (the therapist directly confronts our distortions) and through other techniques. Some of us can never overcome them, however. We all have emotional memories. We might still remember at the age of sixty, being bullied at the age of fourteen and looking like the fool in front of the other kids. Incidents like these can affect our interactions with others for years or even our entire lives. Our fear of being vulnerable in social situations can be automatic and enduring.

Freud asserted that these emotional memories, which comprised a significant portion of the metaphorical "id," our subconscious, have no sense of time, awareness, or logic.

In my book *Battling the Inner Dummy*, I told the story of Sarah Reinwald, someone of my acquaintance, who at the age of eighteen was in a terrible elevator accident. The elevator she was exiting began to slip, and somehow she got caught between the door and the front wall of the shaft; it crushed her arm and leg. After almost a dozen operations, Sarah was able to resume her life. But from then on and up through today, now at the age of sixty-seven, she will go to extraordinary lengths to avoid riding in an elevator. When she has no other choice but to use an elevator, she experiences intense pangs of fear. This type of memory has no sense of *time, awareness, or logic*, as Freud said. No one at all, including family, friends, and a string of therapists, has been able to rationally resolve her fear.

"Look, Sarah," we might say to her today, standing with her in the lobby of a high-rise office building, facing a bank of elevators, one of which she must take to visit a dentist on the twenty-third floor, "That accident happened to you over forty-nine years ago; it is time to get over it."

"I know that," she would likely reply.

"You realize that the odds of this ever happening to you again are simply infinite. You realize that, don't you?"

"Yes, I realize that."

"So you know that if you step in an elevator car today, it is practically impossible that any harm can come to you."

"Yes, I know that."

"Well then, good. Let's get on the elevator and leave all this nonsense behind you, once and for all."

"Not on your life. I'm going home." And she'd find a new dentist on the ground floor.

This is what the mind knows, but isn't telling us. Her mind knows she would be just fine, but it can't penetrate the strong neurological connections that hold the emotional memory.

In his book *Emotional Intelligence*, Daniel Goleman metaphorically calls this type of display an "emotional hijacking." He also uses the metaphors "neural hijacking" and "limbic hijacking."

Joseph LeDoux theorizes that it's the hippocampus, a limbic component of the brain, as noted, that mediates our emotional memories. He conjectures that it also harbors what he calls our "emotional sentinel."[17] This is the system that constantly checks to see if whatever we are experiencing in our lives at the moment matches emotional memories that have upset us in the past. If so, it signals the amygdala, which then may trigger the neural circuitry that unleashes anger, fear, and other such emotions.

Interestingly enough, our frontal cortex—that part of the brain just behind our forehead—was the last portion of our brain to evolve. When viewing reconstructions of primitive man or watching higher animals, such as the chimpanzee and gorilla, you'll see flatter foreheads on them. The frontal cortex found in *Homo sapiens*, modern-day humans, is considered our "executive center." One of its purposes is to receive or intercept impulses from the amygdala or other brain components that mediate emotion, and then to determine if the impulse makes rational sense. If we are at a party with our significant other, with whom we have a great relationship, and someone who is extremely sexually attractive makes a pass at us, our frontal cortex, if operating normally, will reject the impulse to take the next step. If it is not operating normally, we might take the next step, which could lead to all sorts of complications. "Oh well," we might rationalize to ourselves, "another unfortunate hijacking," but then we'd pay the price.

Another vivid example of an "emotional hijacking" happened to a young woman named Jennifer, whom I came across while channel surfing one night and stopped to watch on a rerun of the *Jenny Jones* television show. Please, forgive me, it was late, there was nothing else to watch. Also, if you are a student of human irrationality, as I am, these programs are a perfect showcase for the craziness of apparently normal people. Okay? Anyway, Jennifer was a beautiful model in her early twenties who said that she was unable to have a satisfying relationship with any man because she couldn't trust men.

She traced this anxiety to an experience she had in the eighth grade, when she said she was tall, ungainly, and unattractive. A plot was hatched by her schoolmates who told her that the most attractive boy in the class, the idol of most of the girls, was asking questions about her and wanted to take her out.

Jennifer said she could still remember the thrill of the expectation and the even greater feeling of exaltation when, as she was surrounded by her schoolmates, the boy walked up to her during recess, as if he were going to ask her out. Then the boy said something mildly insulting and walked away. Her schoolmates doubled over in laughter, considering it a schoolyard prank. But, for Jennifer, the "traumatic moment" became a strong emotional memory, distorting her perception of men. Despite the fact that years later Jennifer turned into a beautiful model, her hippocampus continued to hold onto the memory of the insult, complete with the experience of being perceived as unattractive. At the first opportunity in a new relationship with a man, her emotional sentinel would apparently seek out any words or actions that would match the memory of the trauma. Without any intelligence or "logic," the system would mistakenly perceive an experience in the relationship as matching up with the schoolyard prank. It would then trigger the neural circuits that create fear and anxiety, awakening anew the "emotional hijacking." Thus, the relationship would soon end.

On the television show, the producers tracked down the boy who had caused the schoolyard trauma, who was now a young adult with a family. He couldn't remember the prank and seemed only vaguely to remember Jennifer. Whether confronting the perpetrator who had caused her an emotional hijacking would allow her anxieties about men to dissipate remains to be seen. The point is that her emotional reaction, each time she was with a new man, was automatic. There was nothing she could rationally do, just as Sarah was unable to handle getting into an elevator without being terrified.

Traumas seem to produce at least three levels of punishment.

The first level of punishment would encompass the painful emotions that we have just described, which we might have to endure for minutes, hours, days, years, or even a lifetime to varying intensities, depending on the strength of the traumas and our vulnerabilities to them. Still, for the most part, the majority of us remain rationally grounded in carrying out our lives. We might be grief stricken, heartbroken, terrified, enraged, frustrated, angered, vindictive, jealous, or whatever, but most of us could still go to work or raise our kids and get through the day.

The second level of punishment would be the infliction of *neuroses* that can make us irrational in specific or general behavioral areas. *The Oxford Companion to the Mind* describes neuroses as "more or less fixed and resistant to modification through the normal processes of learning."[18] Neuroses, in a sense, are an overreaction of the mind to traumatic events, in that they change our outlooks for the worse and can be extremely difficult to neutralize. They include, in the most simplistic of descriptions:[19]

Clinical Depression—A state of severe depression that endures over time. It prevents any sense of pleasure or joy. Instead, we experience overwhelming sadness. We feel hopeless, wasted, desperate, and despondent. We find it extremely difficult just to get out of bed in the morning and to carry on with our lives. The feelings can be so disturbingly dark that we may consider suicide.

Phobias—Irrational fears, such as those exhibited by Sarah and Jennifer. *The Encyclopedia of Phobias, Fears and Anxieties*[20] lists over one thousand phobias, including irrational fears of heights, peanut butter, crossing streets, and spending money. There is even a fear of the northern lights called auroraphobia and a fear of the color red called erythrophobia. "False Alarm" has frequently been used as a metaphor for describing phobias.

Anxiety Disorder—Persistent feelings of apprehension, worry, and tension with no apparent external cause. It is the feeling of worry, but out of control. We need feelings of anxiety, just as we need fear when there is a real impending danger. It is when the anxieties have no basis in fact and begin to overrun and take control of our lives that they become a disorder.

Obsessive-Compulsive Disorder—A repetitive act or thought that is clearly excessive. "Clearly excessive" is the operative phrase. Many of us are obsessed with activities in our lives, which may be helpful in performing them. Obsessive-compulsive disorders go far beyond this. The two most common behavioral compulsions are washing and checking. We may wash our hands dozens of times a day. We may check the lock dozens of times at night. Obsessions are thought rituals. If we have obsessive thoughts about auto accidents, we might ask the question, "I didn't hit anyone with my car, did I?" dozens of times a day. And we might not have even been in the car that day.

Posttraumatic Stress (or Syndrome) Disorder—Many of the survivors of the World Trade Center attack suffered this syndrome, which is similar to what used to be referred to as "shell shock" among afflicted soldiers who had been in battle. The syndrome may include tremors, sleep disturbance, restlessness, heart palpitation, and increased perspiration, among other problems. It may last a few months or a few years after the event, or throughout lifetimes.

These neuroses are mood disorders that distort reality. And they may be further warping our virtual realities, which may already be distorted by attachments to specious facts and convictions.

Then there are the *personality disorders*, which are not formally included under the definition of neurotic disorders, but should, however, be included at this level of punishment, because, at their extremes, they can cause as much distortion in our outlooks as the neuroses. Among the personality disorders are the following, which I've defined here by simple descriptions.[21]

(By the way, if you've been wondering about the strange behavior of your neighbor across the street who never comes out of the house, or who wears gaudy clothing, or is a megalomaniac, you might find some answers below. Neurotics and people with personality disorders are not confined to any one location. They are free as birds, sometimes seeking professional help, more often not. They might include one or both of your parents, a sibling, friend, coworker, or anyone. Even if you are close to them for whatever reason, you may be more of a victim than they are.)

Paranoid Personality Disorder—If we have this disorder, we are mistrustful of others, even in the most benign of situations;

we see people essentially as devious, deceptive, treacherous, and covertly manipulative, even when in reality they are supportive of us. When subject to this disorder, we expect to be harmed or demeaned by others and bear grudges or are unforgiving of perceived insults and slights.

Avoidant Personality Disorder—If we have this disorder, we view ourselves as inept or incompetent and avoid people, as a general rule, who we think might hurt or demean us through comments or actions. We are easily hurt by criticism or disapproval and have no close friends or confidants. We exaggerate the risks of doing something ordinary, anything outside the regular routine. (We may frequently cancel social plans because we anticipate we'll be exhausted by the effort of getting there.)

Schizoid Personality Disorder—We don't view ourselves as inept, but we avoid close relationships with anyone; we see ourselves as self-sufficient and prefer to be alone. We have no close friends or confidants. We almost always choose solitary activities and are aloof, cold, and rarely reciprocate gestures or facial expressions such as smiles and nods.

Antisocial Personality Disorder—We lie, cheat, and steal, and feel chronic anger. We have had patterns of irresponsible behavior since the age of fifteen or earlier. Lacking remorse, we feel justified in having hurt, mistreated, or stolen from another. We repeatedly fail to honor financial obligations, including support for our children. We are irritable and aggressive. There is a focus on criminal behavior in this disorder. (More about this in the next chapter.)

Dependent Personality Disorder—We function properly only when there is a strong dominant person in our lives on whom we can depend. We are unable to make everyday decisions without an excessive amount of advice or reassurance from others. We tend to agree with people even when we think they are wrong. Frequently we are preoccupied with feelings of being abandoned and feel devastated or helpless when relationships end.

Narcissistic Personality Disorder—We view ourselves almost as princes and princesses. We consider ourselves superior and entitled to special favors and favorable treatment. We have a grandiose sense of self-importance and are preoccupied with fantasies of unlimited success, power, brilliance, beauty, or ideal love. We feel we are above the rules that govern others, and we react to criticism with feelings of rage, shame, or humiliation.

Histrionic Personality Disorder—The key descriptive word here is "expressiveness," which embodies the tendency to emotionalize or romanticize all situations. We continually try to impress and captivate others. We view ourselves as glamorous, impressive, and deserving of attention. Often inappropriately sexually seductive in appearance or behavior, we express our personality with incongruous exaggeration.

Passive-Aggressive Personality Disorder—We procrastinate and don't meet deadlines. When asked to do something we don't want to do, we become sulky, irritable, or argumentative. We believe that we are doing a better job than others. We resent useful suggestions, obstruct the efforts of others by failing to do our share of the work, and unreasonably criticize people in positions of authority behind their backs. When with them, we may be fawning.

Borderline Personality Disorder—Our moods are unstable and turbulent. We are extremely impulsive. We usually don't know what we're going to be doing next. One minute we want to be with people, the next minute we don't. We frequently display temper and anger. We have chronic feelings of emptiness or boredom. We may take to mutilating ourselves, cutting our arms or wrists, or burning and biting ourselves.

There has got be a better name than borderline for this disorder.

Did you recognize anyone you know with these disorders?

To complicate matters, if we have one diagnosable personality disorder, we usually have others as well. For example, 48 percent of people with borderline disorder also have paranoid disorder, 55 percent have narcissistic disorder, and 50 percent also have dependent disorder.[22] Further, as with any disorder, each may afflict us on a scale ranging from mild to moderate to extreme.

We can be a real mess.

The third level of punishment would be an infliction of *psychoses* that take us out of reality, such as schizophrenia and psychotic paranoia, in which we are frequently unable to distinguish between fact and fantasy. (One might imagine that in the brutish world where the limbic system reigns, Freud's metaphor of the id, that a psychosis might be a crude device for providing us with comfort, since we may no longer know what is going on in the real world.) But, in the real world we live in, these afflications can be devastating for those who suffer from them and for their loved ones. The most severe psychoses are described as follows:[23]

Schizophrenia—The simple type is distinguished by gradual and insidious reduction in external relationships and interest. Emotional expression becomes flattened; thinking tends to be disorganized. The sufferer's general level of activity diminishes; he shows progressively less and less use of his inner resources and retreats to less demanding or stereotyped forms of behavior. For example, a skilled industrial designer who develops simple schizophrenia may retreat to routine factory work. The catatonic form is characterized by striking changes in bodily movement; sufferers may become almost completely immobile, often assuming statuesque positions. The paranoid type, usually appearing later in life than the others, is characterized by unrealistic, illogical, hallucinatory thinking, and by bizarre delusions of being persecuted or of being a great person (e.g., of being Jesus Christ or the "emperor of the world").

Bipolar Disorder—This psychosis is characterized by recurring, sometimes cyclic, attacks of depression and manic (excited) behavior. During the depressive state, the sufferer typically looks unhappy, says he feels hopeless and worthless and that he considers life a torment. Evidence of suicidal thinking is observed in about 75 percent of these people, and actual suicide attempts are found to be made by at least 10 to 15 percent. In fact, suicide constitutes the greatest risk in manic depressive psychosis. A small percentage of sufferers (especially females) kill their small children, whom they seem to consider parts of themselves, immediately prior to their suicide attempts. When manic, the individual typically shows unrestrained good humor; however, he may change to sarcastic, irritable, and hostile when he comes into conflict with his environment. He may consider himself rich, strong, and very healthy, and make grandiose plans; he may dissipate large amounts of money in a few days. He cannot concentrate on any topic more than briefly and his speech is rapid. During depressive or manic episodes, the psychotic patient shows no insight into the abnormal nature of his mood.

Psychotic Paranoia—This condition is characterized by apparently logical systems of delusions (false beliefs). The person nourishes beliefs that appear to be absurd to others; nevertheless, he can provide convincing and apparently plausible arguments to support them. The psychotically paranoid sufferer does not resort to primitive ways of thinking to demonstrate the validity of his delusions (as schizophrenics do); rather his thinking is generally logical, once the false premises are accepted. Often, mere possibilities and coincidences are considered as conclusive evidence; the sufferer feels persecuted or imagines plots and conspiracies organized against him or against parts of society with which he identifies. At times he sees himself as a savior of society whose mission it is to unmask the obscure plotting of clandestine agencies. The sufferer becomes so sure of the validity of his beliefs that he may go to the extent of killing the alleged persecutors; more often, however, he may become the plaintiff in an almost endless array of legal suits.

As noted, it is generally agreed that traumas (which might include inordinate emotional or physical neglect) in our life are a primary cause in the development of these and other mental disorders. Many of these traumas happen when we are young. They may become magnified in our minds and may still be affecting us well into our adult years. Further, between two siblings, a trauma that both experience may affect one severely and the other hardly at all. The prevailing theory is that we each have our own genetic predispositions for vulnerability that apply to mental as well as physical characteristics. Among the major studies of identical twins reared apart, particularly the ongoing study at the University of Minnesota, which at this point has registered thousands of identical twins reared apart, it has been concluded that about 50 percent of our mental characteristics are inherited. Thus, there is a 50 percent chance that at birth both twins may have a genetic predisposition for shyness, for example. Whether the shyness continues to express itself as the twins age would depend on the strength of the predisposition and how they were raised. Those of us who are parents recognize the innate differences between the children we raise. (A description on how genes shuffle themselves at fertilization is found in chapter 12.)

The key word for traumas that lead to neurotic, personality, and psychotic disorders appears to be *vulnerability*. How vulnerable are we at the time to a specific form of trauma? Even with schizophrenia, when we are taken out of reality for periods at a time, it is generally agreed that we may have a genetic predisposition to the disorder and that it may take a series of traumas to trigger it.

To make things even more complicated: persons with all

these disorders, even those with paranoid schizophrenia, may act perfectly normal when they are walking down a beach or when they are not confronted with stress. This is one of the reasons why making psychiatric diagnoses is not an easy task. The potential patient who is making life difficult for himself and everyone around him arrives at the clinical psychologist's or psychiatrist's office and acts perfectly natural. Even extreme psychopaths can fool for a time the most skilled of psychiatrists.

The reward system in our brains—also called our "pleasure center," "reward circuit," "reward pathway," and "dopamine reward system"—was apparently designed to motivate us with internal rewards for eating, drinking, having sex, and being nurtured. The idea of being given pleasurable feelings for doing these things was obviously to reinforce the behavior. This way it would be repeated and we would continue surviving and reproducing.

The area in the brain that relates to the reward system is part of the limbic system and is called the *nucleus accumbens.* The neurotransmitter most closely associated with the reward system, dopamine, helps stimulate the firing of the neurons of the nucleus accumbens. In a nutshell, without the nucleus accumbens and the dopamine that helps trigger it, the act of having sex would feel about the same as doing the laundry.

The great majority of us have reward systems that have been able to adapt to modern experiences. We drink alcohol and we feel good; we may even feel a strong "high," but that's it. Most of us can control our intake level. Others of us, alcoholics, are more vulnerable to the feelings of pleasure that alcohol gives us and so begin to drink increasing quantities of it. Still others of us can control our alcohol level, but become addicted to chocolate or Dove bars and so our waistlines grow.

Or worse, we might become addicted to substances such as cocaine, which leaves dopamine awash in the synaptic gaps of our nucleus accumbens (just as Prozac leaves serotonin awash in the gaps), reinforcing its ability to fire the neurons there. And so we feel tremendous highs. We can beat the world, we think, while on cocaine. Our self-esteem soars, our energy is high, our mind is working in ways we never experienced. We can party through the night. But as time passes, the dopamine receptors become clogged, and it takes increasing amounts of coke to achieve the same highs. Our health, already jeopardized, is now at increased risk. If we realize the peril of our situation and attempt to diminish our use of cocaine, our punishment system kicks in and we feel intense waves of depression—the signature symptom of withdrawal. Further, we find that our natural feelings of pleasure that derive from food, sex, and nurturing have been overrun, and it is only through resuming our use of cocaine, or more addictive drugs such as heroin, that we can restore our highs, our sense of pleasure.

We literally can become trapped by a reward and punishment system that, once out of control, takes no prisoners.

Prehistoric man, as far as we know, didn't have alcohol and other addictive substances to tempt him. Adam and Eve ate apples and that was about it. Eating, drinking, having sex, and nurturing offspring were the important things. But enter the temptations of civilized life and, for some of us, our reward system goes topsy-turvy. We become addicted to substances and activities that give us highs, even though they have negative effects on our lives, or as the National Institute on Drug Abuse puts it, we "engage in compulsive behavior even when we are faced with negative consequences."[24] Compulsive shoppers, for example, who become addicted to the highs they feel when acquiring unnecessary things, may drive their families into bankruptcy. Compulsive gamblers, who feel highs only when they are playing blackjack, poker, or the slot machines, frequently end up with broken families and become unemployed.

Unlike flies, which can become drunk and stumble about

when they are fed alcohol but don't really know they're drunk, we humans have rational awareness of ourselves, our lives, and our surroundings. This awareness is one of the major characteristics that differentiate us from other, higher animals. If we become addicted to substances and habits that are causing us great harm, we should be able to recognize what is happening to us and seek treatment. We should be capable of observing the harm that is being inflicted on us. However, part of the insidiousness of the reward center, when we are addicted, is that it may distort our outlook so that we think our addiction is perfectly normal and natural.

Many years ago I knew an executive who could work only during mornings because he drank heavily at lunch. Although he didn't appear drunk, he couldn't really function. One day a group of us confronted him about his problem, and here is his answer as best as I can recall:

"I am not addicted to alcohol, as you might think. I guarantee you I am in complete control; I drink simply to relax. There is a problem with my stomach, however, that part I know. It isn't absorbing the alcohol properly, too much is remaining in my stomach overnight. Regarding treatment, I just can't do it. I know I am not an alcoholic and going into treatment will only embarrass my family."

He was soon asked to leave the company. Experts in drug and other addictions point out that denial is the largest part of the problem. Many addicts find rationalizations that explain away the problem, and so the problem remains with them until they are utterly overwhelmed. Then they may admit that they have a problem, although some cling to their rationalizations until the bitter end.

Some of the offshoots of Alcoholics Anonymous, a form of support group therapy, attest to the reward system's overzealousness. Here are some of them: Horse Addiction Anonymous, Adrenaline Addiction Anonymous, Altoids Addiction Anonymous, Webaholics Addiction Anonymous, Shoplifters Anonymous, Video Gamers Anonymous, Debtors Anonymous, and the list goes on.

Another insidious characteristic of our reward system is that it may give us highs when we hurt other people—that is for the bullies and sadists among us. In his paper "Hatred as Pleasure," Otto F. Kernberg says: "It is of course, well known that hatred, a derivative of rage, may give rise to highly pleasurable aggressive behaviors, sadistic enjoyment in causing pain, humiliation, and suffering; and the glee derived from devaluating others."[25]

Glee seems to be the operative word here. Kernberg describes how during World War II, groups of local civilians would gather near German concentration camps, looking gleeful as families of new inmates were led inside and slicing their fingers across their throats to indicate imminent death.

In the business world, I have seen some executives who look jubilant when they fired people. It gave them their highs for the day. Do you see what I mean about the flaws and craziness of this system?

Then there is the use of the reward system in molding the attitudes and outlooks of children. The Yanamamo of Venzuela is one culture that encourages high levels of aggression. They reward children for fighting and hurting one another. Fortunately, there are other cultures, such as the Semai in Malaysia, which have a fear of a disciplinarian god and raise their children to be gentle and nonviolent.[26]

I think the world needs more Semai.

There is one additional aspect to the reward system. Apparently, all of us have our own "pleasure threshold," a base feeling of pleasure—what it takes for us to feel happy. This includes the pleasure that bullies feel when they get a chance to terrorize others.

Norman Doidge, in a paper included in *The Pleasure Principle*, describes the pleasure threshold as being a level at which the chemistry of our brains begins to allow us to experience pleasure.[27] If we have a lower pleasure threshold, it is easier for us to derive pleasure from the positive situations we encounter. If we have a higher threshold, it is more difficult for us to derive pleasure from positive experiences, and so we might more readily turn to artificial substitutes such as alcohol and drugs, or we may become a compulsive shopper, or we may look for people we can demean.

I have known people who seem to be on a relatively constant and natural high. They rarely feel depressed, and when they do, it is short lived. They apparently don't need alcohol, drugs, or other damaging addictions or experiences to make them feel better; still, I have known people who are so naturally down they suck energy from every room they walk into, and yet they are not alcoholics or other addicts. Maybe they think being down is the way they're supposed to feel. Maybe that is all they can feel.

On a much more positive side, there is a relatively new field of study called "positive psychology." Its objective is to determine what we can do in our lives to induce greater happiness. Martin Seligman, professor of psychology at the University of Pennsylvania, is a leader in this field. In his book, *Authentic Happiness*, he wrote:

> The belief that we can rely on shortcuts to happiness, joy, rapture, comfort and ecstacy, rather than be entitled to these feelings by the exercise of personal strengths and virtues, leads to legions of people who in the middle of great wealth are starving spiritually. Positive emotion alienated from the exercise of character leads to emptiness to inauthenticity, to depres-

sion, and, as we age, to the gnawing realization that we are fidgeting until we die. . . . The positive feelings that arises from the exercise of strengths and virtues, rather than from the shortcuts is authentic.[28]

Time thought enough of this concept to devote a special mind and body issue to it titled "The Science of Happiness" in January 2005. An article by Claudia Wallis pointed to the virtues of kindness, gratitude, and the capacity for love as stimuli for making us happier. She writes:

> Why do exercising gratitude, kindness and other virtues provide a lift? "Giving makes you feel good about yourself," says Peterson [Christopher Peterson of the University of Michigan, a collaborator of Seligman]. "When you're volunteering, you're distracting yourself from your own existence, and that's beneficial. More fuzzily, giving puts meaning into your life. You have a sense of purpose because you matter to someone else." Virtually all the happiness exercises being tested by positive psychologists, he says, make people feel more connected to others.
>
> That seems to be the fundamental finding from the science of happiness. "Almost every person feels happier when they're with other people," observes Mihaly Csikszentmikalyi [psychologist and author of *Flow*]. "It's paradoxical because many of us think we can hardly wait to get home and be alone with nothing to do. But that's a worst-case scenario. If you're alone with nothing to do, the quality of your experience really plummets."[29]

Richard Davidson, a professor of psychology and psychiatry at the University of Wisconsin, who I mention a number of times in this book—he cofounded the HealthEmotions Institute at the university with Professor and Chair of Psychiatry

Ned Kalin—was also featured in this *Time* issue. He was recording the brain activity of a Buddhist monk in the institute's lab as the monk sank into "deep meditation, when he noticed something that sent his own pulse racing . . . electrical activity in the prefrontal lobe of the monk's brain was shooting up at a tremendous rate. . . . It made clear, says Davidson . . . that happiness isn't just a vague, ineffable feeling: it's a physical state of the brain—one that you can induce deliberately."[30]

Maybe there is hope.

6.

EVIL IN PEOPLE
IS A PSYCHIATRIC DISORDER

Evil is driven primarily by the wish to inflict harm merely for the pleasure of doing so.
   Roy Baumeister[1]

A reasonable account of evil must recognize that much evil is caused not by moral monsters but ordinary people going about their ordinary lives.
   Steven Mintz[2]

Hannah Arendt found evil to be banal, not radical or demonic.
   Jewish Virtual Library[3]

The world has been struggling with the concept of good and evil since the beginning of recorded history. It has been the subject of philosophers and religionists and, in modern times, of psychologists, sociologists, criminologists, and moviemakers, among others.

In essence, it has been the study of why some of us are good and others of us are bad. The word "evil" is both a noun, in which the word is used to describe wicked and pernicious activity in general, and an adjective, to describe it as a trait in people.

I found this unattributed quote on the Internet that I thought summed up the issue:

> It's not always a wonderful world. So what is evil? Where does it come from? How can it be reduced? Bad things and nasty people get called evil. Sex crimes, or Hitler's genocide seem to demand the language of evil. . . . But if God is good and full of power, then why's the world so full of evil? From George Bush to Friedrich Nietzsche via Harry Potter and *Star Wars*, the questions keep on coming. Can you escape evil through the Christian atonement? Does a faithful Muslim life lead to an evil-free future in Allah's paradise? Or does the Darth Vader story offer a better myth of good conquering evil? Is an evil person a demon, or a monster, or an animal? Or just a human being, such as any of us could become? And will evil win in the end, or does good triumph? Is evil in all of us?[4]

During the writing of *Power Freaks*, I immersed myself in the study of psychopaths, particularly white-collar or corporate psychopaths, because in positions of power, they can become the ultimate bullies. The term "psychopath" was first used in 1891 to describe a whole range of personality disorders. The term was narrowed during the years that followed and fully defined in 1941 by Harvey Cleckley, in his seminal book on psychopaths, *The Mask of Sanity*, which was reissued in updated editions through 1988.

The term "sociopath" was introduced in 1968 because it was thought at the time that the term "psychopath" disproportionately reflected biological and genetic origins. "Sociopath," it was then believed, would reflect many of the social forces and early experiences in one's upbringing that might create the personality previously described as psychopathic.

Then also in 1968, the term "antisocial personality" was

introduced and subsequently antisocial personality disorder was listed in the *DSM*, the *Diagnostic and Statistical Manual of Mental Disorders*—the bible of psychiatry.

As Cleckley pointed out in his book, the three terms—"psychopath," "sociopath," and "antisocial person"—can today be "used as . . . synonym[s] to designate patients with this specific pattern of disorder."[5]

Robert D. Hare, an emeritus professor of psychology at the University of British Columbia, is today considered the world's leading authority on psychopaths. He wrote the best-selling book *Without Conscience: The Disturbing World of the Psychopaths Among Us*, authored hundreds of articles on the subject for scientific journals, and developed the Psychopathy Checklist, which is used worldwide by trained diagnosticians to determine if a person is psychopathic. In his book he said, "The same individual therefore could be diagnosed as a sociopath by one expert and as a psychopath by another."[6] In other words, we would just be splitting hairs in attempting to define the three terms as other than synonymous.

However, certain segments of the academic and clinical world prefer one term over the other. In general, it appears that the term "psychopath" is preferred by most psychologists, "sociopath" is preferred by most sociologists and criminologists, and "antisocial personality" is preferred by most psychiatrists.

Here are some of the characteristics of psychopaths:[7]

- *Lack of empathy for other human beings:*

  They have no concern for the feelings of others. They don't need approval. Other people are there just to be used; they are pawns. Psychopaths find it extremely difficult to feel any kind of love.

- *Lack of remorse, guilt, or shame:*

  They have no conscience. They lack the social emotions. They will do whatever they deem necessary to make others suffer and then feel no compassion for their victims. This is one of the outstanding features of psychopaths. Many of us when angered and lashing out at others may feel no remorse or guilt at the time. But later, when we calm down, we regret our actions. Psychopaths don't have the capacity to regret, even when they torture or murder.

- *Cunning, callous, and manipulative:*

  They will do anything it takes to reach their objectives. They may make promises this week that they break next week. Any strategy at all is fair play. They are usually pathological liars and predisposed to take what they want and do as they please, with little or no feelings of anxiety or fear. They are totally uninhibited.

- *Grandiose sense of self-worth:*

  They have an exaggerated sense of entitlement, feeling that the ordinary rules of life don't apply to them. They believe that the whole world revolves around them and the views of others are irrelevant.

Doesn't this sound like the beginnings of a good description of evil to you? They also have these characteristics:

- *Superficial charm and high "intelligence":*

  When you are first with them, you may not notice anything disagreeable about them. They appear to be genuine and can have high levels of intelligence.

They can be professors, mathematicians, bankers, doctors, and so on, with superb credentials.

- *Absence of delusions and other irrational thinking:*

  A psychopath doesn't hear voices and doesn't have actual delusions. In other words, he doesn't think he is the king of England. Psychopaths may be sane in how they project themselves. As Harvey Cleckley said, "He is pleasant and affable during his normal phases, which make up the greater part of his time."[8]

In other words, on the surface, psychopaths can act perfectly normal, even charming, warm, and captivating, which is why so many of us can be drawn in by them. In his early days as chancellor of Germany, Adolph Hitler, probably the ultimate psychopath, was literally worshiped by tens of millions of Germans, who believed in him as they would a messiah. While millions lost faith in him when he led them into war, death, and ruination, others continued to idolize him until the very end, and some do to this day.

Unlike Antisocial Personality Disorder (described in the last chapter), psychopaths do not have to be criminals, although many of them are. Psychopaths are believed to have a genetic component that can reflect psychopathic characteristics at the age of four or earlier, and they can be diagnosed by the age of seven.[9] Sociopaths, in contrast, may have led early normal lives but acquired their psychopathic tendencies through experience, after being inducted into a gang, for example, or being abused by parents or siblings, and even after serving a term in the military, where they were literally trained to be psychopathic in combat.

Bob Hare estimates that approximately 1 percent of the world's population is psychopathic, a percentage considered modest by others.

After quoting him widely in *Power Freaks*, I met Bob Hare (he likes to be called Bob, a wonderful man) at a conference on psychopathy held during the summer of 2003 at the University of Wisconsin–Madison, which I helped sponsor. He is close to my age (we both are eligible for Social Security), and I told him as I shook his hand that meeting him after reading his books and papers was like meeting John Wayne. From then on he frequently called me "Pilgrim," Wayne's favorite movie term for a follower, and I called him "Duke."

We struck up a friendship, and it was during a dinner in early 2004, with his associate Paul Babiak, whom I also quoted in *Power Freaks* (an industrial psychologist with a focus on corporate psychopaths), that I brought up the subject of how President Bush was constantly using the terms "evil" and "evildoers." Didn't Bob think that he should use the term "psychopathic," instead—that the term "evil" had too much of a religious connotation?

Bob replied that the term "evil" had been around so long that it really was metaphoric and that he used the term himself, from time to time. He referred me to a paper he had written on the subject, which he subsequently sent me, titled "Psychopathy and Sadistic Personality Disorder." It equated evil with the combination of these two disorders. As he put it to me, an evil person is "someone who is psychopathic, sadistic, and sane."

The paper, which he cowrote with others, observes that:

> Sadistic Personality Disorder is underpinned by a cruel, demeaning and aggressive approach to interactions with other people. As with all other personality disorders, it starts early in life, it is long lasting, and it pervades most of the individual's interactions with others at school, work, socially and within family relationships. . . . Sadists share many of the critical

features of the psychopath: they lack remorse for their controlling and exploitative behavior, they do not experience shame or guilt, and they are unable to empathize with their victims. They are cold-hearted.[10]

The two key characteristics of this disorder as defined in *Diagnostic and Statistical Manual of Mental Disorders-III*:

- Humiliates or demeans people in the presence of others
- Is amused by, or takes pleasure in, the psychological or physical suffering of others (including animals)[11]

The physical basis of evil, psychopathy and sadism, would appear to encompass the lack of social emotions for starters.

Our core social emotions include shame and guilt. Embarrassment, regret, contrition, chagrin, and other such emotional states are offshoots of these core emotions or may be synonymous with them. Shame and guilt, according to Karen Caplovitz Barret, an expert in human development and family studies, in a paper within the book *Self-Conscious Emotions*, are designed to motivate people to follow society's guidelines. She implies that these feelings are included in our emotional portfolio as an aid to hierarchal harmony.[12]

In other words, we apparently have an evolutionary predisposition to be equipped with these emotions to help us get along with one another. In this sense, shame and guilt may be part of our reward and punishment circuitry. In *Emotions in Social Psychology*, the point is made that "generally, people will feel guilty when they benefit inequitably at a partner's expense, or inflict harm, loss, distress, disappointment, or other misfortune on a significant other person. . . . Guilt is an unpleasant emotional state."[13]

The same book asserts that the feeling of shame is more unpleasant than guilt. While guilt is felt over doing a "bad thing," shame is experienced as a "reflection of a 'bad self,' and the entire self is painfully scrutinized and negatively evaluated."[14]

I don't know, that may be cutting it a little thin.

In any event, the evolutionary idea behind the two emotions and their correlates appears to be that we will make a stronger attempt at behaving ourselves to avoid the punishing feelings that guilt and shame will inflict on us if we do not.

This may be why the neural circuitry that harbors these emotions is also apparently present in other higher animals. The books written by primatologists are full of examples of the shame and guilt felt by chimpanzees and gorillas. A chimp attempts to sneak food away from another chimp much higher on the clan's hierarchal scale, but then the higher-ranking chimp spots him. A quick scuffle ensues or a harsh sound or gesture is made, with the result that the lower-ranking chimp "slumps" away, obviously ashamed. Then he comes back and grooms the higher-ranking chimp in apparent expiation of his shame or guilt.

Dogs, like chimpanzees, are among the higher animals. Those of us who have had dogs as pets are well aware of their emotions, including their capacity for manifesting feelings of shame or guilt. In Jeffrey Moussaieff Masson's book, *Dogs Never Lie about Love,* he quotes R. H. Smythe, author of *The Mind of the Dog,* as follows:

> [C]ertain dogs, especially heavy breeds, wag their tails in an up-and-down direction when they are ashamed or feel guilty, or know they are about to be scolded, thumping the floor as the tail descends. A dog who does this is anticipating punishment, and will remain in a lying position, indicating humility. . . . Dogs love to be forgiven. They bear no grudge and are happy when they see that you don't harbor any ill will, either.

[In addition,] every dog is extremely susceptible to ridicule. It enjoys laughter providing one is laughing with it. But it becomes extremely embarrassed and unhappy if it even suspects that it is being made fun of, in other words being laughed at.[15]

With regard to guilt alone, Masson adds, "many dog caretakers report that they believe that their dogs experience excessive guilt."

There are a number of scientists, according to neuroscientist Jaak Panksepp, author of *Affective Neuroscience: The Foundation of Human and Animal Emotions*, who continue to deny the existence of emotional feelings in other animals. It is "clearly a popular scientific stance," he wrote. Perhaps it's because this notion allows the scientists to experiment with the brains of higher animals without feelings of guilt or shame.[16]

One of the differences between the social emotions and our more primal emotions is that the frontal cortex of our brains, our "executive center," appears to be more involved in social emotions, whereas primal emotions are mediated more by the organs of our limbic system.

Research appearing in the May 21, 2004, issue of *Science*, as reported by MedicineNet.com, found that "when the region of the brain known as the orbitofrontal cortex was damaged, people no longer experienced regret, and couldn't anticipate the consequences of their actions."[17]

The same article also quoted Dr. Elkhonon Goldberg, a neuropsychologist at New York University Medical Center and author of *The Executive Brain: Frontal Lobes and The Civilized Mind*, who says:

Orbitofrontal damage robs people of the ability to anticipate the consequences of their action. . . . The orbitofrontal cortex is not alone in processing com-

plex emotions, such as regret . . . if the authors had
studied other parts of the prefrontal cortex they likely
would have noted differences there as well.[18]

If we cannot feel shame or guilt—or their correlates, remorse, regret, and contrition—due to damage to our frontal
cortex, a genetic inadequacy, or some other organic cause, we
basically can become totally uninhibited, the hallmark of a
psychopath. We can be nasty, mean, and bullying; we can
demean or even kill our own parents, our siblings, or anyone
in our path, if we think it will advance our cause, and we will
not feel the slightest regret. If we also have sadistic personality
disorder, we will not only act this way to advance whatever
cause we have at the moment, but we will seek out targets of
opportunity, because demeaning them, or physically harming
them, if we can, will give us a high. We see someone new at our
place of business, someone who looks like an easy target for our
psychopathic/sadistic urges, and we will work to degrade and
disparage him. Day after day we won't let up.

If we are capable of applying a mask of civility over these
urges, we might charm him at first. And only when he thinks
he has a friend do we begin our campaign of degradation and
disparagement. If a mask of civility allows us to rise into positions of political power, we may satisfy our urges further by
attacking the country next door with our armies or commiting
genocide among the minorities in our country whom we were
taught to hate since childhood. And yet, when we are interviewed by print and broadcast journalists, or by diplomats we
are out to impress, we can act perfectly innocent and engaging.
Perhaps we learn to create this façade because we have watched
others do it successfully, and so we try our hand at it. Moreover, it can get results. Many of us can recall watching the tele-
casts of Saddam Hussein bouncing children on his knee, trying
to impress the world that he was a nurturing sort.

Yet are these people sane? This is the third aspect of the evildoer as defined by Bob Hare. Recall that psychopaths don't hear voices and don't have genuine delusions, they don't think they they're the king of England or Jesus Christ reincarnated. Psychopaths can project an image of sanity.

John Wayne Gacy, the serial killer who killed thirty-two young men, is an ultimate example of how this mask of civility can be worn. In his earlier years in Waterloo, Iowa, Gacy managed a string of Kentucky Fried Chicken restaurants, was chaplain of the local Junior Chamber of Commerce, and organized the group's first communitywide prayer breakfast. He volunteered to shop for Christmas presents for underprivileged children and joined the Merchant's Patrol, a volunteer group that helped to police area businesses. He was married and had a seemingly normal home life, including inviting neighbors over for barbeques. But he began having sex with teenage boys and was soon caught and imprisoned.

After his release from prison, he moved to Des Plaines, Illinois, and began a new life, where he quickly became a respected trade contractor and was named a Junior Chamber of Commerce "Man of the Year." He entertained children at numerous civic and other events in costume as "Pogo the Clown." People who knew him, by and large, genuinely liked him. He was glib and entertaining, which helped him attract young men in bars, whom he lured to his home and forced sex on them. Then, in a turn from his Iowa experiences, he murdered them so they couldn't later testify against him in court. He buried them, thirty-two in all, in his basement crawl space.[19] Gacy, though considered evil personified, was judged sane enough to stand trial.

All of us have been nasty and mean at times. The propensity for it varies between individuals. In the book *Power Freaks*, I called this being in the power freak or bullying mode. It might occur when we are intensely angered by someone that we lash back with crude and hurtful statements. During that relatively brief interval, we become impervious to reality. If we are short tempered, we are easily transformed into the mode. The slightest unfulfilled expectation, including the smallest of slights, can set us off. But in an hour or by the end of the day, we resume our normal personalities and feel guilty about our actions. If we are narcissistic and arrogant, we may be nasty and mean to those we consider below us in social rank and obsequious to those we believe may help us in the future and not feel guilty at all for these attitudes.

For those of us at the bottom of the scale of nasty and mean, it would likely take an intense event to set us off. We would be at peace most of the time, but if we were to catch our spouse with a lover, we might be transformed into a bludgeoning mode. Most of us would be in the middle of the scale. It would take a little effort to get us into the mode; someone would have to really work at getting to us, before we turned nasty. When it would be over, we'd likely feel guilt or shame because we weren't able to control ourselves. At the top of the scale, however, would be the psychopath/sadists, who are almost always in the mode, which is often disguised by the mask of civility. Under the mask, they have no feelings for others or a conscience. They don't have to be angered to hurt and maim. They are simply watching for the right opportunities to unleash their nastiness, and after they strike they feel no guilt or shame, allowing them to be all charged up looking for the next target.

There also appears to be a "directionality" to the characteristics of nasty and mean. People who are racist may become intimidating and nasty when they are in the company of members of a minority ethnic group whom they detest. They feel no guilt or shame at the time or later. In a sense, they reflect psychopathic and sadistic tendencies only directionally. At the country club over lunch with their friends, they may appear apparently normal.

People who are messianic may become nasty and mean only when dealing with a challenge to whatever mission obsesses them. A fundamentalist cleric in a Middle Eastern country may beat women with sticks on the street, who, in his perception, aren't properly covering themselves. Or these messianic people may laugh with glee when they learn that their perceived enemies, people of another persuasion, are killed. But they act apparently normal with colleagues in a local coffee house.

We read about suicide bombers in the Middle East who come from apparently normal homes and engage in pleasant social interactions with relatives and friends. But then they strap on explosives and go on buses and into cafes where they blow up hundreds.

The directionality of psychopathy/sadism isn't fully recognized by academics who study the subject. As Bob Hare pointed out in the preface, psychopaths "are what they are and I don't know if the mechanisms that control their behavior are similar to those that prompt psychopathic and sadistic behavior in otherwise normal individuals."

Nonetheless, those who harbor this directionality can be just as deadly as the full-blown psychopath/sadist. Steven Mintz, professor of history at the University of Houston, has a quote at the start of this chapter that takes on greater validity under the concept of directionality: "A reasonable account of evil must recognize that much evil is caused not by moral monsters but ordinary people going about their ordinary lives." Or what Hannah Arendt referred to as the "banality of evil." In other words, we are all capable of mimicking psychopathic and sadistic traits under certain circumstances. In essence, it's a battle between our frontal cortex—which theoretically harbors our social emotions and a keener sense of reality—versus our limbic organs, which have no sense or logic or awareness and

may impel us to be abnormally aggressive, full of rage, retaliatory, and phobic. We have all felt this mental conflict. At times
our limbic brain components win, at which time we become
total jerks, or worse; at other times our frontal cortex wins and
we reflect tolerance and wisdom.

Isn't it too bad that at times we can't get in there with a
screwdriver?

It is unfortunate that our social emotions are apparently not as
strong as our primal emotions that drive us toward status,
power, territory, and sex. Unless we are very high on the scales
of nurturance, attachment, and social bonding, we are vulnerable to the desensitization of our human feelings of shame,
guilt, and their corollary emotions. The most striking example
of this, I thought, was the reports of the late Iris Chang in her
book, *The Rape of Nanking*, about how Japanese soldiers in 1937
raped, tortured, and murdered more than three hundred thousand civilians during a six-week period in Nanking, China. This
number included thousands of babies and older children, who
were bayoneted.[20]

These were not the Huns overpowering a city that refused
their demands in the third century and then performed barbaric
acts when they took the city by force. This was the Japanese
army of 1937, consisting of soldiers born into a culture that was
perceived as being among the most nurturing in the world. The
fact that this intense cultural conditioning could have been so
easily overthrown exemplifies the vulnerability of our social
emotions. As Chang illustrates in her book, new Japanese soldiers entering Nanking felt horror at what they were seeing and
asked to do. They had to be "desensitized" by their officers
within days. This was usually done by Japanese officers, who
would kill children with bayonets in front of the soldiers to
show how easy this was to do, because, they would assert,
"these people are subhuman." And then they were given direct

orders to carry out the carnage. Some Japanese soldiers began to admit that it was easy for them to kill.[21]

Hideo Kojima of Nagoya University, in a 1986 paper titled "Becoming Nurturant in Japan: Past and Present," explains:

> Perhaps due to the Buddhist precept against killing animals, a traditional Japanese conception was that human beings and other living things were basically similar to each other, and the Japanese were led to have a sympathetic attitude toward all living things, for each of us was a member of them.[22]

Given the above, it is shocking but true that our feelings of guilt and shame are so vulnerable that, under certain circumstances, they can be quickly overpowered. This is exemplified by soldiers or terrorists, who are told to kill other humans and are able to do so comfortably within weeks or even days; or by members of political or tribal cults, who believe it is okay to exterminate humans they are led to believe are inferior or subhuman. This weakness can be considered one of the greatest problems of the human condition. In this sense, from the days of Attila—who himself was a nurturing leader of his people, but who led them to commit atrocities in the cities they had conquered—nothing much has changed today. After the campaigns of carnage were over, the Huns went back to their hunting, quilting, and other normal pursuits, just as the Japanese did after the war.

Chang interviewed a Japanese doctor, forty years after he eagerly took part in the carnage, who said, "There are really no words to explain what I was doing. I was truly a devil."

We all sense our vulnerability to this form of desensitization. As parents, we worry that our children may become influenced by gangs or other negative influences, who might desensitize them and turn them into sociopaths. We read today of parents who actually become terrorized by their own once-nurtured children.

What is being done about the problems of psychopathy and sadism? Not much at all, if you consider the enormity of the problem. As of this writing, $600 million per year is being spent on research for depression, $400 million for schizophrenia, and less than $6 million on psychopathy.[23]

The major therapeutic intervention for psychopathic sadists—the "evil" people among us—is the threat and actuality of prosecution and prison. I recall one evening talking to David Spiegel, a renowned psychiatrist at Stanford University and author, after a symposium. I asked him if he ever attempted to treat a psychopath and said I had read that therapy was of little use. He said he had treated two psychopaths, but would never do it again. "They draw you in, over weeks or months of therapy. You think you are making progress, then one day they let you have it, and it's a depressing experience."

What he meant by drawing you in, is that they let the therapist think he or she is making progress. They play the game. Then one day, they tell the therapist something like, "Doc, do you think I'm really going for all your bullshit?" and take off from there.

In reality, evil, as a combination of psychopathy and sadism, is a mental dysfunction, a disorder that robs us of our social emotions and gives us a high when we do something malicious. Yet it leaves us sane enough to talk about sports or politics and such and to stand trial if we are caught committing a crime.

We need to spend more than $6 million a year on psychopathy research to learn if there is a more effective fix for this problem than the threat or use of prisons.

7.

WE HAVE HUNDREDS, IF NOT THOUSANDS, OF METAPHORIC NEURO-DVDS STACKED IN OUR HEADS

Consider that a man's brain originally is like a little empty attic, and you have to stock it with such furniture as you choose.
Sir Arthur Conan Doyle[1]

W hen scientists and science writers try to describe the brain to the public, the *Washington Post* points out, "they are too easily satisfied with feeble metaphor. Receptors are locks, for example, neurotransmitters are keys . . . shorter term memory is a mental scratch pad, the cortex is our thinking cap."

The *Post* observes in the article that a bad metaphor can do more than just befuddle. It can give a reader the wrong description of how nature works.[2]

Well, I've developed a metaphor for the neural circuits of the brain that may take the cake. Yet from what we know so far from the Humpty-Dumpty dilemma (as described on page 60), science has worked very hard in deconstructing the brain, but is struggling mightily when it comes to putting it back together to make sense of a larger behavior.

Science knows a great deal about the workings of the neurons and how they combine themselves into neural circuits or systems that represent emotional and cognitive systems. Jaak Panksepp sums this up nicely in his book *Affective Neuroscience:*

> The human brain, like all other mammalian brains, has circuits that are designed to seek out positive rewards in the environment; the innate tendency can promote excessive materialism and greed. The brain also has systems that can induce anger toward perceived offenders to our liberties and freedoms, which can lead to deep animosities among groups forced to compete for common resources. The brain mediates fear to detect those agents of change that threaten our safety and comfort; this can lead . . . to the stigmatization of groups that do not share our interests. We have brain systems that aspire for social pride and dominance, leading to the types of power politics that have been the hallmark of human history down through the ages.
>
> Our mammalian brain also has systems that mediate social and sexual bonds, including parental nurturance and the despair of being isolated from our fellows. . . . The brain also contains circuits for social play and dominance, and no successful social system has stifled the dictates of those circuits.[3]

Circuitry is apparently the key to our functioning, and different neural circuits have the capability of operating in parallel. We have all experienced being in the midst of making a perfectly rational decision when suddenly some irrational anxiety takes hold of our consciousness, which compounds the difficulty of making the decision.

Further, our emotions appear to merge during times of extreme traumatic circumstance, becoming basically one feeling out of several. For example, our wife, one night, who we've been extremely happy and in love with, tells us as we enter the door of our home after an extended business trip that she wants a divorce, that she is in love with another man, and that she has already moved out her things. She then walks by us to her car. Very quickly we are afflicted with depression, jealousy about the other man, guilt that we could have done more to make her happy, sadness over the kids we had hoped to have, despair over being lonely, fear about starting a social life anew, anxiety about how our assets will be split, concern what people will think at work, and worry what our friends will think. We also feel spiritless, empty, demeaned, dejected, devalued: the punishing emotions overtake us in full force. Yet they appear to forge together so that we more or less simply sink to the lowest state of misery, feeling them individually only when our thoughts turn specifically to the other man, our kids, the money situation, and so on.

There are apparently brain circuits that mediate all of these emotions, as well as those that are rewarding. For example, two days later, our wife, whom we still love, returns to the house, falls on her knees, admits she made a terrible mistake, will never do it again, and that she now appreciates us and loves us more than ever. Now the neural circuitry that mediates forgiveness and happiness kicks in and we suddenly feel exhilaration, delight, glee, euphoria, energy, contentment, delight, zest, and on and on. We may not experience all of these individually, but in general we feel a supreme state of joy.

Earlier, we described Daniel Goleman's use of the phrase "emotional sentinel." This comprises the components and circuitry of the brain that are viewing independently what is happening in our lives at any moment, mediated primarily by the hippocampus and the amygdala. If these components sense danger, such as the imminent and unexpected announcement by our wife that she wants a divorce, the amygdala and the system of related brain circuitry begin the process that leads to our feeling all those punishing emotions, as described above.

Then when she changes her mind, our dopamine reward circuitry is turned on, filling us with the joyous emotions, as also described above. Similarly, if we meet a potential mate, a neural system triggers the romantic emotions that we need to pursue the relationship. Or when we become parents, we are inundated with nurturing emotions that enable us to bring up a baby with a healthy mind and body. After a peaceful day in the park, if we happen to walk on a volleyball court and a ball comes our way, our emotional drives of determination and resoluteness may be sparked, and we may be transformed from feeling peaceful to joining the game and becoming a heated competitor. Or if we are promoted at work and are given a corner office, we may come home to a family and friends that our status system now views as beneath us, and we may be overwhelmed with an attitude of arrogance. When we return to work the next day and meet with our new boss, however, feelings of submissiveness may be turned on once again.

Recall that the triggering of strong emotions can nonetheless last over time. Both great successes and great defeats can be traumatic in the sense that our basic outlooks and attitudes may be changed—if we are highly vulnerable to the events at the time. The operative words here, as described previously, are *trauma* and *vulnerability*. A monumental defeat can cause a severe loss of self-esteem and confidence. We may go from being outgoing and extroverted to becoming avoidant. It may now be hard to get us out of the house, and once at work, we may now keep our office door closed. Similarly, a great success may transform us from your average nice person to someone who is arrogant and disdainful. If we are vulnerable, successes can overtake us as much as traumas. These new outlooks cover our consciousness like a shroud, but they usually affect our outlooks only when we are interacting with others, or when daydreaming, as we savor our new station in life. If we are lost in reading a book or watching a movie, we may basically remain in neutral.

There are apparently brain circuits that mediate all of these emotions, motivations, temperaments, and more. But as Panksepp emphasizes in his book, "[M]any [highly specific] human emotions—from avarice to xenophobia—are almost impossible to study in the brain even with modern brain-imaging techniques, not to mention in animal models."[4] But we do know that they are there, although—in a phrase favored by neuroscientists—"not fully understood at this time." And we do know a great deal about such negative emotions as fear and anxiety.

Then there are apparently neural circuits that mediate our cognitive skills such as our ability to learn, as well as to converse and to read and write in a language. Or even in two languages, or several. Language is processed in the neural circuitry located in what are known as the Broca's and Wernicke's areas of the brain.

Damage to the Broca's area causes what is called Broca's aphasia, a condition in which people have trouble producing and shaping speech. Damage to the Wernicke's area results in Wernicke's aphasia, in which people produce sentences that are grammatically correct but contain no meaningful content. They also have difficulty in comprehending speech.

According to Brian Butterworth, author of *The Mathematical Brain*, the circuitry for math appears to be located primarily in the left parietal lobe of the brain, the part of the cerebral cortex that is thought to harbor the multiple intelligences that separate us from the higher animals. (See figure 1, page 14, for the location of Brocas's and Wernicke's areas and the left parietal lobe.)

Butterworth's study of a patient, Signora Saldi, an alert, fifty-nine-year-old Italian woman, who had suffered a stroke that damaged this part of the brain, found that it left her: "hopeless with arithmetic. She cannot read, write, compare or calculate with any numbers other than one, two, three or four. Even with numbers below four, she is not performing normally."[5]

We can presume that there are neural circuits in sections of the brain that mediate all of our intellectual capacities. It is Howard Gardner, a professor of education at Harvard, who in 1983 developed the theory of multiple intelligences. He delineated them as follows:

- Linguistic or word smart
- Logical-mathematical or number/reasoning smart
- Bodily-Kinesthetic or body smart
- Musical or music smart
- Interpersonal or people smart
- Intrapersonal or self smart
- Naturalist or nature smart[6]

I watched a twelve-year-old boy named Jay Greenberg, a musical prodigy, who was featured on *60 Minutes*, on November 28, 2004. He has already written five full symphonies, and he asked for a cello at the age of two. Sam Zyman, a symphonic composer who was interviewed, compared the boy to Mozart and Felix Mendelssohn. Neither of Jay's parents are musicians. Obviously, the circuitry of his "musical or music smart" intelligence is constructed differently from most of ours.

The idea of multiple intelligences with their individual neural circuits has appealed to me as a general theory, although I believe that there are many more than Gardner has listed. Moreover, I disagree with tying mathematics always to logic. Logic and reasoning are two of the most important intellectual skills that one can have. Some of us come by them easily. Others of us have to work hard at them, forcing ourselves to think through complex steps. I have known many people who were poor in mathematics but could think and write logically, and vice versa, and so the two need not always be tied together. I have also known many people who could begin a track of logical reasoning but would get lost in the middle and end up confused.

I recall at an early age that my sister belonged to a congregation that I would visit on special occasions. When it came time for the sermon, the rabbi would begin wonderfully. We would all sit back in our seats, expecting an inspirational speech. But then, at some point in the sermon, he would lose his logic and trod on aimlessly, while we all looked at each other questioningly. He would do this almost every time, and each time, his audience would hope that something would change—that this time he would deliver a message cogently. But to the best of my knowledge, it never happened.

Years ago, I hired a man with an intellectual capability that would qualify him for membership in Mensa. His IQ was in the top 2 percent of the spectrum. Yet he couldn't get organized. He would give a presentation and walk in front of the screen, obscuring his most important talking points and even knocking over the projector. Worse, he was unable to multitask. If he had one job in front of him, he couldn't be interrupted to look at something else, let alone do three or four other projects that might need his immediate attention. He would get angry and look at the people who came to him for help and say something like, "Don't you see I'm busy?"

I have known engineers who could deliver flawless presentations on how a product could be better modeled or how a certain piece of machinery could take costs out of a process. But those engineers also thought that their expertise automatically qualified them as experts in other areas, such as accounting and marketing. And thus they made inappropriate comments at planning conferences that drew the same questioning stares as those regarding the rabbi.

I have known accountants who could look at intricate financial statements and deliver within minutes a succinct summary of the condition of the company or institution but who couldn't program a VCR.

I knew a superb classical pianist who could memorize

elaborate scores of music but couldn't remember anyone's name.

Then there are the savants, who may have low IQ levels, but may be extraordinarily talented in a specialized pursuit. Neurologist V. S. Ramachrandran in his book with Sandra Blakeslee, *Phantoms in the Brain*, discusses savants who have an IQ level less than 40. He described one who "could come up with the cube root of a six-figure number in seconds and could double 8,388,628 twenty-four times to obtain 140,737,488, 355,328 in several seconds. Such individuals are a living refutation of the argument that specialized talents are merely clever deployments of general intelligence."[7]

It would appear that the mental intelligences that Gardner delineates, as well as all of our mental aptitudes, including those of savants, are all part of the circuitry of our cerebral cortex, including many of our memory circuits where our individual skills and areas of expertise are stored. There are probably dozens, if not hundreds, of cognitive, mental capabilities, including creative ones, that could be extrapolated from Gardner's thesis. As in the case of our emotions, they are brought into our consciousness as we perform our jobs and avocations. When employed, they become synthesized with our moods, temperaments, emotional feelings of the moment, and motivations in a process of consciousness that is still unknown to science (as pointed out in chapter 4).

Nonetheless, we can experience our consciousness, and what we are seeing, feeling, hearing, and thinking, and reflect on them. Thus, in this sense, we know we have a theater of the mind, even though science doesn't know where it is precisely located or how it operates and comes together; in other words, the process is "not fully understood at this time."

It is probably a gross simplification to compare a neural circuit to a digital DVD disc, simply because both use the binary system of on-off. Still, as a metaphor this comparison can enlighten us as to what really happens in our minds on a daily basis.

While many references to the brain describe it as analogue, like the wave streams of our earlier television sets, one scientist, John R. Searle, philosophy professor at the University of California at Berkeley, in an address to the American Psychological Association, referred to the possibility of the brain being likened to a digital computer on which DVDs can be played. He said:

> To find out if an object is really a digital computer, it turns out that we do not have to actually look for 0's and 1's; rather we just have to look for something that we could treat as or count as or could be used to function as a 0's and 1's. . . . This machine could be made out of just about anything. As Johnson-Laird says, "It could be made out of cogs and levers like an old-fashioned mechanical calculator, it could be made out of a hydraulic system through which water flows, it could be made out of transistors etched into a silicon chip through which electric current flows; it could even be carried out by the brain. Each of these machines uses a different medium to represent binary symbols."[8]

Thus, let's use the phrase "neuro-DVDs" as a metaphor for our neural circuits, and let's go back to our example of the husband whose wife told him when he returned from a business trip that she wants a divorce, that she is in love with another man, and that she has already moved out her things. If we identified with the husband and viewed each of the emotions we felt at that instant as a neural circuit, represented metaphorically as a neuro-DVD, we could say to ourselves, as we felt them, "Well, there goes the depression neuro-DVD; I can feel it beginning to spin." Then, as we envisioned the other man, the jealousy DVD would be begin to spin; then as we thought about the things we didn't do to keep the wife happy, our guilt

DVD would begin to spin; then the sadness DVD would play when we thought about the kids we had hoped to have; the despair DVD would follow when we thought about being lonely; the fear DVD would spin when we thought about starting our social life anew; and the anxiety DVD would play when we thought about how our assets would be split, what people would think at work, or what our friends would think. We would also visualize the neuro-DVDs beginning to spin that trigger feelings of being empty, demeaned, dejected, and devalued. Our limbic system would throw in these additional punishing emotions for good measure, ostensibly to reflect its displeasure at our not being tied to a woman with whom we could raise and nurture offspring.

We might envision all these neuro-DVDs that have entered our theater of consciousness as being on a tall, metaphoric spindle, each of them spinning away to make us miserable.

Then, two days later, our wife returns to our home, falling on her knees, admitting she made a terrible mistake, will never do it again, and that she now appreciates us and loves us more than ever. We can now feel the neuro-DVDs that created all those miserable feelings being withdrawn and deactivated. Then our neuro-DVDs, representing our rewarding emotions, would kick in, evoking forgiveness, happiness, joy, exhilaration, delight, satisfaction, contentment, delight, zest, and so on. They would now be in place, spinning happily away on the metaphorical spindle.

Traumatic memories and events might also be seen metaphorically as DVDs, ready to come out of their hiding places and spin into our consciousness when we are faced with a situation similar to the one that caused the emotional memory. Remember the story of Sarah Reinwald, who at the age of eighteen was in a terrible elevator accident that caused severe injuries. Now, at the age of sixty-seven, she still goes to extraordinary lengths to avoid riding elevators. She knows rationally that they are safe. But she sees an elevator in front of her, and her DVD that contains the memory begins to spin, instigating feelings of panic. There is no way she'll get into that death trap.

Then there was Jennifer, who while in the eighth grade had been set up in the schoolyard by her schoolmates who told her that the most attractive boy in the class, the idol of most of the girls, wanted to take her out. Later in the schoolyard, when she was surrounded by those schoolmates, the boy walked up to her during recess as if he indeed was going to ask her out. Instead, he said something mildly insulting and walked away as her schoolmates doubled over in laughter. Now in her twenties and a beautiful model, she admits to not being able to have a trusting relationship with any man, because she can't trust men as a whole. Apparently, as soon as she sees a man as a potential serious partner, the DVD holding the emotional memory of her schoolyard trauma begins to spin, distorting her outlooks and creating anxieties and tension. So a healthy relationship never develops.

Then there was pop music star Karen Carpenter, who reached the zenith of her nationwide popularity in the late 1970s. One day someone made the simple statement to her, "Karen, on television you look thirty pounds overweight." From that point on she became anorexic and literally tried to stop eating. She lost weight and was hospitalized several times. We can assume that the DVD representing the emotional memory of that innocent comment began to spin in her head whenever she looked in the mirror, distorting her outlook. So she still believed she was fat. Despite reason or logic, no one could convince her, or others like her, otherwise. She eventually died from the disorder.[9]

Ted Turner, the founder of CNN and other network channels, was interviewed on July 28, 2004, by Charlie Rose on his PBS program. Despite all the successes Turner had with his television networks, his ownership of the Atlanta Braves baseball team, his ownership of the MGM motion picture studio, the championships he won sailing in the America's Cup, and his possession of millions of acres of land, you could tell he was obsessed with being fired by Jerry Levin, CEO of AOL/Time Warner, four years earlier. That was soon after Time Warner had purchased CNN. Turner had been given a five-year contract as an officer of the newly merged company.

You could see the agony that Turner was feeling as he described that phone call to Charlie Rose: Levin had fired him over the phone, having reached Turner on his cell phone, while driving in his car. Turner berated Levin for not only firing him, but for doing it over the phone, and told him he would sue. Levin replied all he could win was his salary for the remainder of the contract, and that if he wanted to sue, he should sue. Although Turner's net worth had sunk considerably after the merger of AOL and Time Warner, and the stock plummeted, he admitted to still being worth around two billion dollars at the time of the Charlie Rose interview and was the largest individual land owner in United States, owning nearly two million acres—roughly the size of Rhode Island and Delaware combined. Yet he was as bedeviled by the emotional memory of that firing while in his sixties as Jennifer the model was from her schoolyard taunting she had experienced at the age of twelve. Clearly, when Charlie Rose asked him about that firing, you could tell his neuro-DVD containing that emotional memory was instantly spinning at full speed.

All of us have traumatic memories that were formed from events early or late in our lives that have altered certain of our outlooks and may have created mild or even extreme variations of the personality disorders described earlier. Psychological and psychiatric literature are full of examples of them. Though many of us are unaware or have forgotten about these traumas, most of us remain aware of them and what these traumas did to us. They are emotional memories—mental assaults upon our minds that continue to haunt us. But they are mental only metaphorically. They are basically *physical*, embodied in the neural circuitry of our brains. We can attack them, if we are aware of them, just as we might remedy persistent eczema on our arms or impaired hearing. We might not always succeed, but if we know that these memories have a physical basis, they are easier to deal with than if we consider them ghosts in the night or lingering spirits.

The same holds true of irrational emotions that are triggered without any logical reason—a jealousy of a wife that has no basis in fact, for example—but which may beleaguer us and make our lives at times miserable, as well as the lives of those around us. These irrational emotions are all physical, represented by neural circuits, creating at the instant they are triggered one single feeling, such as anger, and at other times, an ensemble of feelings, such as those described in the man whose wife told him she was leaving him.

A representation of the neural circuitry in our brains, which involves our basic emotions, temperaments, motivations, and multiple intelligences, is listed below. You might want to picture them metaphorically as neuro-DVDs—a graphic representation of the neural circuitry within our brains.

BASIC DRIVES, MOTIVATIONS, AND URGES

Food and Water	Nurturance	Religion-Ritual-Spiritual
Sex	Status and Power	Territoriality

BASIC EMOTIONS AND REACTIVE FEELINGS

Painful/Punishing Feelings:

agitation	agony	anger/temper	anxiety
depression	despair	desperation	disappointment
discouragement	disgust	disillusionment	distress
distrust	embarrassment	envy	fear
frustration	grief	guilt	hate
heartbreak	hostility	humiliation	infuriation
insult	irritation	jealousy	mournfulness
offense	pain	regret	rejection
repugnance	resentment	sadness	shame
sorrow	suspicion	tearfulness	terror
torment	vengeance	victimization	

Rewarding Feelings:

agreeableness	amicability	amity	animation
cheer	delight	dominating	ecstacy
empathy	exhilaration	gladness	glee
good-humor	gratification	happiness	joy
jubilance	laughter	love	mirth
satisfaction	sympathy		

EMOTIONAL MOODS AND INTERMITTENT MOODS AS WELL AS GENERAL FEELINGS THAT MAY PERSIST

abrupt	blue	bored	cantankerous
confident	cross	determined	disgruntled
dissatisfied	down	grumpy	happy
irritable	peevish	rebellious	restless
saddened	shy	sulky	sullen
tentative	testy	uncertain	up
vulnerable	wary		

PERSONALITY CHARACTERISTICS
THAT ARE GENERALLY ROOTED OVER TIME

aggressive	altruistic	ambitious	bad-tempered
brusque	cerebral	charismatic	charitable
charming	cheerful	civil	close-minded
cold	compassionate	concerned	congenial
considerate	contrarian	controlled	cooperative
cordial	courageous	decisive	demanding
detached	detestable	difficult	disagreeable
disciplined	dishonest	driven	eager
ego-driven	elusive	empathetic	energetic
enthusiastic	extroverted	fearful	fearless
flexible	forgiving	friendly	funny
generous	gentle	good-hearted	gracious
greedy	gregarious	hard	hesitant
honest	hot-tempered	humane	humble
ill-tempered	impatient	impulsive	indecisive
indulgent	insatiable	insightful	intolerant
introverted	involved	irresponsible	kind
lascivious	listless	loathsome	lustful
magnetic	malicious	mean	merciful
nasty	obliging	open-minded	optimistic
passionate	peaceful	perceptive	pessimistic
petty	pleasant	polite	possessive
prideful	promiscuous	rash	reasonable
reliable	repulsive	responsible	rigid
ruthless	selfish	shameless	sociable
soft	solemn	stiff	stubborn
sympathetic	tentative	thoughtful	tolerant
treacherous	understanding	undisciplined	unforgiving
unfriendly	unpleasant	unreasonable	unreliable
unscrupulous	unsociable	vexatious	vulgar
warm			

COGNITIVE CAPACITIES

Capacity for creating and/or implementing art, music, literature.
Leadership capabilities.
Long-term memories.
Physical capacities.
Skill capacities.

Capacity for appreciating art, music, literature.
Capacity for logic and reasoning.
Linguistic ability.
Mathematical capacity.
Short-term memories.
Other aptitudes.

Eastern cultures apparently recognized long before others that there is a physicality to the emotional makeup and personality of the brain. Eastern teachings of authors and lecturers such as Deepak Chopra would urge us to get in touch with our feelings—to work hard to experience where in our heads and bodies we are sensing punishing feelings like anger, for example, so we can ease their intensity.

Many years ago I attended a New Age seminar on headaches. There were about twenty-five people in the group. It was an evening session, and after the introductions, we were put through a set of complex mental exercises that were intended to give us headaches. I definitely got one. We were then asked to lay on the floor, to get to work on our headaches. The first thing we were asked to do was to work out the shape of the headache as it resided in our heads. If we had to cut out a piece of paper to apply outside our heads to cover precisely the area of pain, we were told, try to envision precisely what it would be shaped like. It could be elliptical across our forehead, it could be in the shape of goggles, it could have no symmetry at all. Once we had the shape down pat, we were asked to envision that shape as a piece of metal pressing against the pained areas. My headaches were almost always behind my forehead. Then we were asked to judge how thick the metal was. The more pain we felt in a specific spot, the thicker the metal would be, and vice versa. Finally, we were asked to describe what the color of the metal was.

Then we'd start the process all over again. Each time we began anew, you could feel the shape of the pain shifting, and so we'd have to imagine new shapes. We would keep doing this until the pain was barely perceptible.

This simple process has now worked for me for more than thirty years.

Eastern and natural cure advocates might get some use out of the neuro-DVD concept because it allows you to visualize the physicality of the neural circuits in your brain that may be overrunning your consciousness, be they those of anger, upset, or vengefulness. By visualizing them as spinning in your brain, and working figuratively to slow them down, you may have success. I have found this works with small upsets: getting cut off by a car, being reprimanded by an authority figure, being mildly insulted by someone, or having irrational fears of engaging with certain people or groups of people. But it does not work so well with the bigger upsets: losing a major customer or watching a job promotion we wanted go to someone else. But working hard at the visualizations, you might at least mitigate the misery. This visualization and the process of journaling (writing on a sheet of paper with four columns: in column one, what the upset was; in the second column how you felt; in the third column how you should have felt as a rational person; and in the final column how you feel now) are the only two things that have helped get me through some pretty bad upsets. You can find various formats for journaling on Google under "emotional journaling."

Each of us probably has some propensity for each of the basic urges—the primal motivations, emotions, and moods, in varying degrees from mild to moderate to extreme—which depends on our individual personality and the situation of the moment. In addition, we all have some combination of the above-listed personality characteristics and cognitive abilities, which are represented in our neural circuitry. It is thus no wonder that all of us who comprise the human race are so different from one another.

Ted Turner said another interesting thing during his interview with Charlie Rose that others who have worked themselves up from humble beginnings have similarly said. He admitted that he had never considered himself intellectually gifted, but he was determined to succeed. He did so primarily by working hard to exercise his brain by reading books on subjects that weren't necessarily easy to read, by exercising his ability to think, and by attacking his weaknesses. These steps, in general, helped him attain the intelligence and the skills he needed as he moved along with his life and career.

He pointed to his brain on the show and said that the brain is like a muscle. "You need to exercise it."[10]

It would appear that too many of us stop exercising our brains at certain times in our lives, thinking we have reached our limits. But we'll never know what they are until we have batted our heads against them enough to know that maybe we should try something new. By the same token, if we are haunted by anxieties, phobias, compulsions, and personality or other disorders, which we are aware of and which are making our lives needlessly difficult, we need to continue reminding ourselves that these are physical problems—that they are controlled by neural circuitry in a brain that is never the same two minutes in a row. It is terribly hard work to mitigate any mental dysfunction, even the mildest of them, but there is always the possibility that we might succeed.

Maybe I should use a podium.

8.

WE ARE LOST IN A MEGA-UNIVERSE THAT IS INCOMPREHENSIBLE TO US: THE TRAGEDY IS WE ARE UNABLE TO PERCEIVE IT

If an object in space is 400 light-years away, it would take a spaceship traveling at 100,000 miles an hour, 2,800,000 years or so to get there. If we could get beyond our limited brains to fully comprehend that piece of information we would probably say something like: "What, 2,800,000 years? How big is this universe, anyway? What is this all about? I cannot visualize spending 2,800,000 years trying to get anywhere."
Henry Heiman[1]

If we break down all the very basic statistics that we have discovered about the size and nature of the universe and look at them again and again without any preconceived notions of religion, ideology, or culture, we would likely be incapable of absorbing that vast amount of information. Apparently a barrier in our minds allows us to recognize the information, but disables it from sinking in, from registering. Our minds may know, but they won't tell us.

For example, let's examine the concept of the light-year. The nearest star to Earth is Proxima Centauri, which is 4.1 light-years away. I can recall an article in the *New York Times* a few years back that described this star as a "neighbor." But the reality is that one light-year is basically an acronym for

5,865,696,000,000 miles, and so Proxima Centauri is 20 trillion miles or so away. This means that if we were able to travel in a spaceship at the speed of 400,000 miles per hour, which is about sixteen times the speed of our current space shuttles (which travel at about 25,000 miles per hour), it would take us about 7,000 years to get to Proxima Centauri.

In other words, if Alexander, Julius Caesar, Cicero, or Jesus Christ were able to board a spaceship traveling 400,000 miles an hour during their lifetimes, heading toward Proxima Centauri, our nearest neighbor, they wouldn't even be halfway there.

Then there is the Milky Way, the name that we've given to our own galaxy of stars, which is about 100,000 light-years across. It would take our same spaceship, traveling at 400,000 miles an hour, about 100 million years to cut across just our own galaxy. Even if we discovered a way to travel near the speed of light, 670 million miles an hour, it would take us 100,000 years.

Can you grasp this? How can we comprehend a span of 100,000 years, against our own life span of usually under 100 years.

Then in our Milky Way galaxy alone there are approximately 200 billion stars, each of which has some basic equivalence in its atomic structure to our sun. And many of them could have planets orbiting about them like ours.

Furthermore, beyond our own galaxy, should we ever manage to reach its edges, the nearest galaxy, the Andromeda galaxy, is 2.2 million light-years away. To get there at 400,000 miles per hour would take over 2 billion years. And beyond Andromeda, there are about 140 billion additional galaxies, each with approximately 200 billion stars, all with the same basic atomic structure of our sun and many of which may also have planets orbiting them—some of which may be capable of sustaining life.

If untouched by religion, the average, rational person,

when faced with facts like these, might conclude that we are basically lost in the universe and that, amid it all, we are presumably insignificant. If someone were lost in space floating around in a galaxy that was quadrillions upon quadrillions of miles from Earth, he or she would have no idea where the Earth was, should someone else float by and ask directions. In other words, we still don't know how big the universe is as of this writing. Though we do know it's getting bigger, we haven't mapped out the estimated 140 billion galaxies. The number comes from estimates that astronomers interpolate from small samples of the universe they are photographing.[2]

So until we map out all the galaxies and their quadrillions of stars, if that is ever possible, we won't know our precise location against this massive universe. We are basically lost, and there is no living thing out there who we've found that might provide directions, let alone some insights.

We'll read facts like those above, but they make no difference in our lives. In a doubles tennis match with my partner, Joe Farago, I'll frequently say when we're behind, "Why are we getting so excited? We don't even know where we are in the universe. We are lost in space. We are insignificant." And he'll usually reply, "Forget the universe, I want to win this set." One time over lunch he said, "So let me tell you what you are really telling me, when you boil it all down. It means I'm not ever going on a tour of the Milky Way. Look, I haven't seen Mongolia, either, and it isn't keeping me up at night."

Most of us try to avoid the subject, as Joe does. The facts just bounce off of our virtual realities, without making the slightest dent. Even when some of us make a conscious effort to study the enormity and the makeup of the universe that is known, many of us don't experience a significant change in our perspective, a rational and emotional humbling, for instance, that might improve our outlook on life. We appear incapable of putting our cares and woes within a perspective of a universe that in actuality is mysterious, incomprehensible, and so gargantuan that it emphasizes our insignificance. Instead, we continue to clash with each other, as we have over the centuries in defense of one ideology or another, or one religion or another, or one piece of land or another. Not to mention that we often experience exaggerated torment when we are not doing something perfectly right or when events in our lives are not going impeccably for us.

But the wars and the terrorism that we continue to wage in the twenty-first century amid the enlightenment that astronomers and astrophysicists, among others, have provided are the real puzzlement. It appears that this knowledge has given us no perspective at all about our lives. It is far easier to comprehend all the wars that took place in ancient times, through the time of the Romans, through the Middle Ages, and into the eighteenth and nineteenth centuries. Wars of one kind or another were nonstop. They were thought to be part of the human condition—people expected them. Then in the twentieth century, we began to learn much more about the dimensions of the universe through sophisticated telescopes and began to understand that our planet was not the center of everything, that we were in fact a part of a cosmos that appeared to stretch endlessly. These facts should have been a revelation that would have brought us to our senses. But instead, as we read, heard, and saw reports of these discoveries, nothing clicked. We didn't get it. We humans didn't gain any additional perspective. We remained grounded in our primitive belief systems that were firmly protected by our virtual realities. And so wars and terrorism, and other violence against each other, continued—even after worldwide television networks and the Internet put us in instant communication with each other.

In the twentieth century alone, despite reaching new heights in technology and communication, 90 million people were killed because of the wars we fought. This is incredible. But like the dimensions of the universe, statistics like this one don't sink in, either.

Joseph Stalin once said that one death is a tragedy, a million deaths is a statistic. Many considered this statement as just more evidence that Stalin was the personification of evil, a psychopath, and a sadist—of course he did single-handedly cause millions of deaths in his drive to consolidate and maintain his power. But he was also correct in this statement. It is easier for us to visualize death when it happens in smaller numbers, particularly to one poor soul. During the battle of the Somme in World War I, there were 30,000 casualties in a single day. We can't grasp that statistic as easily as we can grasp the fact that during the Iraq war there were 900 deaths after eighteen months of war and occupation, because most of those deaths occurred each week in numbers small enough for us to comprehend. So certainly we can't intuitively fathom the fact that in World War I, as a whole, there were a total of 8,538,315 military persons killed on all sides and 21,219,452 wounded, not to mention the civilian deaths that occurred as a direct result of the war.

And this was truly a nonsensical war that deserves a moment of examination to reflect on how insular we have remained, in spite of every effort science has made to enlighten us. Many believe that a web of treaties that had one country after another declaring war on each other, following the assassination of a member of the Austrian royal family in Serbia, was the cause of the conflict. But it apparently was caused because Kaiser Wilhelm, who ruled as the monarch of Germany leading the country into the war, had a breech birth. This was noted in a biography of him, *Kaiser Wilhelm II: Germany's Last Emperor*, by John Van Der Kiste. As one result of this birth, Kaiser Wilhelm, according to Kiste, had little discipline, was ruled by his impulses, and was perpetually adolescent. He was described by Sir John Erichsen, a British specialist at the time, as "incapable of forming reasonable or temperate judgements, and some of his actions would probably be those of a man not wholly sane."[3] It was surmised that the breech birth caused damage to his prefrontal cortex, which as you'll recall is our "executive center" and, in a relatively normal person, helps discipline impulsive action. The German people, who adored the kaiser's father and grandfather, both monarchs before him, didn't like Wilhelm at all and gave him the nickname "Wilhelm the Sudden." In the days of the monarchies, the common people were always fearful of who their next king or queen would be, and, if you read any history at all, you would know that they had good reason. To add to the tragic nonsense of World War I is the fact that Queen Victoria of England, which had 3.1 million killed and wounded in the war, was in actuality Wilhelm's grandmother; King George V, of England at the time of the war, was his first cousin; and Tsar Nicholas II of Russia, which had 9.1 million killed and wounded, whom he also fought before Nicholas abdicated, was another first cousin. Nicholas's wife was Queen Victoria's granddaughter.

It was all absurd. The war never involved any noble cause. All the participants in the war were fighting either to expand or maintain their empires. It was the status imperative: the need to maintain, display, or increase status, gone rampant.

In China, from 1916 to 1949, there were 35,000,000 deaths from wars and famine. I found this statistic in the biography *Chiang Kai-Shek: China's Generalissimo and the Nation He Lost*, in which the author, Jonathon Fenby, seemed to report this figure as an afterthought.[4]

The history of the twentieth century and now the twenty-first century is littered with human carnage. Could we have avoided this fate if we had the capacity to absorb the information scientists were uncovering that showed how little we apparently mean in a gargantuan universe? Would it have given us a perspective that would allow even the extreme ethnic and religious fanatics among us to settle our differences without bloodshed? Maybe this is one reason why humans are getting taller. Maybe natural selection has a bigger brain planned for us that might give us a better vision of reality, and, in order for us to carry it in our skulls, we have to be taller and stronger. I hope that's the reason.

In the meantime, we go about our daily lives ignoring facts which offer us a perspective that could make even the most arrogant and prideful among us humble.

Physicists tell us that they have the nature of the universe pretty well figured out, down to its origins. Physicist Brian Greene, in *The Elegant Universe,* explains: "At the moment of the big bang, the whole of the universe erupted from a microscopic nugget whose size makes a grain of sand [about the size of this dot (.)] appear colossal."[5]

Can you comprehend that fact, truly absorb it, get it to register? I can't. I read it, I say aha, then I go do my laundry. "Physics Intelligence" should be one of Gardner's multiple intelligences, because mine, on a scale of one to ten, is less than a two. I have to read books like Greene's, which are written for the general public, at a snail's pace.

I even had some difficulty with parts of Bill Bryson's excellent book, *A Short History of Nearly Everything,* even though he was more successful in dumbing down the facts, I thought, than was Greene, probably because Bryson is a writer and Greene a scientist. By the way, Bryson describes the origin of the universe as follows: "The whole episode may have lasted no more than 10 (to power 34)—that's one million million million million million millionths of a second—but it changed the universe from something you could hold in your hand to something at least 10,000,000,000,000,000,000,000,000 times bigger."[6] It probably turned out to be a lot bigger than that, perhaps taking up pages of zeros.

But can you imagine the universe as something you could hold in your hand—or if the size of a grain of sand, on your fingertip? It's mind boggling, but let's not dwell on this thought because physicists tell us that that little grain was so dense, it weighed billions or trillions of tons. Okay, I see. And then in one blast, the universe began to expand with enormous speed. Alan Guth, another eminent physicist, points out in *The Inflationary Universe* that gravity began to emerge "at one ten-millionth of a trillionth of a trillionth of a trillionth of a second," after the bang started.[7] Then in three minutes, 98 percent of all the matter that the universe is currently composed of was produced.

It is a wonder that physicists have been able to deduce facts like these from their studies of particle physics and cosmology. They apparently are able to reconstruct the beginnings of the universe from, among other things, the nature of the particles that they have recently uncovered in those enormous accelerators used for research. They appear capable of delineating the exact amount of time, down to the trillionth of a second, that certain things happened after the instant of the big bang.

Of course, no one knows what was going on *before* the big bang took place. Stephen Hawking, on his audiotape *Black Holes and Baby Universes*, asserts that "any speculation about what was going on before the big bang is a point where science and religion meet."[8] An article in the *New York Times* in 2001, titled "Theorists Ponder What, If Anything, There Was before the Big Bang," contains the most telling statement: "[M]ost cosmologists, including Dr. [Alan] Guth and Dr. [Andrei] Linde, agree that the universe ultimately must come from somewhere and that nothing is the leading candidate." Linde also notes that this may be a "religious question."[9]

Nothing is the leading candidate? Yes, indeed, that's what he said. In other words, we haven't a clue.

Guth and others have theorized that our universe is only one of several. Try comprehending that, if you can. If it would take about 15 billion years traveling at the speed of light to reach the fringes of our universe, then we'd likely have to spend several more trips of 15 billion years to have grand tours of all the universes that have been produced. Try thinking about that the next time you're upset that you've dripped soup on your shirt.

But then there is the problem of actually traveling about the universe. It was part of Einstein's theory of special relativity that nothing can travel faster than the speed of light. Not only that, but at the speed of light, time stops. (Another mind boggler that we will take up in the next chapter.) Light travels at the rate of 670 million miles per hour, pretty fast, but even if we could approach that speed, we'd still not be fast enough to get us anywhere interesting in the universe. Approaching that speed, we would reach the planet Pluto in seven hours and the star Proxima Centauri in approximately 4.1 years. But remember, it would still take us about 100,000 years to cross our own galaxy, the Milky Way, and another 2,000,000 years to reach Andromeda, the next galaxy over. And remember, there are at least 140 billion galaxies beyond that, each with at least 200 billion stars.

What is going on here?

Some physicists have talked about the theory of wormholes, based on Einstein's theories, a theoretical fabric of the universe that would allow us to escape the impediment of approximately 670 million miles an hour, as the fastest possible speed that we could travel. It is the stuff of *Star Trek* and other science fiction movies and novels, but that's as far as it goes. Then there is the concept of string theory, which may work to alter our notions of distance, if the physicists studying it can ever work it out. The details of the theory are far beyond my ability to comprehend.

The fact remains, however, that we can't even travel around our own solar system, which is an infinitesimal portion of the Milky Way. (As noted, the Milky Way has at least 200 billion stars, many just like our own sun, which is about 26,000 light-years from the center of the galaxy.) We are basically lost in space, as an astronomer I sat next to six years ago on an airplane admitted. If we were able to reach someone on a planet in the Andromeda galaxy on our cell phone and asked him if he knew the address of the planet Earth because we wanted to send ourselves a letter, he wouldn't be able to tell us. Besides, it would take 2,000,000 years between the time we said "hello" and when he answered back "hello," even if he understood English. If we consider the enormity of it all, can we be conceited enough to believe that we are something special on the planet Earth: that in all of the 140 billion galaxies, each with 200 billion or more suns, with perhaps trillions of planets orbiting them, billions of which might be similar to ours, that we are the only planet to harbor life? As a scientist said on a CNN special on the universe, the chances that we are the only planet in the universe to harbor life "is virtually zero."[10]

It would appear to me that, given the enormity of space, we as human beings are fundamentally insignificant. I mentioned this fact between sets to my tennis partner, Joe Farago, who replied, "Insignificant, what do you mean insignificant? We are all significant. Life is significant. You are out of your mind. Besides, have you ever seen an alien from space?"

"No."

"So there you are, we are special."

"But wait a second, Joe," I replied. "There is nothing wrong with feeling insignificant from a galactic point of view. If all of us did feel insignificant in that way, we would be humbled, curious, the fighting and battles would hopefully stop, the small worries, fears, and anxieties we have would disappear. We are nothing, so why worry? If you want to believe in some religion—many of which also attempt to humble us in the face of an almighty God (a spiritual approach to humility and virtue, versus our rational approach)—or ideology to make you feel more comfortable, then go to it, as long as we all understand that there are no ultimate answers. Live life to its fullest, be kind and gentle to make life for all of us more pleasant. What is wrong with that?"

"Why don't you just shut up and serve the ball."

And there is the tragedy of it. Our virtual realities have it all figured out, and we appear to be helpless to penetrate them.

Moreover, the world has barely addressed the three most important questions of our time: First, what was going on before the big bang? Second, what was the idea behind the big bang, why did it happen? Third, whose idea was it? The first question is currently being addressed, as mentioned earlier, but I have yet to find references addressing the second and third questions, aside from those of religious dogma.

We appear to be content either with spiritual answers or with avoiding the subject altogether, for fear of knocking our virtual realities out of balance, or with thinking that the efforts of NASA and its equivalents in other countries will find the answers with their probes to the outer planets. But that wouldn't get us to first base. Tell me we have a probe that can get to the next galaxy in my lifetime, and I'll say we're getting somewhere.

When was the last time you sat around with friends, relatives, or colleagues at a gathering and discussed these three questions? When there is a lull in the conversation and I bring up these questions at gatherings, I get the kind of looks reserved for known psychotics. But then there is my friend, scientist Bob Hare, mentioned earlier, who told me that he sometimes sits in his backyard at night, staring at the heavens, and ponders these very questions. He says he doesn't get far, and neither do I. Perhaps there are thousands of others, or tens of thousands of other humans, who ponder these questions, but until we receive a single message from somewhere in our universe, or better yet, beyond the universe, that all the peoples of the world might immediately understand, the answers appear unknowable.

Until then, we'll undoubtedly continue to terrorize each other.

9.

THE PASSAGE OF TIME, AS WE SENSE IT, DOES NOT REALLY EXIST

With minimal effort, we can make use of the constancy of the speed of light to show that the familiar, everday conception of time is plain wrong.
Brian Greene[1]

Let not the sands of time get in your lunch.
National Lampoon, "Deteriorata" [2]

The passage of time does not exist as we think it does. This was a revolutionary discovery by Albert Einstein, who first published the idea as part of a 1917 paper titled "Cosmological Considerations on the General Theory of Relativity." And yet today, very few of us are aware of its implications, one of which is that the faster we are able to travel, the slower the passage of time will be, and that time literally stops when we are able to travel at the speed of light, 670 million miles an hour. As physicist and author Brian Greene succinctly puts it in *The Elegant Universe*: "There is no passage of time at light speed."[3]

As with noting the dimensions of the universe, try bringing up the fact that time is imaginary at a social gathering, and the conversation will quickly divert to other topics. Most of us don't want to hear about it, unless we are curious about what science is discovering. This interested group is apparently an extreme minority among us humans.

I brought this subject up during a dinner at a restaurant, and the woman next to me said, pointing to my shirt, "I like that color on you."

Einstein actually had two theories of relativity, both of which have now been proved correct. The first, his theory of special relativity, had to do with space, time, and the fact that energy and matter are interchangeable. The latter is represented through his famous formula $E = mc^2$, which was later used as the basis of the atomic bomb. Also tied in with this part of the theory was that time is relative to where an observer happens to be and at what speed he, or someone he is observing, is traveling.

His general theory added gravity, acceleration, and the fact that gravity can be curved in space, which we won't cover here, thank goodness.

It is the space-time relationship that we find so difficult to comprehend, because the speed of light is constant, no matter at what speed the source of the light is traveling. For example, if we put a strong headlight on the front of a space shuttle traveling at 25,000 miles per hour, we would expect that the speed of the light traveling forward from the lamp would be 670 million miles per hour, plus the 25,000 miles per hour the shuttle is moving. But that doesn't happen. The speed of the light stays constant.

Conversely, if we put a headlight on the back of the shuttle, we would assume that the speed of light traveling back from the shuttle would be 670 million miles per hour, less the 25,000 miles per hour we're traveling. That doesn't happen, either. The speed of light stays constant.

Even more puzzling to us humans going about our lives and jobs without giving space and time a second thought is the fact that the faster we travel, the slower time passes. At the speed of light, which is the fastest that anything can go, time actually stops, as Brian Greene pointed out. It would also stop if our space shuttle (were it capable of traveling in the farther reaches of space) happened to get sucked into a black hole. The gravity is so dense in a black hole, that it apparently won't let anything escape immediately, including light. And since light appears to be the mediator of time, time would stop, at least for the persons inside the space shuttle—that is, if they could survive the force of the gravity, which they couldn't. Scientist Stephen Hawking, in *Brief History of Time*, says it's more likely the persons would be "turned to spaghetti."[4]

Bill Bryson, in *A Short History of Nearly Everything*, cited English philosopher and mathematician, Bertrand Russell, in illustrating the phenomenon of speed controlling time from Russell's book *The ABC of Relativity*. Russell asked the reader to envision a train one hundred yards long, moving at 60 percent of the speed of light. To someone standing on a platform watching it pass, the train would appear to be only eighty yards long and everything on it would be similarly compressed. If we could hear the passengers on the train speak, their voices would sound slurred and sluggish, like a record played at too slow a speed, and the passengers' movements would appear similarly ponderous. Even the clocks on the train would seem to be running at only four-fifths their normal time. However, the people on the train itself would have no sense of these distortions. To them everything on the train would seem normal.[5]

And that, in a nutshell, is why the theory is called "relativity." Time is relative, depending on where we are at any given moment and how fast we are going.

Unfortunately, we can't go fast enough on Earth to make any appreciable difference in how we sense time. And so we can't sense the trick of time being played on us by whoever or whatever devised the universe. This might have helped us gain a better sense of perspective about our lives, just as a comprehension of the dimensions of the universe might have helped as well.

I mentioned this concept of imaginary time to my contrarian friend, Bob Schwartz, over dinner one night.

"You're crazy," he said. "Who is telling you that time is imaginary?"

"The physicists, astrophysicists, and other scientists whose books I read."

"How do they know that?"

"They've tested the theory, they know it works. I recall when the astronauts used to make trips to the Moon, the commentators would almost always mention that they were actually younger than they would have been if they didn't make the trip, that the clocks on their wrists were running slower, but that the difference would be infinitesimal."

"Well, those astronauts always looked the same to me, when they returned. This appears to be your usual craziness."

It is extremely difficult comprehending within the sphere of our everyday lives that there is no such thing as real time or absolute time. But the daunting fact is that all time is indeed relative and what we sense as time is indeed imaginary or illusory. If we could travel, as Einstein envisioned himself doing, at the head of a light beam, time would literally stop. If you were wearing a wrist watch, it would also literally stop.

If we were sitting on a spaceship, something out of a *Star Trek* movie, the more speed we'd be picking up, the slower the time we'd be experiencing would pass. And as we would begin to pick up speed up to the rate, say, to one-tenth the speed of light, or hundreds of millions of miles per hour, time would noticeably begin to slow down. We would, in fact, begin to age a lot slower than those we left behind on Earth. If we returned in, say, ten years, after continually traveling that fast, the clocks of those we left behind might be three or four years ahead of the clocks we took on the flight. They would literally be three or four years older than we were at the start of the flight.

This is no longer theory: the concept has been proven. In *Einstein's Brainchild: Relativity Made Relatively Easy*, physics professor Barry Parker describes a number of tests that verified the theory, including one at Harvard using radioactive cobalt:

> The cobalt was placed in the basement of the building and holes were drilled up through several floors to the roof above, which was 74 feet up. An absorber was set up there to absorb the emitted rays. Measurement of the emitted and absorbed frequencies then allowed them to test Einstein's theory, and it was again verified.[6]

Stephen Hawking, in the audio tape for *Black Holes and Baby Universes and Other Essays*, describes another test in 1962 that is easier to understand. Highly accurate atomic clocks were used at the top and bottom of a water tower. After the testing period was up, scientists found that the clock at the bottom of the tower actually ran slower, since it was closer to Earth and not traveling through space as fast as the clock at the top of the tower.[7] The difference in time was infinitesimal, but it was enough to prove the theory of the relativity of time. It's only as our speed picks up to 10 or 100 million of miles an hour, or more, that the difference can become truly noticeable. And then, as noted, at the actual speed of light, 670 million miles an hour, time literally stops.

The reason is that the faster we travel, the more mass an object picks up, which then begins to impede our speed. During a baseball game, for example, if a pitcher throws the ball at 100 miles per hour, as some can do, the ball, by the time it reaches the catcher's glove, would probably have picked up mass—approximately 0.000000000002 grams of mass, according to Bill Bryson in his *Short History of Everything*.[8] And the heavier an object becomes, the more energy it takes to keep propelling it. At about the speed of light, any form of mass becomes infinite in its proportions, and you simply can't propel it any faster.

And would we look just as we look right now, traveling all that fast, you might ask?

Not really. If you used Einstein's famous equation, $E = mc^2$, the mass of objects increases vastly as it nears the speed of light, which includes our bodies, so we probably couldn't nearly reach such a speed as a human, as we know humans to be.

Then there is the issue of black holes. The odds of our ever traveling fast enough to reach a black hole in space are long. But if we were to sail past a black hole and fall into it, time would also stop. So there we go again, another stoppage of time. A black hole is the result of a burned-out star falling in on itself. When this happens, the gravity that it creates is extraordinary, akin to the weight and mass of a mountain being congealed into a particle the size of the nucleus of an atom. That minuscule particle would weigh as much as the mountain. It would be so heavy that if you placed it on the surface of the Earth, it would instantly plunge down to the center of the Earth.

Did you get that?

It turns out that the more mass an object has, the more gravity it creates. So you can imagine the mass and gravity of an enormous black hole. The gravity would be so intense that a beam of light from your flashlight would be drawn back into it. The theory up until very recently was that light cannot escape a black hole and so neither could time, which would stop with it. However, as I understand it, Stephen Hawking said in 2004 that, at some point, information may be capable of escaping, which I found to be an enormous relief.

The upshot is that time is basically an illusion for us, since it is not what we think we are experiencing. It is just part of a big show being staged for us, for whatever the reasons. Our stage is an Earth that is lost in an immeasurable universe but with props such as a pleasant sky and clouds to give us a sense of reality. Human bodies and other organisms form the cast of characters to keep the show going. The illusion of time is to make us think we are moving forward into the next act. We envision, to some degree, our lifetimes as being an infinite series of acts. And all of this and more is synthesized by the neural circuits of our brains in a way that makes us think something important is taking place.

As noted, the fact that time is imaginary has been known by scientists for many years, but its implications have yet to trickle down to the overwhelming majority of us. Further, as with the dimensions of the universe, the fact that time is imaginary appears to be repelled by the barriers that surround our virtual realities. After all, we have been conditioned since youth with the observation that time passes. Clocks move. We see ourselves aging along with everyone we know, and that is our knowledge of it.

The great physicist J. Robert Oppenheimer, the head of the Manhattan Project, said:

> [The apparent paradoxes of relativity] do not involve any contradictions on the part of nature; what they do involve is a gross change, a rather sharp change from what learned people and ordinary people thought throughout the past centuries . . . thought as long as they thought about things at all. The simple facts, namely that light travels with a velocity that cannot be added to or subtracted from by moving a source of light, the simple fact that objects do contract when they are in motion, the simple fact that processes are slowed down when they take place in motion, and very much if they move with velocities comparable to the speed of light—these are new ele-

ments of the natural world and what the theory of relatively has done is give coherence and meaning to the connections between them.[9]

Well, they give coherence and meaning to those who can comprehend it all, but not to most of us. Sir James Jeans, a mathematician, physicist, and astronomer, said the following in an effort to try to comfort us about the fact that we discovered that time is imaginary:

> [The limitations of our own personal experiences relating to time and space] do not of course suggest that we must abandon the intuitive concepts of space and time, which we derive from individual experience. . . . Whatever conclusions the mathematicians may reach, it is certain that our newspapers, our historians and story-tellers will still place their truths and fictions in a framework of time [that is still familiar to us]; they will continue to say—this event happened at such an instant in the course of the ever-flowing stream of time; this other event at another instant lower down the stream, and so on. . . . The theory of relativity merely suggests that such a scheme is private to single individuals or to small colonies of individuals.[10]

In other words, the normal, uninformed among us can ignore the whole thing. We can presume that our virtual realities will continue to judge that time is constant and that our watches, when they're working correctly, will keep regular time. The concept of our staying young through time travel is currently beyond our reach, but one might imagine some of us willing to endure the tedium of a twenty-five-light-year round-trip—if this were ever possible—if we could return years younger because of it.

Another difficulty to tackle is actual space exploration, managing to get out of our galaxy, to Andromeda, for example, about 2,000,000 light-years away. If we could learn to build a spaceship that could travel at speeds approaching 670 million miles an hour, while keeping our body mass at a manageable level, it would still take us more than 2 million years to travel to Andromeda and to explore it. I don't know about you, but I have trouble on really long airplane trips—15 hours is really rough for me, 25 years would seem unthinkable. And so I can't imagine traveling 2,000,000 years to go anywhere, even though traveling 4,000,000 years round-trip, approaching the speed of light, would mean that, in terms of time on Earth, I wouldn't have aged at all when I returned home. And then who would I know? How would I turn on the television?

Maybe the science fiction writers know more than scientists do. Knowing these facts about space, they blindly ignore them and assume that space travel between the galaxies will someday in the future be possible.

The only thing that really bothers me about science fiction is that while these humans of the future have all the technology for space exploration, they are still trying to kill each other in outer space. Does this mean that our limbic system and other brain neural circuitry that creates psychopaths and sadists will continue to haunt us forever?

That is a somber thought.

10.

THE CODING THAT CREATES AND SHAPES US AS HUMANS IS THE SAME FOR ALL LIFE, INCLUDING BABOONS, FLIES, ANTS, AND POTATOES

Wherever you go in the world, whatever animal, plant, bug or blob you look at, if it is alive, it will use the same dictionary and know the same code. All life is one. . . . We all use exactly the same language.
Matt Ridley[1]

We now go from the ridiculously large, the dimensions and nature of space and time, to the ridiculously small, our DNA molecules.

It was the great hope of some of us at the outset of the Human Genome Project—a research project devoted to mapping our genetic makeup—that at its completion, the world would gain insight into the fact that we are all one. We would understand that the coding of all life in all its forms emanates from a DNA molecule that is so tiny that it can't even be seen with our strongest microscopes.

I hoped that the terrorists, the power-hungry, and the violent fanatics of all religions would finally get that there is nothing to be violently fanatic about—that they would come to their senses! The project was completed in April 2003, and the publicity surrounding it was enormous, but nothing happened to alter our outlooks. It was life as usual.

The following is an edited and abridged version of a discussion I first had with a geneticist I met at a cocktail party in 1998. Then we later talked over the phone, after the Human Genome Project was completed, to bring the facts up-to-date.[2]

"First," I began, "I'd like to confirm that our DNA exists in every cell in our bodies, which I understand is about 60 trillion cells?"

"Sixty trillion? Is that how many cells we have?" (This was when we first met.) He pointed to his ample stomach—he was short, overweight, and jovial. "Hey, I bet I have more than that. I've heard the estimate of 100 trillion cells. But the answer to your question is a qualified 'Yes.' Almost all of our cells, with some exceptions, I believe the red blood cells and some immune system cells, have the identical DNA. Of course I'm not counting sperms cells and the female egg, which have only half the DNA, so that when they come together, there will be a full arsenal, so to speak."

"And speaking of chromosomes, might one visualize the twenty-three pairs of, or forty-six, chromosomes that form our DNA as separate threads?"

"Threads? Sure, why not. We use the term 'filament.'" He took a minute to inspect his sport coat and pulled a short thread from the inner lining. "Yes, this is about right and it's on average a little less than two inches long, which is the length of DNA in an average chromosome. Of course, they're all tightly coiled so you'd have to stretch one out to make it look like this, and they all are of different lengths. It would come to about six feet of thread or filament if you were to connect all the filaments from all the chromosomes together in a straight line."

I took the thread from his hand and asked, "As I understand it, if this thread was actually a DNA chromosome, it would be so thin it would actually be invisible to the naked eye."

"Quite correct. It takes a form of sophisticated x-ray crystallography technology called gene or DNA sequencers to examine these threads as you call them."

"Now the term 'gene,' as I understand it, applies to sections of this six-foot thread of DNA, if we just were to imagine that this thread is six feet long," I said dangling the thread he had given to me. "Is that correct?"

"Yes, and the approximate 35,000 genes we have uncovered on the human genome is only a method for classifying sections of the thread, representing what will become different proteins."

"Now here's the hard part, which I find difficult to comprehend."

"Go ahead, test me."

"Well, as I understand it, there are actually 20 billion bits of information on this DNA thread, which converts to about 3.2 billion letters, of which there are only four."

"Four letters, you mean."

"Yes."

"What you said, then, is all quite true. There are approximately 3.2 billion copies of four letters, nucleotide bases . . . that are encoded on our filament or thread, if you like, of DNA, a short and amazing alphabet, but which are the very basic building blocks of everything in our bodies. The letters representing those nucleotides are A, G, C, and T. Astounding isn't it?"

"To say the least. And I read that the Human Genome Project literally copied the sequence of letters on this thread, and when they were through, there was the equivalent of 300,000 pages of those four letters in varying sequences, if it were set in the type of a standard encyclopedia."

"Sounds about right. I've seen the coding referred to as the equivalent of 5,000 average-sized books, or 400 volumes of the *Encyclopaedia Britannica*. And I imagine you know how small that type is. It can take quite some time to read just one page."

"And all from this one six-foot thread." I waved the little thread in the air.

"Yes, yes, quite correct. And I should add that the thread you are holding as a metaphor may also contain the coding for a chimpanzee, or a pigeon, or a butterfly, or an oak tree. Each cell in every living thing contains a filament, such as the imaginary one you are holding, with exactly the same DNA molecules organized into genes, but with different coding for each, so that each can ultimately be transformed into a liver cell, a neuron, a mouse tail, or a rose petal. And so there is not only the human genome, there is the chimpanzee genome, the pigeon genome, and the rose genome."

"So all life starts basically the same as part of these genomes. The DNA is basically the same; the only thing that is different is how it is coded."

I paused for an instant, then pulled a loose thread from the sleeve of my sport coat, and held both threads up. "So you're saying that this one thread could represent a human, and this second thread could represent a pigeon, and before all the DNA molecules go into action and begin following the directions of their codes, their basic DNA filaments would look like this."

"Metaphorically, yes. All life begins with the chromosomes in each cell body, each holding strands of DNA, which if picked apart and tied together would look the same to begin with. You couldn't tell them apart because the DNA molecule, shaped like a double helix, an illustration most of the world is familiar with, is the same in every genome, on every filament, although the length of the filaments may be different. The human genome has over 3 billion letters, while the fruit fly has 137 million, and an HIV virus only 9,700. So the threads, as you call them, of the latter organisms, would be shorter."

"So all living things are indeed all one, at least at the very start of life."

"That is correct."

"So why don't we all know this? Why isn't this being broadcast to us everyday in some way?"

He burst out laughing, bent over to his knees, then looked up and said, arms open questioningly, "Hey, do I own CBS?" Then he gathered himself and said, "This has been well publicized, but the implications are so overwhelming for so many people who are used to demeaning animals and other humans they perceive as below them that the facts just don't sink in."

"Okay, let's digress for a moment. Is it true that as the cells in our body divide—particularly as we are growing, or building muscle, or whatever—that each of those 3 billion letters buried in the nucleus of the cells are replicated?"

"Oh, yes, it is quite a process."

"Now I read this somewhere and it's sort of mind boggling. After the double helix of the molecule is split down the middle as the cell prepares to reproduce itself and divide . . . and a new strand is replicated from the old and spliced together with the remaining strand, is it true that before the cells actually divide, little checkers, so to speak, go down each of the new DNA threads that were just replicated to make sure the replication is accurate, and if mistakes are spotted, these checkers can actually fix them?"

"Checkers, did you say?"

"Yes, checkers."

Again, he broke out laughing. "I never heard them called that before. Science prefers a more sophisticated vernacular. We call them snipping enzymes."

"Then I learned that our cells divide at different rates, with some dividing in under an hour, and in the brain at birth, the cells replicate at 250,000 per minute. So this whole process of creating a 300,000-page volume of human coding can be done that quickly and with checkers making sure that those sequence of letters were all copied correctly. Can you say this isn't true?"

"No, it's true all right."

"So just in this short instant of time, the checkers or

enzymes, which are beyond microscopic in size, can review 300,000 pages of data."

"Yes, in a metamorphic sense that is true."

"Hold on." I took out my pen and a post-it note I had in my pocket and did a rough calculation.

"If we assumed that we could find someone fast enough to read and edit 300 pages of an *Encyclopaedia Britannica* in a single day, it would take that superhuman person twenty-seven years to do what those enzymes can do in hours or even minutes or seconds."

"Are you suggesting that we replace editors with snipping enzymes?"

I laughed, "Hey, I don't want to get my editor mad. This is all just sort of mind boggling."

"It is, isn't it?"

"So the Ultimate Designer has to be some kind of incredible design engineer."

"The Ultimate Designer?"

"You know, the fellow upstairs." I pointed to the ceiling.

"Oh, that's great," he said laughing. "Yes indeed, someone, if it was a someone, a god figure, had to be an engineer beyond all comprehension to design this system. This is monumental biological engineering. On the other hand, the system isn't perfect. Now and again your checkers, the snipping enzymes, overlook a mistake and a mutation occurs, possibly leading to susceptibility to disease. You don't want another drink and some peanuts, do you?"

"I could do with one more, and, yes, some peanuts."

I told him what I was drinking, and he left me staring at the thread. While he was gone, I went over to the hostess, Mimi, and asked her if she had any thread in the house.

"Thread? Are you crazy? I don't sew."

"You mean in this whole house, you don't have one spool of thread?"

She thought for a minute. "You know, I do have some thread in my traveling kit. Do you really want it?"

"If it wouldn't be much trouble. And if you get it, I promise I'll talk to your cousin again." She had been trying to fix me up with her for years.

"Done." She ran off to get the thread and arrived just as the geneticist returned with the drinks and a bowl of peanuts.

She looked at him and said, "He wanted some thread."

The geneticist smiled and said, "So the threads from my coat lining and your sleeve wouldn't do, eh?"

"No, it wasn't that; I just wanted to draw off six feet of thread so that maybe it might be easier for my brain to register these facts."

"Well, go ahead. Do you want a tape measure?"

"No, I'll use my shoe, it's about twelve inches long."

I measured out about six feet.

"There," I said, holding the thread up. "Now the big difference between this thread and our DNA chromosomes, if they were all connected together like this, would be that it would be invisible to the human eye."

"Yes, and to our strongest microscopes as well, at least as of now. You can see them only when they are reproducing and the coils thicken."

"So the threading on a spider web would be thick by comparison."

"Of course."

"Now in the photo reproductions I've seen of DNA, which most of us have seen on television or in the newspapers, it appears to me that when the reproductions of sequences of the four basic letters are enlarged, the markings look very much like bar codes."

"Bar codes?"

"Yes, you know, the bar codes on boxes of cereal and cans of soup and such that they scan at supermarket checkout counters. Or the bar codes you find on all items in a hardware store."

He thought a moment and then started to giggle. "You know, they do look like those bar codes."

"So it wouldn't be inaccurate to say that, metaphorically, all of human life emanates from a series of bar codes."

He continued giggling. "You're not going to quote me, are you?"

"Remember, I promised I wouldn't tell anyone who you are."

"Well, then, yes, you could say metaphorically that we all come from a series of bar codes, which even as a metaphor is quite a stretch."

"All classified neatly on this six-foot string of thread."

"Yes."

"Which in the laboratory might one day be cloned to produce a human being."

"Yes, the possibility exists for that to happen, many, many years from now."

"Which means the possibility exists that we might one day be able to clone each of the 60 trillion cells in our body to create enough humans to populate other solar systems hovering about stars in the Milky Way or nearby galaxies—if we can ever get to them. In other words, from our single body alone, we may have the potential to create 60 trillion new bodies."

"You know," he pointed to his drink, "maybe I should have made this a double."

"So this thread," I stood up, reaching high up and let it hang to the living room carpet, "is composed of three billion letters formed in bar codes, and this is what human life is made of."

"Yes, and before discussing humans alone, let's turn to humans versus animals. To begin with, it turns out that between humans and chimpanzees, the species closest to humans, we share 98.7 percent of our DNA coding. In other words, only 2.3 percent of that string you're holding represents the differences between us humans and chimpanzees. In addition, the only difference between that string you're holding and one for a spider, an orange, or an ear of corn is its length and the configuration of letters."

"And so Richard Nixon, and George Bush, and your mother, and my mother, all came from threads like these."

"Yes, a string of DNA, whose polymorphisms, if you'll excuse the technical term, create the differences between individuals."

"Including mental differences, the variances in our brains that make each of us not only look different, but think and act differently."

"Yes, I would imagine so."

"And now let me ask you the jackpot question."

"Which is?"

"How much difference is there between this strand or thread of DNA, that, say, represents you, a Caucasian, and someone who is African American?"

"Yes, yes, that is an important question. First, it is apparent that there are differences between all humans, just look around this room, different faces, noses, ears, and so forth. But the fact is that, in terms of the human genome as a whole, the differences between any of us, whoever we are on the Earth, are minuscule. It turns out that we all share 99.9 percent of the same genetic code. And that includes people of other colors and other general physical characteristics. Do you have a brother or a sister?"

"I have a sister."

"Well, then, the differences between your DNA and that of your sister are no more different in volume than between you and an African American."

"Amazing. I would ask you why the world doesn't know about this, but then you would probably tell me again that you don't own CBS."

"Probably so. It is a great shame that these kinds of facts

seem to be hidden under a hat for most people. I'll agree with you on that."

"I think it's a tragedy. But let's move on. What about our genetic predispositions for hatred, jealousy, envy, fanaticism, love, and so much more. . . . Are they already encoded on this thread?"

I waved it up and down and drew some stares from others at the party, including Mimi's cousin, who looked at me as if I were just let out of an asylum. "Maybe I don't have to talk to her," I said to myself.

"I can't comment on that. I'm a gene man, not a brain man. But I can tell you that the structure of the brain is definitely encoded on the DNA, so whatever your brain includes, when it first comes out of the womb, is a result of that coding. And now, my friend, it was very nice to meet you." He rose and grabbed my hand as I quickly switched the thread from my right hand to my left.

"I definitely need a double, now."

After I thanked him for his time, and as he was walking away, he turned and said, "Don't call me, I'll call you." Then he laughed uproariously again.

That conversation and the one I had recently with the geneticist to bring the information up-to-date left me in a daze. Like the dimensions and nature of the universe, the nature of the genome doesn't appear to sink into our consciousness. Our mind can know it, but it isn't telling us.

In 1991, when the publicly funded Human Genome Project was being considered at a projected cost of $3 billion over a period of eleven years, it was competitiveness and politics that helped bring it into being. One of the arguments that motivated a skeptical US Congress to allocate the money was that the Japanese would undertake and lead the study if we didn't. We thus needed the threat of Japanese competition, a big rival to the United States at the time, to convince Congress that the allocation of this money was worthwhile. This for a research project that will probably be the most useful for humankind, not only for finding the causes of and potential gene-based remedies for a myriad of diseases it might uncover—there are more than three thousand[3] known inheritable diseases—but for the understanding it will give us in determining who we are, what is life, how we began, and what the mechanisms are for perpetuating ourselves.

The completion of the first draft of the human genome, more than 300,000 pages long, was announced by former president Bill Clinton on June 26, 2000.

One fascinating aspect regarding DNA is the fact that we need to have the coding for our entire body in every cell of our bodies, as mentioned in the discussion with the geneticist. In other words, every cell in the fetus has the coding for an entire body from which to determine what turns into a liver or kidney cell, or a specific muscle cell or neurotransmitter. This appears to be a bit of overkill. Even more humbling is the fact that only about 3 percent of our DNA is composed of proper genes.[4] Tell me what this is all about.

In essence, the 3.2 billion letters on the filaments of DNA are first sectionalized via the chromosomes. Humans have twenty-three pairs, or forty-six, chromosomes in each of our cells (excluding sperm cells and the female egg). Broken down, on average, this would mean that each chromosome would carry about 70 million letters, which comprise our 35,000 genes, which create proteins (as we'll soon see). However, the chromosomes are not equal in size, so some have far more letters clustered into genes than others. Scientists have assigned numbers to the chromosomes. The Number 1 chromosome carries the most genes, 2,968; while the Y chromosome has the fewest, 231. Each chromosome carries different building blocks and functions for the body. If the genome as a whole is a book, the chromosomes can be viewed as its chapters, and its genes its pages.

```
GAGCTCTGATGACTCGGTATTAGTACTTAATCCATCCTTTAGGGATCATGACAATTCCGGATTAC
GAATAATGATGAGCTCGGAATCGATTAACCTGACTGGTACTGAAGGGTTACTGAATGAGAGCTCG
AGTCACGGAATTGACTTACTATTGGAGGAATCATGCATGACTGACTACTGGAAGGCTCGAGTCTA
CGGTATTCCTTAGCTCTATTACTATTCTTAGGATCTTACTTACTTTATATTACGGAGAGTCATAT
TCTTATCCTAGGTCTTACTTGAGCTCTTAACCACATAGCCAGTCATTTAGGGAAGGTATCGTCTA
GAGCTCTGATGACTCGGTATTAGTACTTAATCCATCCTTTAGGGATCATGACAATTCCGGATTAC
GAATAATGATGAGCTCGGAATCGATTAACCTGACTGGTACTGAAGGGTTACTGAATGAGAGCTCG
AGTCACGGAATTGACTTACTATTGGAGGAATCATGCATGACTGACTACTGGAAGGCTCGAGTCTA
CGGTATTCCTTAGCTCTATTACTATTCTTAGGATCTTACTTACTTTATATTACGGAGAGTCATAT
TCTTATCCTAGGTCTTACTTGAGCTCTTAACCACATAGCCAGTCATTTAGGGAAGGTATCGTCTA
GAGCTCTGATGACTCGGTATTAGTACTTAATCCATCCTTTAGGGATCATGACAATTCCGGATTAC
GAATAATGATGAGCTCGGAATCGATTAACCTGACTGGTACTGAAGGGTTACTGAATGAGAGCTCG
AGTCACGGAATTGACTTACTATTGGAGGAATCATGCATGACTGACTACTGGAAGGCTCGAGTCTA
CGGTATTCCTTAGCTCTATTACTATTCTTAGGATCTTACTTACTTTATATTACGGAGAGTCATAT
TCTTATCCTAGGTCTTACTTGAGCTCTTAACCACATAGCCAGTCATTTAGGGAAGGTATCGTCTA
GAGCTCTGATGACTCGGTATTAGTACTTAATCCATCCTTTAGGGATCATGACAATTCCGGATTAC
GAATAATGATGAGCTCGGAATCGATTAACCTGACTGGTACTGAAGGGTTACTGAATGAGAGCTCG
AGTCACGGAATTGACTTACTATTGGAGGAATCATGCATGACTGACTACTGGAAGGCTCGAGTCTA
CGGTATTCCTTAGCTCTATTACTATTCTTAGGATCTTACTTACTTTATATTACGGAGAGTCATAT
TCTTATCCTAGGTCTTACTTGAGCTCTTAACCACATAGCCAGTCATTTAGGGAAGGTATCGTCTA
GAGCTCTGATGACTCGGTATTAGTACTTAATCCATCCTTTAGGGATCATGACAATTCCGGATTAC
GAATAATGATGAGCTCGGAATCGATTAACCTGACTGGTACTGAAGGGTTACTGAATGAGAGCTCG
AGTCACGGAATTGACTTACTATTGGAGGAATCATGCATGACTGACTACTGGAAGGCTCGAGTCTA
CGGTATTCCTTAGCTCTATTACTATTCTTAGGATCTTACTTACTTTATATTACGGAGAGTCATAT
TCTTATCCTAGGTCTTACTTGAGCTCTTAACCACATAGCCAGTCATTTAGGGAAGGTATCGTCTA
GAGCTCTGATGACTCGGTATTAGTACTTAATCCATCCTTTAGGGATCATGACAATTCCGGATTAC
GAATAATGATGAGCTCGGAATCGATTAACCTGACTGGTACTGAAGGGTTACTGAATGAGAGCTCG
AGTCACGGAATTGACTTACTATTGGAGGAATCATGCATGACTGACTACTGGAAGGCTCGAGTCTA
CGGTATTCCTTAGCTCTATTACTATTCTTAGGATCTTACTTACTTTATATTACGGAGAGTCATAT
TCTTATCCTAGGTCTTACTTGAGCTCTTAACCACATAGCCAGTCATTTAGGGAAGGTATCGTCTA
GAGCTCTGATGACTCGGTATTAGTACTTAATCCATCCTTTAGGGATCATGACAATTCCGGATTAC
GAATAATGATGAGCTCGGAATCGATTAACCTGACTGGTACTGAAGGGTTACTGAATGAGAGCTCG
AGTCACGGAATTGACTTACTATTGGAGGAATCATGCATGACTGACTACTGGAAGGCTCGAGTCTA
CGGTATTCCTTAGCTCTATTACTATTCTTAGGATCTTACTTACTTTATATTACGGAGAGTCATAT
```

Figure 3: This is what one of the 300,000 pages of DNA coding looks like, as collected during the Human Genome Project. Change the letters around, and this could be the coding for a baboon, fly, ant, rose petal, or potato.

I frequently wonder about that Y chromosome and the fact that it has the fewest genes. This is the chromosome that determines our sex. Here is how Matt Ridley describes it in his book *Nature via Nurture*: "A single gene, called SRY, on the Y chromosome, starts a cascade of events in the developing fetus leading to the development of masculine appearance and behavior. If that gene is absent, a female body results."[5]

Can you believe it? This one little, tiny event determines whether we'll be male or female? Ridley even suggests that homosexuality may arise "from the partial failure of this prenatal masculinization process in the brain, though not in the body."[6] In other words, there may be a disconnect of our sexuality between what our mind will now be predisposed to think and how our body is constructed. We may think we're male, but our physical disposition may be female.

In a later chapter he clarifies this by stating that the plethora of other genes switched on by the SRY gene may alter the development of the body. Further, many of these other genes may be sensitive to "external experience, reacting to diet, social setting, learning and culture to refract the developing machinery of the person . . . but given a typical middle-class upbringing . . . it is not absurd to call it [SRY] the gene for maleness."[7]

In other words, he is suggesting with scientific nuance that the conditions of our upbringing may also influence our sexual preferences, regardless of the body we are carrying.

Chuck Snowdon, as noted, chair of the Psychology Department at the University of Wisconsin, wrote that it is critical that we understand Ridley's statement that genes may be sensitive to external experiences. He cites a colleague, Anthony Auger, an assistant professor of psychology, "who has found that dopamine can activate genes for estrogen receptors in the absence of estrogen." In other words, we are not always stuck with what our genes have mapped out for us.[8]

What Ridley has done is simplify (and I have simplified his

explanation even further, and it is still not that easy to understand) the explanation of the origination of what sex we become in the womb, including the possibility of a genetic predisposition for homosexuality. It has generally been considered that two chromosomes, the Y and X, are involved in our sexuality. Males have both an X and Y chromosome, while females have two X chromosomes. Ridley has simplified this by stating that if the SRY gene is missing on a Y chromosome, it is not a Y chromosome, but an X, and so the result will be a female.

I can tell you that, throughout my life, this one little gene that creates two sexes has caused me a lot of trouble.

As we've discussed, the genes, in general, are basically the pages of the forty-six chromosomes that are the genome chapters. They are sections of the DNA filament they inhabit. Their basic purpose is to create the proteins that end up as a fingernail cell, the beak of a bird, or the stem of a rose.

The genes do this when the proper time comes by switching "on." Then they use what are called RNA messengers, also embedded in the nucleus of each cell. The RNA, in turn, directs the operation of what is called the ribosome, a protein-making machine also located in the nucleus, which then turns the cell into a fingernail cell or an eyelid cell, or whatever.

I wonder if you can explain to me how all of this not only fits within the body of a cell, invisible to the naked eye, but in the nucleus of a cell, which is infinitesimal in size. Who was the engineer, do you suppose, who could do this and also develop a universe of incalculable size? And where is his office? Better yet, where is his complaint department?

And so when it is time to create a liver cell, the proper letters, comprising a gene on the DNA filament, signal the appropriate sections of the RNA messenger, which, in turn, instruct the ribosome to put together the specialized protein enzymes to make a liver cell. It has been said that the genes are primarily a recipe for making proteins, of which there are thousands of variations. As a matter of fact, the next great body of study following the genome appears to center on proteomics, the study of how our genomic alphabet translates into more than 100,000 different proteins in the human body that need to be individually identified and cataloged.[9]

When I first read about the protein-making capacity of the DNA and RNA messengers some years ago, I couldn't figure out how all this would work in a potato. I wasn't eating potatoes at the time, since I was on the modified Atkins diet. Potatoes, I thought, were completely made up of carbohydrates. It turns out that all plant organisms, even potatoes, have proteins in enzyme form that carry out the functions of the genetic machinery that creates its cells—a fact you can drop at the next PTA meeting.

But let's keep moving along. Among the genes on the DNA filaments are what are called "hox genes." These are the genes that help guide how and where an organ is to be constructed. In that sense, these genes determine in a fetus where the kidney goes, the brain goes, an eye goes, and so forth. When a gene that is to use its coding to become a liver gets into position, it switches on, and the cell becomes a liver cell, and begins to reproduce as a liver cell, until there are enough cells to create the liver as a whole. There are additional types of genes, whose sole job is to tell other genes when to switch on or switch off. In the rib cage of a mouse, a gene switches off the reproduction of rib cage cells far sooner than it does in humans, who have, as we know, larger rib cages than mice.

Stem cells, whose use has generated much controversy, are cells that can be taken from embryos, developed in a vitro fertilization clinic, and then donated.

The benefit of stem cells is that they haven't been switched on to become a specific type of cell. They are thus unspecialized, and they can give rise to specialized cell types, such as neurons. They are also capable of dividing and renewing themselves for long periods. And so science hopes to work with them for use in parts of our bodies that have been damaged or destroyed by accident or disease, to create new cells that will replicate the damaged cells. In other words, in a patient with Alzheimer's disease, the hope is that the stem cells can be actuated in the damaged sections. There the stem cells would be switched on to create the specific, needed cells (recall that there are more than two hundred different neuron types). And so you would have a fresh new neuron cell that can reproduce and create other neurons to replace those that have been ravaged by the disease. And the result, it would be hoped, would be the eradication of Alzheimer's.

However, you can imagine how complicated this type of research is to perform. While we have mapped the genome, how do we find the specific letters among the 3.2 billion on our DNA for the gene that may encode for a specific form of neuron that we need? How do we get the gene to send the right message to the RNA and then get the ribosome to create the new neuron cell? And then how do we tell it when to shut off?

Notwithstanding these difficulties, scientists are making progress in general in the regulation of switching mechanisms in genes. As this book is being written, tests are underway on a number of drugs, including one called RNA Interference, which have the potential ability *to turn off* genes. The *New York Times* reported on September 14, 2004, that the drug RNA Interference was being tested "against the gene that sets off the process of age-related macular degeneration of the retina that is the leading cause of blindness in the elderly."[10] In other words, according to this report, it could "potentially yield a cornucopia of other drugs designed to silence errant, disease causing genes in the body, or disarm an invading virus by knocking out its genes."

A virus is a living thing with its own genome. Not only are we attempting to learn how to turn on a gene in a neutral stem cell, but we are also working to learn how to switch off the harmful, intruding genes of a virus, for example. It makes sense.

There are religionists and others who believe that we shouldn't be tinkering with the genetics of the human body that a higher being created, even though we all recognize that our bodies are not perfect and that our brains and minds, in particular, are not perfect. Through stem cell and other forms of genetic drug research, we may be able to fix many of these imperfections, not to mention the dysfunctions of the brain and mind. For the majority of the people inhabiting the Earth, genetic dysfunctions can create and/or contribute to a myriad of problems, including depression, anxiety, sadism, attention deficit disorder, and thousands of inheritable physical disorders. Fortunately, other governments are supportive of stem cell research and so, in time, we may all greatly benefit from it.

The greatest disappointment for me, as noted, after the results of the Human Genome Project were announced, was that nothing happened to pierce the virtual realities of the least humble among us. There was no toning down of the fanatically sanctimonious, bigoted, disdainful, and smug attitudes that drive the rest of us to absolute distraction.

I was hoping that for a week to two after the announcement people like the Taliban religious police, whose job (prior to 9/11) it was to berate and even whip women on the streets in Afghanistan, who they believed were not dressing properly, would stop. I also hoped that the orthodox Jews in Israel who taunt Jewish women on the streets for the same reasons would end their harassment. I was hoping that those status-obsessed politicians who intone solutions about problems they know little about for the sole purpose of later watching themselves on television would be humbled enough to stop. I was hoping that bullies and terrorists and even psychopaths and sadists might be hit by an epiphany from this singular news—that every single living thing is all one, we are all in this together, we all come from the same building blocks, whether humans, animals, or plants—and thus give us a few days less of torment and misery.

For the information was, after all, on the news. And the media did its best to explain it in a way that we could all understand. Science journalists did wonderful work in attempting to elucidate the meaning of the research. Television newscasters and commentators put together special segments and documentaries that presented the breakthrough in entertaining and exciting formats.

But nothing happened. Less than a month after the announcement was made, the newspapers on which the printed information was communicated were already in the garbage, as the old saying goes.

This view of the public's apathy was reinforced for me when the local CBS radio station in Chicago called me for an interview to be scheduled the next day, to tell their listeners what the Human Genome Project really meant. The producer had remembered my little excerpt from *Battling the Inner Dummy* and called me. I barely had time to run back to my reference books to refresh my memory, particularly on the RNA messenger and the ribosome machine. For twenty minutes, I did my best, wondering why they just didn't call a geneticist. Later, I saw old friends and asked what they thought about the interview. "Very nice, very interesting," was the typical response. I could tell nobody was getting the monumental power of the message.

I took to carrying a six-foot length of string in my pocket. I became a temporary fanatic, but, fortunately, I limited my passion to sharing this vital information to only my friends and acquaintances. My talking about the thread drove them to distraction. Second City, Chicago's famous improvisation group, came to mind. Maybe I could get them to cooperate and do this in a humorous way. Maybe it would take off from there. Nature has apparently been treating us with humor, as in giving us an entire DNA molecule in each of the cells of our body, enough to grow a whole new body, though it takes only 3 percent of it to make our body. And that includes the human brain—what scientists have called the most complex object, living or mechanical, in the known universe. And yet it emerges from a DNA molecule that is thousands of times smaller than a grain of sand, and our entire body, including the brain, comes from only 3 percent of it. It seems odd that the universe before the big bang and the DNA molecule were and are thousands of times smaller than this dot (.). Doesn't this sound like someone is playing a joke on us? Couldn't comedians make something of this? And how hard should it really be, if life emerges from such a tiny mechanism, to improve the design someday soon? Couldn't we, in particular, fix the DNA that creates physical and mental handicaps in humans before they are born? Some people say we shouldn't play God. How would they like to spend their lives in a wheelchair or hear voices that aren't there?

Or maybe we should interpret this news as just plain embarrassing. Maybe some of us should be taken down a peg or two, because, among other things, humans are not only very close to chimpanzees in our DNA, but we are not that far from mice! As Lisa Stubbs of Lawrence Livermore National Laboratory puts it in a paper:

> Mice and humans (indeed, most or all mammals, including dogs, cats, rabbits, monkeys and apes) have roughly the same number of nucleotides [the four letters described in my conversation with the geneticist: A, G, C, and T] in their genomes—about 3 billion base pairs. This comparable DNA content implies that all mammals contain more or less the same number of genes, and indeed our work and the work of many others have provided evidence to confirm that notion.
>
> I believe the number of human genes without a

clear mouse counterpart, and vice versa won't be significantly larger than 1 percent of the total. . . . However, the most significant differences between mice
and humans are not in the number of genes each carries, but in the structure of genes and the activities of
their protein products. *Gene for gene, we are very similar to mice* [italics mine]. What really matters is that
subtle changes accumulated in each of the approximately 30,000 to 35,000 genes add together to make
quite different organisms.[11]

In other words, when you get right down to it, the major
difference between humans and mice and other animals, like
rabbits and squirrels, is not in the number of genes we carry,
but in how those genes are encoded to make different types of
bodies, including brains. Still, all of these genes produce neurons in humans and animals that give rise to basic instinctive
emotional systems that are significantly similar. If all these animals had larynxes and more cortex neurons added in, we could
probably all talk to each other, just as they do in Disney
movies, which, of course, would hurt the hunting, fur, and
extermination industries.

Even some plants have up to 25,000 or so genes (part of a
DNA filament of 125 million letters), and fruit flies have up to
13,600 genes (on a filament of 180 million letters).

But these letters are all the same: A, G, C, T, as just shown
in figure 3. If you only looked at the pages themselves, you'd
never know if you were looking at the coding of a bumble bee,
a geranium, or a human.

Of course, this doesn't sink in, either. We read it, we know
it, but our minds with their virtual reality protective barriers,
are difficult, if not impossible, to truly pierce.

Then there is the fact that the differences between humans
of *every ethnic origin* are no more than the differences between

one human and another—a brother and a sister, for example. We are all different, but our differences comprise only 0.001, or one-tenth of 1 percent of our genes.

But what have all the religious clerics, academics, government leaders, and other people of influence done with this information? Here, finally, was some really "good news" that they could deliver. When it was first announced, why weren't they behind their podiums waving the DNA information at us and telling us that—after centuries of ethnic racism, religious prejudice, and wars fought on their behalf, killing hundreds of millions of people needlessly—it was all a myth. That it was all for naught. That humans indeed are all equal in origin, except for the miniscule differences between us as individuals.

But this never happened. There was never any trumpeting of this news. Even the media that were so responsible for reporting the advances of the Human Genome Project didn't emphasize it. Do you recall ever seeing a headline in a newspaper, magazine, or TV report that said: "All Humans Are Genetically Equal: Racial and Religious Hatred to Stop"? *Has there ever been any more important news?*

As I was watching the 2004 Olympics that took place in Greece, the home of the venerable Greek philosophers, I thought what a great time to reannounce and publicize these facts. There were 202 countries of the world participating and displaying the myriad of human emotions, including laughter, glee, shame, frustration, and regret—emotions that we experience among our families and communities. We could see on our television screens how similar we all are. Yet back in the countries of many of these athletes, more than ninety wars were being fought or threatened. And within every country, some form of racial hatred or discrimination was taking place, wherein one group treated another as beneath them or even subhuman.

Faced with the ignorance that continues to create needless conflicts, I often reflect on the thought that I am nothing more than a string of DNA—that this DNA became fertilized into a temporary human, who lives on a planet that is lost in space.

There are times when one ponders the general craziness of humans—that this fact can be a comforting thought.

11.

THE BIGGEST LOTTERY IN OUR LIVES TOOK PLACE THE INSTANT WE WERE CONCEIVED: WE COULD HAVE BEEN ONE OF 300,000,000 OTHER PEOPLE

The odds of you coming into being from one specific sperm cell out of the trillions produced by your father during his lifetime combining with fertilizing one of approximately 400 eggs produced by your mother during her lifetime are beyond calculation.

Alexander Dixon[1]

Does my little life have any real significance in the grand scheme of things? If my father's sperm had not fertilized that particular egg on that fateful night, would I not have existed, and in what sense, then would the universe have existed? . . . What if my dad had coughed at that critical moment so that a different sperm had fertilized the ovum? Our minds start reeling when pondering such possibilities.

V. S. Ramachandran[2]

The forty-six chromosomes that exist in each cell of your body, and which have the capability of reproducing your entire body, are actually two pairs with twenty-three chromosomes each. That is, of course, with the exception of your sperm cell or egg cell.

Interestingly enough, these chromosomes in a way don't belong to you. One of the pairs came from your biological father and the other from your biological mother. They combined the instant the egg in your mother's womb became fertilized, and then they reproduced faithfully. The cells and the DNA strands within each of them created the codes for hands, feet, a nose, a heart, a blood cell, and so forth. Your own personal DNA will not show up until it is in the cells of your offspring. So if your parents are dead, or you don't see them often, you can take some comfort that the very essence of their being is still alive within you, in each of your approximate 60 trillion cells. If each DNA strand when stretched out and tied together is six feet long, you basically have about 360 trillion feet of your mom's and dad's DNA within you. Of course, if one or the other was an abusive alcoholic or psychopath or both, then this thought can be a bit disconcerting. Recall that psychopaths make up about 1 percent of the population, so the chances that we have or had a psychopathic parent is not out of the question.

All of us look the way we do because of our particular combination of genes that line the two strands of the DNA that make up each chromosome. As with other elements of the subject of genetics, most of us have read or heard about dominant and recessive genes, but we rarely give the subject a passing thought. And yet this is an astounding process of nature that creates both our physical and probably our basic mental characteristics as well.

Do you have brown eyes? If both of your parents have brown eyes, then you will have brown eyes, because the gene that creates brown eyes is dominant over the one that creates blue eyes.

There is a large body of study covering dominant and recessive genes in humans and plant life. The creation of hybrid forms of plant life, including corn, roses, and tomatoes, depends on an understanding of which genes will be dominant when two different forms of the same plant species are mated. It was with plant life that we had our first inkling of recessive and dominant genes, courtesy of the work of Gregor Mendel. He was a monk who lived during the mid-1880s and bred hybrid pea plants in the gardens of his monastery.

Dominant and recessive genes play a major role in our heredity. As with most other aspects of life on this planet, a form of competition takes place in the fertilized egg between our maternal and paternal genes. Your mother's and father's genes and their alleles—the term that describes the human characteristics they carry—are basically at odds in the fertilized egg to determine who you will become.

What makes this interesting is that both the maternal and the paternal genes that encode for a specific characteristic are opposite each other on the strands of DNA. And so your mother's gene on her strand for eye color is located exactly opposite your father's gene on his strand for eye color. However, the competition or rivalry between the two is automatically resolved by nature's innovation of dominant and recessive.

Making this process more complex, however, is that both parents carry *two* alleles for the same characteristic. If you took botany or biology classes, you might recall the terms "homozygous," which means that the two alleles on a given gene for a specific characteristic are the same, either dominant or recessive,[3] and "heterozygous," meaning one is dominant, the other recessive.

If brown eyes are dominant and an allele expressing it is on one of the two strands, the brown eyes automatically win. It doesn't matter if the opposite side is coding for blue eyes. The only way you will have blue eyes is if both strands carry the gene coding for it.

Or as Charles Snowdon put it to me: "Maybe a better example is do you have blue eyes? This can only occur if both parents have blue eyes or if one is carrying the recessive gene for blue eyes and you happen to inherit it. If my mom has blue eyes and my dad does not and both his alleles are dominant in him, I can never have blue eyes. And if he does have both a dominant and a recessive allele, my chances of being blue eyed are only fifty-fifty."

Complicated? It is for me.

So let's simplify by saying the same process in general takes place for every other human characteristic. Broad lips, for example, are dominant over thin lips. Freckles are dominant over no freckles. A full head of hair is dominant over baldness. Curly hair is dominant over straight hair. Normal vision is dominant over nearsightedness. Farsightedness is dominant over normal vision, and normal vision is dominant over color blindness. Double-jointedness is dominant over normal joints. Normal hearing is dominant over congenital deafness. Normal blood clotting is dominant over hemophilia (a disorder that hinders blood clotting). Among many other items on an obviously long list, immunity to poison ivy is dominant over a susceptibility to poison ivy.[4]

If I walk within three feet of a poison ivy plant and my legs are exposed, I will get an irksome reaction. Since I can't scold my parents, who have both passed away, for giving me recessive genes for susceptibility to poison ivy, I'll just have to live with it.

Looking over this brief list of dominant and recessive traits, I can see that it's no wonder that certain families might have a preponderance of a specific characteristic such as dominant farsightedness, if the alleles align. It is constantly being passed down through generations, and because it is dominant, there are far greater chances that the offspring of the family unit in general will ultimately become farsighted. When spouses come into the family carrying the gene for normal vision, it is, in essence, overruled by the dominance of the farsighted gene. Most of the older members of the family will be seen either wearing bifocals or carrying reading glasses around their necks.

Now and then, however, in a family where baldness is predominant, a full head of hair with matching alleles emerges out of what scientists describe as the "gene pool" and is matched with a full head of hair of matching alleles of a spouse, and the resulting child ends up with a full head of hair. The odds are long, but here you have a child with a healthy head of hair in a family that is predominately bald, and the result may be that the family begins looking suspiciously at the female who bore the little boy.

While some scientists contend from studies of identical twins reared apart that approximately 50 percent of our mental characteristics are inherited—passed down through our genes—scientists have done little research in studying dominance and recessiveness of *behavioral* genes. Is a predisposition for extroversion dominant over introversion? Is a predisposition for empathy dominant over lack of empathy? Is aggressiveness dominant over gentleness? Is being bad-tempered dominant over mild-tempered?

In a 2003 article in *Knight Ridder Tribune Business News*, Robert S. Boyd describes the results of a conference on behavioral genetics—the term given to the study of genes and human behavior. The conference included a panel of geneticists, psychologists, philosophers, and legal experts. The article states:

> The consensus was clear: Genes strongly influence behavior but do not control it. Neither does a person's environment—family, upbringing, life experiences—completely determine who he or she will turn out to be.
>
> "Genes make certain behaviors more likely, but genes don't automatically lead to actions," said Gregory Kaebnick, co-director of a National Institutes of Health–sponsored project on genetic ties and the future of the family. "We still can believe in free will."
>
> "Genes set the stage, but our brains—not our

genes—ultimately control our behavior," said Stephen Hyman, former director of the National Institute of Mental Health in Bethesda, Maryland. "We should not use the genome sequence as a bar code," said Hyman, now the provost of Harvard University. "There is no such thing as a gene for grumpiness or for a serial killer."[5]

Of course, it may be a little too early in the study of behavioral genetics to come to Hyman's conclusion. Genes may predispose a behavior, which our early upbringing may reinforce or soften. Hyman also said, according to the article, that "your brain builds a complex web of personality traits by combining internal genetic instructions inherited from your parents and external signals received from your surroundings. Personality is shaped and *re-shaped over a lifetime* [italics mine]."

Not that I want to disagree with the former director of the National Institute of Mental Health, but I respectfully feel that the latter may or may not be true. I've known people, over a course of fifty years or more, whose very basic personalities have changed little, if at all, over time. Recently, I spent a weekend with a childhood friend of mine after a long absence, and it was as if nothing had changed between us. His views, habits, and quirks were the same as I had remembered them, and I told him so. He replied that he thought the same of me. It was as if the years hadn't passed, except for our experiences.

In addition, I recall attending a recent seminar given by Jerome Kagan, a research professor at the Department of Psychology at Harvard University, at a HealthEmotions Research Institute symposium held at the University of Wisconsin. Kagan unveiled a study that ranged over more than twenty years, which followed two individuals from a point shortly after birth until they were in their early twenties. One was introverted, the other extroverted. They were videotaped intermittently over the years. In their cribs, the introverted baby would become upset and cry when it saw a stranger; the extroverted baby would smile.

As they grew older, the babies, now young children, remained respectively introverted and extroverted. Kagan showed their reactions to different types of controlled situations as they grew older. He concluded his presentation by saying that both children grew up to be successful happy adults, even though their personalities remained significantly different. I recall specifically his comment that the introverted child became a nuclear engineer, I believe it was, and put his penchant for avoiding social interaction to good use.

On the other hand, my son Andy was introverted and shy in his childhood but grew out of it as an adult.

In any event, there is little doubt that both genetics and the experiences of life shape our personalities, but researchers in the field still have much work to do in clarifying both of their effects.

Even more fascinating is how our physical characteristics, and our mental ones as well, are sorted out in male sperm cells and in the female egg.

The six feet of DNA that exists among our twenty-three pairs of chromosomes is reproduced faithfully in a process called "mitosis" each time a cell divides. The enzymes, or checkers as I called them, move down the strands policing their sections of more than 3 billion letters to make sure that the new strands are absolutely correct. Errors are extremely rare.

While this process is mind-boggling enough, particularly at the speed with which it happens, even more dumbfounding is the process, called "meiosis," which is used to create a female egg and a sperm cell with only twenty-three chromosomes each.

Reducing the number of chromosomes by half in these special cells is necessary in order to produce a fertilized egg with forty-six chromosomes combined from both the male and the female. In other words, the sperm cells that move up the vaginal tract are the only cells produced by the male body that have twenty-three chromosomes. The winning sperm cell then combines with the female egg, which is similarly the only female cell produced with twenty-three chromosomes. And so when combined, the newly fertilized egg now has the full complement of forty-six chromosomes that is needed to create a live body.

In a process called "crossover," the twenty-three chromosomes, in both the sperm cells and the egg, and their individual genes are selected at random. Remember that chromosomes are like chapters of DNA, while the genes are the pages. And while 35,000-odd genes have been identified by the Human Genome Project, there are smaller units within these genes, genetic units, that might be selected in the random shuffling of the meiotic process. Even more amazing is the fact that each sperm cell has its own unique pattern of genetic units making up its twenty-three chromosomes. *In other words, each sperm cell has the capability of creating a different person!* This is one reason why some siblings hardly resemble each other.

Here is how eminent biologist Richard Dawkins summarizes this process in his celebrated book, *The Selfish Gene*, which is one of my favorites.

> Therefore, every sperm cell made by an individual is unique, even though all his sperms assembled their 23 chromosomes from bits of the same set of 46 chromosomes. Eggs are made in a similar way in the ovaries, and they, too, are all unique. . . . It means that if you got out your microscope and looked at the chromosomes in one of your own sperms (or eggs if you are female) it would be a waste of time trying to identify chromosomes that originally came from your

mother. . . . Any one chromosome in a sperm would be a patchwork, a mosaic of maternal genes and paternal genes.[6]

So the lottery of our lives actually begins at this point. The patchwork of genes in both the sperm cell and the egg that eventually unite is apparently a mix-and-match process akin to the numbered Ping-Pong balls ejected at random during lottery drawings. Or maybe it's like an extended bingo game, which also uses Ping-Pong balls blown around in a cage. The bingo leader picks out number five and announces: "Number five, this child will have short legs. Number eight, this child will play the piano at the age of three," and so on.

But that's only the beginning of the lottery. In an additional act of what I consider to be overkill, nature can create upward of 300,000,000, and at times, as many as 800,000,000, sperm cells in a single ejaculation. Doesn't this seem high to you? However, it turns out that it makes perfect sense, given the circuitous nature of the reproduction process as a whole, which relies on high sperm counts to increase the odds of a successful fertilization. The number of sperm in a single ejaculation can vary, depending on such factors as time since the last copulation or masturbation; whether you suspect your partner has been with another man—which may cause the sperm being manufactured and stored in the testes to multiply enormously, so that there is enough sperm to override what another man might have deposited—the temperature of the testicles; and other factors. These facts are all charted out and detailed in a remarkable book called *Human Sperm Competition* authored by scientists R. Robin Baker and Mark A. Bellis. Of course, after a full night of lovemaking, the male sperm count per ejaculation can drop dramatically. At this point in life, I can barely remember those nights. Did they happen at all?

All of these sperm cells are living, moving things. If you've seen them in a documentary—such as *The Miracle of Life*, a PBS production that I have on tape and watch frequently—you see the sperm enlarged as much as four thousand times and looking very toadlike. With rapidly swishing tails, they swim up the vaginal canal in a desperate effort to reach what they are obviously programmed to believe is an awaiting egg. Can you imagine a single race of 300,000,000 living things of any kind? It would be like lining up the population of the United States along the mouth of an enormously wide river and seeing who can swim fastest to a finish line two or three miles away in a narrowing channel. Janet Hyde, former chair of psychology at the University of Wisconsin, estimates in *Understanding Human Sexuality* that a sperm—the smallest cell in the human body— may swim three thousand times its own length, which would be "comparable to a swim of over 3 miles for a human being."[7]

Making things harder, brackish waters surround them, similar to what we find in an ocean. The vaginal tract is not a warm, cozy place. Acids and other substances are released that are apparently aimed at quickly killing off the weakest of the sperm cells. And, as a matter of fact, almost all of them are eventually killed off. About 25 percent are killed off almost immediately, according to the *Miracle of Life*, because they are defective or deformed.[8] Others fall out of the vagina as a result of gravity, lose their way, or mistake another organ for an egg.

Anywhere from fifty to upward of one thousand sperm cell contestants may reach the egg. Then for no apparent reason we know of, one sperm cell successfully penetrates the egg for conception. And the instant it does, a membrane is created around the egg that keeps all the remaining sperm cells out. They now join the other 300,000,000-odd sperm cells who have already died. Or if it's the second ejaculation of the night, or if the male has a low sperm count to begin with, maybe it's only 80,000,000.

How do we reach such high sperm counts? According to the authors of *Human Sperm Competition*, there are more than seven hundred feet of microscopic tubing within the testicles that are capable of producing 12.5 million sperm cells per hour,[9] in addition to maturing and storing them. It was difficult to substantiate these facts. Melissa Rosenkranz, my University of Wisconsin graduate student, found data that suggested a proliferation of 40 to 50 million sperm per day, or 4.1 million per hour. We also asked Sijo Parekattil, a urologist and specialist in infertility at the New York University School of Medicine, to comment, and he said:

> We always tell men to abstain from ejaculation before giving a specimen for about 2–3 days. Let's assume that when a man ejaculates three times he would clear out all his stores and mature sperm and then gets a three-day rest period before he is back to normal. Let's say his first ejaculate was normal . . . 100 million sperm. Let's assume that two successive ejaculations will have exponential decreases in total sperm count, so ejaculate 2 would have 50 million and ejaculate 3 would have 25 million.
>
> So the total for the three ejaculates is 175 million. Let's assume that in three days, he gets fully replenished, so that is 72 hours. We could make a rough conservative estimate that the average production/ replenishment of mature sperm in a young male could be . . . 2.43 million/hr. Although one has to remember that sperm is actually being continuously produced in the testes and stored/processed in the epididymis, so this replenishment rate may be an overestimate or underestimate of the testicle's true potential that probably varies based on need.[10]

And so the estimates vary as to how many sperm are being produced per hour in the male testicles from a low of 2.4 million per hour to a high of 12.5 million. Even at 4.1 million an hour, that is 68,000 a minute, which should give pause for thought to anyone who thinks her husband is lazy.

But remember as well, if we assume an ejaculate of 300,000,000 sperm for an average, young, healthy male, as described in *Human Sperm Competition* and from research sources reviewed by Melissa Rosenkranz, each one of those sperm cells has a different combination of genetics—the potential to become a unique human being.

Am I mistaken? Do facts like these indicate that life is of no great value? Is this why we need to build our own virtual realties, full of beliefs, convictions, and values, to ward off the frightening possibility that, if we absorbed the facts, we might conclude that indeed life is irrelevant? And if so many of us are protective of the life in the womb that may have been a 300,000,000-to-1 shot on any given night, why is there no public anguish over the killing of quadrillions of living, squiggling sperm cells each night on the planet, in perhaps a billion or so wombs? Each of those sperm could have created a life, if there were enough eggs in vitro to accommodate them. (Although the Church does frown upon masturbation and the unnecessary waste of sperm.)

And what does this process of the testes say for people who think that they are products of human destiny? Napoleon, for example—his father may have been capable of producing as many as 12.5 million sperm per hour, in the more than seven hundred feet of microscopic tubing in his testicles; after all, Napoleon had four brothers and three sisters. On the night of the eventful copulation that created Napoleon's embryo, each one of the hundreds of millions of sperm cells released by his father into his mother's womb was capable of producing a person other than the one Napoleon became, even a girl. One hiccup or belch before the ejaculation might have done the trick and saved millions of lives that were lost during Napoleon's battles. Think of the tens of millions of lives lost because the fathers of Kaiser Wilhelm and Adolf Hitler didn't belch or hiccup just prior to the ejaculations that resulted in these two men. We all appear to be random accidents of a sperm race, which includes the many nights our parents had intercourse spilling out billions of sperm cells that raced to nowhere, when eggs weren't in the right position or simply didn't become fertilized.

I can understand how so many people of the world today and in history began to think they were products of destiny when they achieved great successes or even moderate successes in their circumscribed worlds. They became full of themselves, vain, and even megalomaniacal as part of our *status imperative*—our biological propensity to maintain, increase, or display our status (as will be described in the next chapter). I could understand the concept of destiny better if these people were the products of only one single sperm cell released by their fathers, which quickly migrated to an egg that quickly became fertile and retreated to a deep part of the womb where it began to reproduce. That would seem more like a product of destiny than the trillions-to-one odds of creating a fertile egg that became us, which includes the many nights when a father's sperm was released to find an egg, but none was available. And then, out of nowhere, one night, one sperm cell hit the jackpot. When you go back one thousand, or five thousand, or ten thousand years, with all those quintillions upon quintillions of sperm cells used in the line of our direct parentage, the odds of each one of us being here today are beyond calculation. We appear to be an absolute matter of chance, unless some higher being has some supercomputer for Earth that uses magnetics or some other system to penetrate the womb at the fateful moments and guides the right sperm in at the right time. Some people I've talked to actually think something like this happens. But why would this god make this so complicated, when the reproductive system, if it wasn't to be the world's greatest lottery, could have been greatly simplified for humans? One sperm, one egg—bingo. The odds of our being fertilized to be destined for some great endeavor is a tremendous long shot.

Bill Bryson did some mathematics of his own, in his *A Short History of Everything*. Go back eight generations of your family, and there are:

> [O]ver 250 people on whose timely couplings your existence depends. Continue further to the time of Shakespeare and the Mayflower Pilgrims and you have no fewer than 16,384 ancestors earnestly exchanging genetic material in a way that would, eventually and miraculously, result in you.
>
> At twenty generations ago, the number of people procreating on your behalf has risen to 1,048,576. Five generations before that, and there are no fewer than 33,554,432 men and women on whose devoted couplings your existence depends. By thirty generations ago, your total number of forebears—remember, these aren't cousins and aunts and other incidental relatives, but only parents and parents of parents in a line leading ineluctably to you—is over one billion (1,073,741,824, to be precise.) If you go back to the time of the Romans, the number of people on whose cooperative efforts your eventual existence depends has risen to approximately 1,000,000,000,000,000, 000, which is several times the total number of people who ever lived.[11]

Bryson explains this anomaly by contending that there were times in your background when incest was performed, "a relative from your mother's side of the family procreated with some distant cousin from your father's side of the ledger." He pointed out that most of the people we know and see are probably distant relatives—"In the most literal and fundamental sense we are all family."[12] (I was dubious about Bryson's figures, and so I asked a friend, Steve Herkes, to use a large pad of paper and a calculator to trace back generations of parenting for twenty generations of thirty-five years, and the figures do pan out.)

Further, the sperm that are released into the vaginal tract seem to mirror human behavior, engaging in fierce competition to win the great lottery of life. In *Human Sperm Competition*, the authors advance the contention that some sperm are programmed to be defensive in nature, others offensive, almost like players on a football team. Here is what they observe:

> Briefly, the Kamikaze Sperm Hypothesis suggests that animal ejaculates [humans included] consist of different types of sperm, each programmed to carry out a specific function. Some, often very few, are "egg-getters," programmed to attempt to fertilize the female's eggs. The remainder, often the vast majority, are programmed for a "kamikaze" role. Instead of attempting to find and fertilize eggs themselves, their role is to reduce the chances the egg will be fertilized by sperm from any other male.
>
> We envisage two primary categories of kamikaze sperm: "blockers" and "seek-and-destroy." Blockers take up strategic positions en route to the egg, become relatively immobile, and bar passage to any later sperm. Seek-and-destroy sperm roam around appropriate areas of the female tract, seeking out and attempting to incapacitate/and or destroy any sperm from a different male. . . . Whether sperm competition is a lottery, a race or warfare, it is likely that the more sperm a male enters for the competition, the greater his chances of winning. . . . The sperm competition would seem only, therefore, to favor males who ejaculate as many sperm as possible on every occasion.[13]

When it comes to the concept of fierce, irrational, and often savage competition in this world, I don't know which is worse: parents of players on competing Little League teams or sperm cells fighting it out in the womb.

Then, as part of the status imperative, there appears to be a predilection among certain higher animal males for insisting on having only their own offspring in their family, even to the point of some species, such as lions, killing off the current offspring of new female mates. So why not start the male battle early to assure that it is only his offspring in the womb by ejaculating millions of sperm, some of them programmed to kill off the sperm of others? It makes perfect sense in a crazy world.

Not only are we as humans the result of an unlikely accident, but our influence on future generations appears to be limited. In his book *Nature and Nurture*, Robert Plomin describes how our genetic relatedness to our offspring continues to decrease with the birth of each new generation. He describes how parents and their offspring are considered "first-degree relatives" and have a genetic relatedness of 50 percent. In other words, each parent has supplied half the genetic units on the forty-six chromosomes. Plomin continues:

> Genetic relatedness would then decrease among grandchildren to 25 percent, great-grandchildren to 12.5 percent, great-great grandchildren to 6.25 percent, great-great-great grandchildren to 3.12 percent and among great-great-great-great grandchildren to 1.06 percent.[14]

As an interesting aside, in many cultures of the past and some to this day, girls marry at the age of twelve and have a child at the age of thirteen. If in one such family each succeeding generation of first borns were women who married at twelve and had a child at thirteen, a woman could become a great-great-great-great-great grandmother at the age of ninety-two. When she looked at the most recent offspring of her family with a genetic relatedness of just above one-half of one percent, she'd be hard pressed to find much similarity to herself.

So tell me, what is all this concern many of us have about keeping our names and heredity alive when, at the age of ninety-two, we could be looking at offspring who might be almost as remote from us as our next-door neighbor—who could have descended from our same family tree, but who our forebears just lost track of?

As a matter of fact, it is Richard Dawkins's contention that we as humans, along with other higher animals, are nothing more than "survival machines." Our job is simply to carry genes long enough to pass them onto the next generation, thus the title of his book *The Selfish Gene*.

He points out that the smaller the genetic unit on our chromosomes, the fewer the letters, the easier it is to pass that same gene down through several generations. He contends that each of us may be carrying a genetic unit that may be millions of years old. He asserts:

> A gene can live for a million years, but many new genes do not even make it past their first generation. The few new ones that succeed do so partly because they are lucky, but mainly because they have what it takes, and that means they are good at making survival machines. . . . For example, a "good" gene might ensure its survival by tending to endow the successive bodies in which it finds itself with long legs, which help those bodies escape from predators.
> . . . Individuals are not stable things, they are fleeting. Chromosomes too are shuffled into oblivion, like hands of cards soon after they are dealt. But the cards themselves survive the shuffling. The cards are the genes. The genes are not destroyed by crossing-over,

they merely change partners and march on. Of course
they march on. That is their business. They are the repli-
cators and we are their survival machines. When we
have served our purpose we are cast aside. But genes are
denizens of geological time, genes are forever.[15]

He concludes that those of us who don't have offspring
have little to worry about in our failure to pass on genes. There
is no failure, he contends. Maybe our siblings passed the genes
on for us, or maybe others in our family, or maybe our remote
cousins even did. And if you go back a few generations, we all
shared in a similar gene pool.

So, apparently, we are all part of the scheme of things,
including old, maiden aunts. Stigmatized in the past, they can
now take comfort in knowing that their genes have been
passed along somewhere. On the colder side of the selfish gene
concept are the many living things in nature that die right after
conception—salmon and spiders, among them. They pass their
genes on and it's "so long, pal."

According to Dawkins's theories, even adoptive parents will
share a considerable amount of genetic material with their
adopted children from our overall gene pool. Dawkins's theories have been well accepted but do remain somewhat controversial. Spirituality aside, the idea of selfish genes simply intent
on passing themselves on to the next generation, and to all
those that follow on a future road, does appear to make empirical, rational sense as a mechanism for sustaining life. As physi-
cian and medical historian Sherman Nuland succinctly says in
How We Live, "Empires fall, ids explode, great symphonies are
written and behind all of it is a single instinct that demands
satisfaction."[16] Our selfish genes, in other words, create good
and bad in our lives—we may lead an orchestra, overthrow a
government, or build a bridge. In the grand scheme of themes,
however, this is apparently only playtime. The main objective

collectively for us appears to be simply gene survival. We live, we play some form of cowboys and Indians, and then we die.

So on those days when you feel down and out, when you believe your life has no meaning, you can content yourself with the fact that you are at least a human survival machine, who may or may not pass your genes along, and if you do or you don't, it doesn't make any difference anyway.

Is this what existentialism or extreme reductionism is really all about? Maybe so, but as we'll see in the next chapter, for most of us, the neuronal circuitry of our brains doesn't allow us to dwell on these concepts for very long. The cold, hard world doesn't give us much time or leeway to ponder them. Moreover, the need that many of us have for a spiritual belief can shut out this type of thinking entirely.

Our virtual realities, in other words, provide barriers against these thoughts, just as they block out the concept of imaginary time. If you're seeking a greater sense of reality, you really have to work at it.

12.

OUR STATUS IMPERATIVE IS ONE OF THE MAJOR CAUSES OF HUMAN IRRATIONALITY AND CRAZINESS

I believe there is no one principle which predominates in human nature so much in every stage of life, from the cradle to the grave, in males and females, old and young, black and white, rich and poor, high and low, as this passion for superiority.

John Adams, second president of the United States[1]

The territorial imperative is as blind as a cave fish, as consuming as a furnace, and it commands beyond logic, opposes all reason, suborns all moralities, strives for no goal more sublime than survival.

Robert Ardrey[2]

Robert Ardrey's description above of the territorial imperative sums up what I've referred to as our "status imperative," a primal urge to defend, display, or increase our status. Territoriality is unquestionably a part of this.

Ardrey, a playwright, became a self-taught science reporter. In 1968 he wrote *The Territorial Imperative: A Personal Inquiry into the Animal Origins of Property and Nations*. It quickly became a best-seller. Among other things, he described the territorial characteristics of the higher animals and compared their behavior to that of humans. Interestingly, he noted that the higher animals appear to live more peacefully with each other than humans and questioned whether the cultural achievements of humans will ever be enough to override our penchant for war. He continued:

> It is the darkest of questions for all those who have placed their faith in cultural evolution as a means for accomplishing the pacification of man. . . . And unless nature saves us by an unexpected surfeit of earthquakes, volcanic upheavals, tidal waves and swarms of locusts, we are caught in the most encompassing of trips. I have no suggestion of shaking penetration to offer beyond that most obvious of comments: that we must know ourselves better in the future than we have in the past.[3]

We seem to have made little progress in knowing ourselves since Ardrey presciently wrote those words. The human attraction to violence, terrorism, and warfare continues to this day among large segments of the world's population. And one of the primary reasons appears to lie in the same neural propensity that ultimately allows higher animals, such as gorillas, chimps, and baboons, to live in relative peace within their groups—the propensity to form "dominance hierarchies."

The field of academic study that covers this is called "social dominance." Within those animal societies that live in groups, each individual has his or her place, a status, in the group's hierarchy from the dominant alpha male to the omega who lingers at the bottom. Females in these societies have their own dominance hierarchy, and in some societies it's the females who rule the entire roost. It would appear that nature provided this obvious genetic propensity to develop dominance hierarchies to establish a sense of order, reduce disorganization, and promote tribal defense and survival.

As humans, we appear to have the same biological propensity to develop dominance hierarchies, but instead of creating order among us, this urge, combined with the human ability to think and strategize, all too frequently leads to chaos, violence, and tragedy. In the case of animals, it's mostly eye stares or scuffles or other such devices that create the hierarchy. Among humans in most "civilized" societies, or to be more specific, in democratized societies, it is the ability to think, become knowledgeable in pertinent subjects, strategize, convince, and lead that are the primary devices for determining hierarchies. However, these devices can also be perverted, enabling warped, charismatic alpha leaders to manipulate the more vulnerable among us to follow some irrational cause. For example, in 1997 Marshall Applewhite, a former minister, convinced thirty-nine followers of his Heaven's Gate cult group to commit suicide because it would propel them to a new life on a spaceship following the Hale-Bopp comet, which at that time was about to pass near Earth.

Hello?

As with any other psychological characteristic, the status imperative resides in each of us on a scale. Those low on the scale feel little or no desire to seek and display status. Most of us have known people like this, who don't want any leadership responsibilities. They just prefer to do their jobs and that's it. Most of us are in the middle of this scale. We have a healthy level of ambition, we want more for ourselves and our families, and we'll accept positions of leadership, but we try not to abuse others when we're in such a position. Those high on the scale are obsessed by their urge for power and status, and no matter how high they climb, no matter how much money and power they acquire, it is never enough. Worse, they look down on those they perceive as beneath them, and may take pleasure in causing them misery.

If you're interested in seeing where you stand on the psychological scale of status and power, go to http://www.reality

checkbook.com and take a simple quiz. This power quiz has been taken by more than 700,000 people since it was first posted in 1996. The quiz was developed with the help of two graduate students in psychology from the University of Wisconsin. The results show that the scale of power and status is on a bell curve, with 2–3 percent near the bottom of the scale and 2–3 percent near the very top. The great majority of us, fortunately, are in the middle. But as will be described shortly, even the most mild mannered among us can be transformed into a "power mode" when we perceive that our jobs, relationships, or other aspects of our lives involving status are being threatened by others, or when we are thrust into a competitive situation.

The irrational outcomes of the status imperative in its more extreme forms have been chronicled in books, movies, and the news. One of the primary manifestations of the imperative is the belief that asserts: "I am better or smarter than you." Subconsciously or consciously, we appear to gauge our status against not only new people we meet but also those whom we see everyday or even live with. A sister may do something irrational like taunt her brother about the appearance of his new date to gain a brief status boost. A husband who has worked all day in a law firm may offer a sarcastic remark to a wife who is struggling to find a new job—"Do you ever do anything but watch television?" This may satisfy his urge for a brief status boost, vis-à-vis his unemployed wife. "I am better than you are," he thinks, as he puts down his wife. Like a crayfish successful in a challenge match, as described shortly, he walks out of the room strutting in triumph, while his desperate wife is slumping and cringes, having had her status deflated.

One night on public television, I watched the coverage of a small firm called Hoosier Bats, which makes about 50,000 baseball bats a year. It competes with Louisville Sluggers, the dominant bat company that makes more than 1,000,000 bats a year. "Our bats are double-dipped," an owner of Hoosier Bats said. "Theirs are not," he said in an instant of pride, deriving a momentary high from his display of status.[4]

My friend Bob Schwartz called me the day after both of us coincidentally sponsored groups at Chicago's beautiful new Millennium Park, which opened to the public in July 2004. "Did your tour cover the whole park?" he asked.

"Yes I replied."

"Did your tour visit the new Harris theater?"

"Yes," I said.

"Was your group allowed to see backstage?"

"Yes," I said.

"Did your group see the dressing rooms?"

"No," I said.

"Aha," he declared in a moment of apparent triumph. He had won in this mini battle for status.

How many times have we seen small battles like this between two individuals. Did you read the new book by Philip Roth? No? I'm surprised. You don't have a subscription to the Shakespeare Theater? You don't support the Lyric Opera? I don't see a wedding ring, are you divorced? You actually shop at K-Mart and wear their clothes? You say you live where? That's a suburb? Never heard of it. "Put downs," as we call triumphs of status between humans, are like viral infections and may cause more damage than viral illnesses, depending on our vulnerability to them.

Channel surfing one evening, I stopped to watch a talk by Joel Osteen, the Houston minister. He uses experiences based on his own human flaws to make the points of his sermons to his congregation and to a wider television audience. His apparent theme that night was the subject of pride and how it can hurt our relationships. He described how he and his wife, Victoria, when driving back from an event in downtown Houston, had problems finding an entrance to the freeway that would lead them home. They were waiting at a stoplight at an intersection, not far from the event they had attended.

"I thought we should turn left, and she thought we should turn right," he said.

The discussion became heated, and he made the arbitrary decision to turn left. He then described how the unspoken hostility in the car began to grow. Hostility can frequently grow quickly when a person's status is demeaned. Victoria's certainly was, because she lost status through Joel's stubborn decision. It then shortly became obvious to Osteen that he had made the wrong decision. They were lost. And so he decided to try to make his way back to the intersection where the confrontation took place, which he was able to do. This time he turned right, and he described how he was secretly hoping that they would get as lost as when he originally turned left, but he found the freeway entrance and was actually unhappy about it.

Here was apparently another mini battle for status. "I know more than you know. I am better than you, and so I *know* that turning left is correct."

Osteen made the point in his sermon that during the confrontation he should have given up his pride. He gave into a status-driven reactive feeling. This kind of arrogant and stubborn behavior can lead to irrational outlooks both during and after the conflicts, no matter who wins. How often do many of us do the same thing? Would it make any difference if we knew we were being driven by a biological status imperative while in an argument over something basically trivial? For some of us, maybe it would. For others of us, doing anything to boost our own status at the expense of someone else is indeed an absolute imperative.

The higher our drive on the scale for dominance and status, the more we appear to be compelled to find others whom we can look down upon, even if it's our own children or family pets. This drive can also manifest itself in whom we'll associate with and whom we won't; what designer labels we'll wear; what we say and do in status-charged situations; where and how we'll live; what our vocations and avocations will be; where and how we'll vacation; as an employer or a supervisor in the workplace, how we'll treat those reporting to us; and the list goes on. Our sense of our status may even be associated with athletic teams.

The rabid fans that attend football, baseball, and other athletic events may paint their faces in the team colors or wear the jerseys of their favorite players. If their teams win, they may be just as exhilarated as the players, and if they lose, just as dejected—maybe more so. When Bobby Knight, longtime coach of the University of Indiana basketball team, was fired in 2000 by university president Myles Brand for physically and mentally abusing some of his players, demeaning many of his assistant coaches, and intimidating others, thousands of supporters, students, and alumni marched on the home of Brand that evening shouting: "Hey, hey, ho, ho, Myles Brand has got to go."[5] For these rabid fans, the winning ways of Bobby Knight and the team was a status booster. It made them feel better, happy; this was much more than just a game of basketball. Now their status was threatened, and they felt hostile and retaliatory.

During the time of the Bobby Knight affair, an English professor at Indiana, Murray Sperber, had been critical in general of how Indiana and other universities were being more lenient with student athletes in class work, and he later wrote a book about his experiences titled *Beer and Circus*. When Knight was fired, Sperber was singled out as another target by rabid students and alumni, who wanted to protect the winning ways of the team at all costs. Here is what he wrote: "I was threatened and it was made impossible for me to teach this fall. Hardcore fan Web sites, people who worship Knight, had me on their 'enemies' list with many vilifying postings."[6] This action came from the educational product of our university system—students and alumni, whose status was now diminished because Bobby

Knight and his record of championships were gone, and who *forced Sperber out of his classroom.* Sperber had thought, as many of us do, that teaching and learning are why universities exist.

Was this irrational outlook and craziness caused by the status imperative? Of course.

Bobby Knight and the thousands of high school, college, and professional teams in the nation might be considered status symbols to their fans and followers. And it is not always fun and games, as Professor Sperber learned. Even at Little League baseball games, fathers and mothers shout obscenities at opponents from the stands, sometimes get into fist fights with umpires and other parents, ridicule the other team's children, and abuse their own children when they are not doing well. In Chicago, on October 8, 2004, a father of a young hockey player was convicted of misdemeanor battery for sticking the head of his son's teammate in a locker room toilet because the thirteen-year-old boy was whistled for a penalty in a game that was just concluded.[7] The status of these frenetic individuals is reflected by their teams, and if their children are on the teams, it's also in how their children perform.

Then there are status symbols, such as Harley-Davidson motorcycles, leather jackets, and body jewelry. Even beards are a status symbol, because they can reflect intelligence and wisdom. The symbols may be different for all of us, but the one thing they have in common is that they're used to boost our status. Jean Godden of the *Seattle Times* described some of Seattle's top status symbols during the 1998 heyday of the dotcoms, which included an unwashed blue Volvo station wagon, Microsoft stock options (how quickly some status symbols can change), reservations for Table 24 at Stars restaurant in Pacific Place, and even the burial of relatives in Lake View Cemetery.[8]

We are basically beset with symbols of status wherever we look. Their use is affected by what George Simmel, a respected professor of sociology, wrote around the turn of the century. His paper reported by the National Research Council Institute of Psychology said: "When social groups are ordered by rank, agents imitate symbols designating the higher hierarchal levels and abandon those designating the lower level ones."[9]

This means that as soon as existing status symbols favored by those higher within specific groups are copied by others, those higher in the group quickly find new and better status symbols to take the place of the old ones. This was soon labeled the "Simmel Effect" and is a phenomenon that we all recognize, even as much as we are baffled by it.

We have watched the tattoo craze and wondered why some people start with one or two tattoos and eventually end up with them covering almost every area of their bodies. The Simmel Effect would apparently dictate that as soon as all the members in that social group have one or two tattoos, they will thirst for more—or more body rings, or a bigger and blacker motorcycle, or more chest muscle, or whatever.

Presumably, Simmel understood that some of us may define our status by the symbols we display. If we're one of these people and our neighbor down the street buys a newer and better-grade car than we have, the Simmel Effect will kick in. At first, we may feel angered and dejected. But soon, as noted earlier, we may be transformed into the power mode, and, thinking aggressively, we may buy an equivalent or better car, even though we can't afford it. Someone once told me that in Los Angeles, you are what your car is.

If our bodies are laden with tattoos and have jewelry adorning every conceivable fold of our skins, we may believe that this will enhance our status among our peers. If we were to see someone who is even more impressively covered and whom our peers admire even more, we would feel crestfallen, defeated. Not until we'd find even more outlandish tattoos and "bling bling" jewelry might we again feel rewarded. By fulfilling the new round of expectations of our status imperative, we would feel good again, at least for the moment.

I have known corporate executives who have upgraded their corporate jets because too many of their executive peers or those they perceived as beneath them began flying the same jet model as theirs. I have also known high-ranking executives who outfitted their offices with outlandish decor, at exorbitant costs—with steam rooms and exercise areas, and, in one case I know of, a lap pool—to set themselves apart from the rest. The Simmel Effect had made the private office bathroom—once the highest symbol of an executive who had arrived—much too common. Interestingly, the most successful executives I have known, however, did none of this, some having offices you couldn't distinguish from their subordinates.

The status imperative even exists among many academics, who should know better. Among these academics the imperative manifests itself primarily in fierce, competitive battles for resources and recognition, including the need to be the first published with new research data. How many times have we read how one academic has tried to sabotage or demean the studies of another so that his paper will be the first in print? The purpose is to give him status over his rival—whose status is then diminished among his colleagues in the field of study. How many of us watched in amazement the bitter rivalry that existed in the quest to sequence the human genome, between the privately owned Celera and the publicly funded Human Genome Project? Bitter charges and countercharges flew between them, each believing that the other was threatening its status. And yet, as discussed earlier, this was considered by many scientists to be the most important study ever conducted. Moreover, the bottom line of this study showed that we're all connected.

Frequently, the main benefit of a work becomes subjugated to the need to be recognized and the status boost that accompanies that recognition. Research scientist Candace Pert, in her book, *Molecules of Emotion*, alluded to the fact that her jealousies undermined the dreams of a Nobel Prize for two of her research laboratory associates. She apparently thought they were using too many of her ideas about opiate receptors in the brain, without including her name on the application.[10]

The battle for status may be between siblings in families and even parents versus children. One famous battle for status and dominance took place between Sara Roosevelt, the mother of Franklin Delano Roosevelt, our thirty-second president, and his wife, Eleanor. Sara made it a point to humiliate and exert dominance over Eleanor in front of the family with enough frequency that a separate house had to be built for Eleanor on the family's Hyde Park estate.[11] Think of mothers and fathers we have known who have never been able to give up control of their children, no matter how old they became.

In the business world there are any number of managers and executives who look for someone to demean in order to get a daily status boost. Or they refuse to mix with subordinates under any circumstances. They will not eat at the same table with them in the company eating facilities. If forced to do so, they look uncomfortable. Executives like these may thrive in those corporations whose culture encourages this type of snobbery, believing that only the tough, aloof, and insensitive can move things forward. However, in my experience, most of the best CEOs and other managers in the business world are those who cultivate climates of teamwork and innovation among their employees, who work to submerge their own roles, which, oddly enough, gives them even greater status.

In recent years, status among many CEOs has been focused not on the earnings they create for the companies they run but on their compensation packages, which have become unreal. One evening some time ago, I brought up the subject with one of them.

"You don't understand," he said. "Our compensation as CEOs of public companies is public knowledge. The details are published in our annual reports and then frequently by the media."

"But what does that have to do with it?"

"It means that if we are invited to dinner or a party in Cape Cod, or Palm Springs, or the Hamptons, we feel uncomfortable if we know that the host has a compensation package much higher than ours. I've even turned down invitations for that reason."

I remember him thinking for a moment.

"And let me tell you," he continued. "Compensation differences can also get in the way of working out mergers and acquisitions, or even serving on the same board of another company or nonprofit institution. The CEO with the higher compensation has more status, and thus more leverage."

Apparently the same compensation status battles exist in the world of sports. In the spring of 2001, Frank Thomas, the then star of the Chicago White Sox baseball team, threatened to walk out of spring training camp, if his contract, which paid him $9 million annually, wasn't voided and a new one wasn't drawn up. Thomas was upset at the time because another player, Alex Rodriguez, was given a ten-year, $25-million-per-year contract by the Texas Rangers. Thomas felt demeaned because he thought he was as good as Rodriguez. Thomas actually had some sportswriters sympathizing with him.

Phil Jackson, former coach of the Los Angeles Lakers basketball team, said in *The Last Season: A Team in Search of Its Soul* that one of the reasons his contract wasn't renewed after the 2004 season was because he wanted more money. He was already making six million dollars per year. He wrote, "Six million dollars five years ago . . . isn't six million dollars today. . . . To me it's a matter of respect more than the money."[12]

Okay, I see.

The upshot is that the salaries paid to sports stars, CEOs, movie stars, and others whose compensation is public knowledge is not necessarily based on talent, but on the status it reflects against others in the same category.

The status imperative can be found in individuals or even in small groups. One family may feel superior to a family that lives next door or a family that one of their children has married into. The members of one church or synagogue may feel superior to the members of another church or synagogue, even in their own denomination. On a factory floor, it is not unusual for one group of workers to feel superior over another down the line. In cities, there are thousands of deaths and injuries every year caused by the rivalry of gangs: "Yo, you, you stepped on my block, this is my territory, so I will now shoot you."

Rivalries of status can encompass entire communities, cities, and nations—Pakistan versus India, for example—as well as cultural, political, and religious groups, and practically any group organized to promote a cause.

The status imperative might in certain circumstances be harnessed and put to good use, as will be discussed. But, in general, its influence is insidious, causing both mental and physical abuse to those whose status is being demeaned.

For example, in their book *Social Dominance*, psychologists Jim Sidanius and Felicia Pratto chronicle the class divisions that continue to plague the world. They discuss in detail the caste system in India, described as being relatively intact after three thousand years, even though it is "no longer part of the legal order of Indian society and 'untouchability' was outlawed after Indian independence in 1947 . . . and yet it remains an extremely important aspect of Indian social and political life." They further say:

> For example, most marriages are still made within castes, politicians rely on the "caste vote," castes continue to act as economic and political pressure groups,

castes are still ranked in terms of purity and pollution,
and intercaste violence continues to the present day.

While the United States is a more socially
dynamic nation than India and is, of course, not
nearly as old, the U.S. version of the caste system
shows every sign of being highly stable as well.
Despite intense efforts to eliminate racism from U.S.
life, the relative dominance of Euro-Americans over
African Americans has remained unchanged since the
European occupation of the New World more than
400 years ago.[13]

The authors state that class hierarchies may be based on
"such characteristics as clan, ethnicity, estate, nation, race,
caste, social class, religious sect, regional grouping, or any
other socially relevant group distinction that the human imagination is capable of constructing." They point out that these
systems of "group-based hierarchies abound . . . in modern
nations on every continent."

They offer a "partial list of modern nations including Mexico,
Japan, Sumeria, Nigeria, Germany, Israel, France, Canada, the
United States, Taiwan, Zaire, Korea and South Africa. . . . One is
truly hard pressed to find a society anywhere in the world that
does not have an arbitrary-set stratification system."

In his book *Japanese Etiquette and Ethics in Business*, author
Boye De Mente describes how Japanese society, in general, is
based on a ranking system:

Everything and everybody is ranked, within whatever
school they attend or organization they work for, first
on the basis of their educational background, then on
their seniority, and finally on their ability to get along
with others, their personality and their talent. . . . The
higher ranking the employer is, the higher the status
will be. This status is visually exhibited by the com-

pany or organization lapel button worn by employees
of most major corporations and government bureaus.[14]

Even in the old Soviet Union, a creation originally based on
the ideas of Karl Marx's classless, utopian society, the more
privileged had access to such things as the best apartments,
houses in the country, and well-stocked grocery stores, while
the remainder of the "classless people" had to live several to a
room, stand in long grocery store lines, and suffer other incon-
veniences spared those of higher status. We might safely conjecture that our natural, biological imperative for status was the
primary enemy of communism.

Children who are born into families that support the ideology of caste may be more readily imbued with the family's
prejudices and domineering attitudes because this is part of the
culture and because their own status imperative may be
helping them absorb these attitudes. Those cultures that recognize and work hard to repress strong drives for status, such as
the Amish, may escape with their attitudes for the most part
undistorted, but look at the work and effort they need to invest
to be free of these prejudices. And even they may feel superior
to outsiders.

Then there are the status-driven parents who may attempt
to mask their need for status with a "we're just plain folks"
veneer. In actuality, they insist that their children go only to
the "right" schools and befriend only the "right" children.
They continue to dominate their children with their demands
to do the right thing, even after they become adults. They must
marry the "right" person, have the "right" job, and so on. Any
sublimation of the status of the children would result, in their
minds, in a diminishment of their own status or a curtailment
of their efforts to gain and defend a higher status.

Further, some of these status-obsessed parents are unable to
give their children credit for anything they do at any age, even

if they do all the "right" things, because the admission would diminish the parents' own status. In their minds, only they are capable of achievement. And so the children, if they are needy of parental nurturance, become ripe for a personality disorder of their own.

At the conference on psychopathy I helped sponsor in 2003, I asked Jordan Peterson, a clinical psychologist, neuroscientist, and professor at the University of Toronto, where in the brain does this propensity for social dominance and ranking exist. He told me he had touched on the subject in his book, *Maps of Meaning*, which is considered a landmark work. He then summarized it by stating that this propensity was controlled by the levels of the neurotransmitter serotonin in the brain. He described experiments that showed how the addition or reduction of serotonin in a species of monkey actually enhanced or reduced status. My thought was how could this be so simple? But apparently Jordan's contentions have been corroborated elsewhere.

For example, Matt Ridley, in *Genome*, writes the following:

> Monkeys are not people, of course, but as Michael McGuire of the University of California, Los Angeles, has discovered, any group of people, even children, can immediately spot which of the monkeys in his captive group is the dominant one. Its demeanor and behavior—what Shelley called the "sneer of cold command"—are instantly familiar in an anthropomorphic way. There is little doubt that the monkey's mood is set by its high serotonin levels. If you artificially reverse the pecking order so that the monkey is now a subordinate, not only does its serotonin drop, but its behavior changes, too. Moreover, much the same seems to happen in human beings. In university fraternities, the leading figures are blessed with rich serotonin concentrations, which fall if they are

deposed. Telling people they have low or high serotonin levels could become a self-fulfilling prophecy.[15]

Catherine Marler, professor of psychology at the University of Wisconsin, alerted me to several studies, while I was writing *Power Freaks*, involving the hormone testosterone. She reports, for example, that "there is a study demonstrating that testosterone increases in fans supporting the winning team and decreases in fans supporting the losing team."[16] More recently, she has found evidence of winning effects in mice. "The more one wins the more successful and the higher the testosterone. In contrast, a mouse with a history of losing simply gives up when faced with a more confident winner, so often fights don't even happen."[17]

And so it is apparently our serotonin system, in some combination with testosterone, among other components, that appears to be a primary factor in the human primal or natural urge for confronting challenges, and which influences our place in the social hierarchies in which we are immersed, at home, at work, on church committees, in group athletics, and so on.

In *Power Freaks*, I also reported that the key to the dominance rankings in the higher animal world is apparently a system of challenges followed by submission or capitulation. Among the higher animals, including chimpanzees, gorillas, orangutans, and baboons, Jane Goodall and other primatologists have noted in detail the constant struggle for dominance and status within the colonies they observed and studied.

The fact that "human beings share the general primate tendency to seek high social rank" is an assumption that is "uncontroversial," asserts Jerome H. Barkow, professor of anthropology at Dalhousie University, in *The Adapted Mind: Evolutionary Psychology and the Generation of Culture*.[18]

On the other hand, Charles Snowdon, who, as mentioned, is also a primatologist, reports that while Jane Goodall is correct about chimpanzees:

there are other species where the status imperative is not very clear. In my cooperatively breeding tamarins [monkeys] where everyone in a family works together to rear infants, we cannot induce fighting over scare resources. And my colleague, Karen Strier, Professor of Anthropology, studies a remarkable monkey in Brazil, the muriqui, where she cannot see any evidence for dominance in a group. If there is a receptive female, males patiently wait in line until it is their turn to mate, often hugging and embracing each other while waiting. Males in a group are related to each other, and may not lose much if their brother or father is the one successful in fertilizing an egg. More important is that they work together and cooperate with each other.[19]

They patiently wait in line for sex?

Apparently, like all other mental proclivities, there is a scale among animal groups that measures the strength of dominance hierarchies, and the muriqui's would probably be classified at the lowest end of that scale.

For most of the animal world, the drive for social dominance and internal ranking is intense, and it is frequently called the pecking order—a phrase that originated from watching the behavior of chickens. Chicken A pecks chicken B, who pecks chicken C, and a social hierarchy is quickly formed and maintained. A variation of this system exists throughout most of the animal kingdom. In their book *Shadows of Forgotten Ancestors*, Carl Sagan and Ann Druyan describe the following:

> In crocodiles, dominance is established by slapping the head into the water, roaring, lunging, chasing and biting, pretend or real. . . . A toothless, brightly colored Central American frog, genus *Dendroates*, intimidates intruders by performing a vigorous sequence of push-ups. . . . When hermit crabs introduce themselves, they

devote a few seconds to taking each other's measure—
by stroking one another with their antennae; the
smaller then promptly submits to the larger.[20]

In the modern world of humans in democratized societies,
things aren't this cut-and-dried. We don't need to be big and
brawny, and physically brave, to have the ability to climb our
way to dominance, as do the higher animals and probably the
alpha cavemen. Maybe being a big, strong bully pushing,
shoving, and hitting in poorly supervised elementary and high
school yards will help in establishing dominance; but among
adults, it may get us arrested. What does the trick today for
carving out dominance is intelligence, organizational skills,
and leadership skills, although looks and stature, when added
to these characteristics, can help.

I thought that David M. Buss, professor of psychology at
the University of Texas, in *Evolutionary Psychology*, made an
excellent point when he said: *"[I]n the battle for status, our
behavior actually changes when we gain or lose status* [my italics].
. . . If a cricket tends to win a lot of fights, it becomes more
aggressive in subsequent fights. On the other hand, if it loses a
lot of fights, it will become submissive (much like the mice of
Catherine Marler)."[21]

The physical manifestations of winning or losing apparently show up vividly in crayfish. Buss states:

> More than one male crayfish cannot inhabit the same
> territory without determining who is the boss. The
> crayfish circle each other cautiously, sizing up their
> rivals. Then they plunge into a violent fray, trying to
> tear each other apart. The crayfish who emerges victo-
> rious becomes dominant, *strutting* [my emphasis]
> around "his" territory. The loser *slinks* [my emphasis]
> away to the periphery, avoiding further contact with
> the dominant male.[22]

Most of us know innately that behavior changes when status changes, because we've seen it happen. However, we might not have known that *this behavioral change may be a biological, automatic reaction.* Apparently, there is more to this shift in our reactions than the levels of our serotonin and testosterone. During a presentation I attended by Huda Akil, professor of neurosciences in psychiatry at the University of Michigan, she showed one slide that illustrated an actual change in the neurons of a higher animal after a "social defeat."

One half of the slide showed the amygdala in relative repose. The other half showed an amygdala prepared immediately after the animal suffered a social defeat. The neurons appeared to be firing in every direction. Here was the biology of defeat.[23] There is little relative difference in physical structure between the amygdala of the higher monkey I saw on the screen and the one in our human brains. The amygdala mediates fear. So a social defeat after a challenge apparently creates a level of fear that can sap our confidence. In humans, as in crickets and mice, after a series of defeats, some of us become too fearful to try again. Professional basketball coach Phil Jackson, in *The Last Season*, said that a basketball player "can easily lose confidence in his shot if he misses two or three in a row."[24]

Interestingly enough, Dr. Akil also mentioned that social defeats in mice not only induce submissive behavior but also activate drug-taking behavior—they are then more apt to imbibe stimulating intoxicants. This reminded me of a local softball team that would quickly migrate to the nearest bar after a loss and drink twice as much as the winning team, reflecting an old, apocryphal saying that "alcohol medicates depression."

Professional sports team coaches like Phil Jackson intuitively understand the neuronal behavior that changes our attitudes after victories and defeats more than most of us. If their team loses a series of games, the confidence of the players on the team in general is lowered. Their serotonin and testosterone levels drop, and their amygdalas create fear, presumably in a primal effort to discourage them from trying again to protect their self-esteem; or these physiological changes may be mechanisms to keep them peacefully at a lower rank. In any event, they begin to act like losers. Their bodies slump on the sidelines, with a self-defeating attitude, just as a crayfish or crickets do after a series of defeats. On the field of play, their bodies tighten and they play tentatively. In close games, they believe they are going to lose. Professional coaches know that confidence is the key ingredient for any team as a whole, just as important as sheer talent. And once that confidence is lost, it is usually only a series of strong wins that can get it back, no matter how many sports psychologists and motivators they bring into their locker rooms.

I play singles tennis from time to time with my friend Herb Weintraub. If he is winning, he struts about the court like a winning crayfish, chest out, happy, and enthusiastic, slinging taunts, like "You're on the way out, buddy." If he is losing, he slumps, looks depressed, and says little.

"You know what you're doing?" I said to him one day. "You're displaying the crayfish effect. You win, you strut; you lose, you slump. Your serotonin is going up and down like a yo-yo."

In other words, he is feeling the full effects of the neural chemistry that mediates his feelings of winning and losing, but he is unable to display a "poker face" (he admits he is a terrible poker player), a mask that some of us can contrive that conceals the confidence levels of our minds at any given instant. This makes it exceedingly difficult for others to perceive what we are really thinking. The psychopath, hiding behind a mask of compassion and interest, is obviously expert at this.

Herb, by the way, in response to my statement, said, "Why don't you just shut up."

The chemistry of the status imperative is involved in every competitive situation in which we find ourselves. It's apparent between lawyers in a criminal trial, for example. Or between architectural firms in a competition to win a new high-rise building or new municipal library project, or between ad agencies in a competition for a major new account, or even a small account or between two or more managers in a company vying for a higher level job. The winners strut in their own ways, and the losers slump.

In his book *The Ape and the Sushi Master*, zoologist and ethologist Frans de Waal, a leading expert on primate behavior, compares human behavior to how chimpanzees react when they lose status. He quotes from the Bob Woodward and Carl Bernstein book *The Final Days* on how President Nixon reacted to his loss of power:

> Between sobs, Nixon was plaintive. . . . How had a simple burglary . . . done all this? . . . Nixon got down on his knees. . . . [He] leaned over and struck his fist on the carpet crying, "What have I done? What has happened?"

The book then describes how Yeroen, a dominant chimpanzee in the world's largest chimpanzee colony at the Arnhem Zoo in the Netherlands, was being challenged by a younger male in a series of scrapes. Yeroen started to realize that he would lose, and began to throw tantrums similar to Nixon's.

> [He] would in the middle of a confrontation suddenly drop out of a tree like a rotten apple and writhe and squirm on the ground, screaming pitifully, waiting to be comforted by the rest of the group. The expression "being weaned from power" is particularly apt because Yeroen's relapse into childlike behavior was the same as that of a juvenile being weaned from its mother's milk.[25]

If a neuroscientist could have measured the serotonin and testosterone levels of Nixon and the chimpanzee at the moments of their being deposed from power, he would probably have found a proportionate lowering for each.

As with other higher animals, we humans do not spend every waking hour fighting to defend or raise our status. We find ourselves in a power mode most often when we are being challenged, or perceive we are being challenged, by others. After the situation normalizes, usually so do we.

In many instances it would be akin to the reactions of one chimpanzee in a chimp colony challenging another. Among chimps there will be "charging displays"—hair rising making their bodies look deceptively large, foot stomping, loud hooting, climbing into trees, and sharply swinging branches. Eventually, the challenge will usually culminate in eye stares and sometimes a struggle, before one of them turns his behind to the other and submits. Once it's over, it's over. In other words, they each transform out of the power mode and return to relative normalcy. Jane Goodall describes the aftermath of one such encounter in her book *In the Shadow of Man*:

> From then on it seemed that Goliath accepted Mike's superiority, and a strangely intense relationship grew up between the two. They often greeted one another with much display of emotion, embracing or patting one another, kissing each other in the neck. . . . Afterward they sometimes fed or rested quite close to each other, looking peaceful and relaxed *as though the bitter rivalry had never been.* [My emphasis][26]

Goodall also relates examples in her books where the dominant male, once fallen, not only becomes sulky and grim, but also remains an outcast, much like the loser in a battle between two stallions. The loser may spend the rest of his life looking at the herd from outside its circle. Nevertheless, the point is that once it's over and the chimps or horses are out of their power mode, they return to relative normalcy.

It is possible that this behavior is also part of the general design of the system of challenges that creates dominance hierarchies. In humans, just prior to a major challenge by another in our lives, we are prompted to become as ruthless and determined as our brain chemistry will allow, to give us the greatest possible odds for a victory. Goodall conveys the story of one chimp named Hugo who transformed as follows in a charging display:

> [H]e would sit, with hair on end, his sides heaving from exertion, a froth of saliva glistening at his half-open mouth, and a glint in his eye that to us looked not far from madness.[27]

Perhaps the characteristics that humans take on in a challenge is the human version of a "charging display." Certainly we have observed glimpses of madness when the linemen of two professional football teams face off together. After the game, the devout Christians from both teams will frequently gather in a huddle with arms about each other and pray together, resuming their normal temperament.

The charging display is plainly manifested among us humans when we feel we have been wronged and we are about to retaliate. Our tempers flare, our faces turn red, the adrenaline flows, and we "charge." If another car cuts us off, we may charge to a position adjoining the offending driver and scream and gesture. If someone at home, work, or elsewhere insults us or makes statements that we feel are deeply demeaning, we may blast back with psychological venom, aimed at inflicting the greatest mental damage on our adversary. If we are purposely pushed down hard on a basketball court, although we may ordinarily be calm in the heat of games, we may quickly pick ourselves up and physically charge the offender.

Given this theory, we may envision the system of challenges and their effect on our temperaments as on a continuum. Our "charging display" characteristics would manifest themselves in the preparation for the "conflict segments" of the continuum. Once the challenge is over, the effect would manifest itself in driving us to become puffed up if victorious or dejected if defeated. In any event, when the competitive match or challenge is over and we have made the transition out of the challenge mode, most of us are capable (if assuming the challenge was nontraumatic) of resuming our normal temperament.

Our "charging display" characteristics can apparently take more subtle forms as well. We are invited to attend a formal dinner and may instinctively feel that we will be in a competition for status. And so we dress to the nines and surreptitiously view the dress of others to determine how we rank against them. Perhaps we talk about a lavish new home we're building. "It isn't much, only 20,000 square feet." Or we talk about an acquisition we made. "My wife, Jane, is too shy to mention it, but the acquisition she engineered for Bostwick Labs—you know she was recently named CEO—is the largest the firm has ever made . . . and then she went right out and bought a Picasso for over the mantle to celebrate. Isn't that great?" Or we talk about the accomplishments of our children. "It's hard to believe, but our little Richie won the annual math prize at Friends School, and he's only six."

If we see a demeaned look in the faces of people we're challenging with our status-charged remarks, we consider it a victory, just as if we were a chimp in battle.

Of course, we don't need to be at a power dinner to set up a competition. In any number of circumstances, the accomplishments of our children may be the strategy we turn to if we see that we may be outranked by other situational factors or we need their accomplishments as a coup de grâce: "She's too modest to tell anyone, but our daughter Emily just led her school's soccer team into the state finals. We're all driving down next week for the game. Isn't that exciting?" Or, "We're so proud of him, Irwin was just admitted to Harvard. Where did you say your son, Jim, was accepted? Bumblebee University? Well, he should have a marvelous experience there."

Humans don't need to puff up their muscles and get their hair to stand on end and create a terrifying look, complete with frothing saliva, as the chimp Hugo did to challenge and demean a potential opponent. The aggressor may be a teenage ticket taker at the Bijou movie theater, who tells us imperiously while smirking that the movie we had hoped to see is all sold out. Or he may be the one next to you on an airplane, monopolizing the armrest. I recently made the mistake of offering a newspaper to a passenger sitting next to me on a flight, and before I knew it, I had to listen to an excruciatingly detailed description of the accomplishments of each of his five children. This was his way of conveying his status ranking to me.

I, on the other hand, was thinking of that Woody Allen movie in which his character is punished in prison, I think it was, by being locked in a hole with a life insurance salesman. That's sort of how I felt.

In the military, there is no subtlety at all when it comes to forming a pecking order, a dominance hierarchy. Each rank in the military is delineated by markings on the uniform, which from the bottom up includes noncommissioned personnel—privates, corporals, and several rankings of sergeants—and commissioned officers—lieutenants, captains, majors, colonels, and generals. The officers are considered "officers and gentlemen," which implies that noncommissioned officers are not—a throwback to the time when officers in the military, in the United States, Europe, and elsewhere in the world, came primarily from a more elevated, educated class.

To reinforce that noncommissioned officers are submissive, they are obliged to salute any commissioned officer they pass.

Further, we appear to be able to compartmentalize our power mode. We may be sweet and gentle in some situations and vicious in others. The Discovery Channel recently showed the biography of Cecil B. DeMille, the famous Hollywood producer and director of epics such as *The Ten Commandments*. His son described how on the sets of his movies he could be vicious, nasty, and relentless—humiliating people who were not meeting his expectations or in other ways disturbing him—all in front of a large cast and crew. Yet when he came home at night, he was a gentle, caring parent.

We might assume that when he walked on a movie set where he was directing a film, he perceived it as a competition for complete control and transformed into a power mode until it was over. He then resumed his normal temperament in his office or at home.

There also appears to be a status imperative in what and how we believe. Fanatical Christians, Jews, or Muslims will assume a higher status and feel morally superior in their rock-solid beliefs. "I know that the Bible is correct in every way." "I know that the Koran is correct in every essential." "I know that the Torah is God's word." The people who insist that theirs is the only true religion appear to receive a status boost as they put down the beliefs of other religions, agnosticism, or atheism as being misguided or dead wrong.

The same would appear to hold true in the political world of ultraconservatives and ultraliberals. Once they come to the conclusion, at whatever age, that their beliefs are correct and all others are wrong, they feel infused with a higher level of status. We watch them on television talk shows arguing with each other. When they are called on to talk, we can see the crayfish within them strut, as the camera covers them and they cannot wait to espouse their next opinion and belief.

In his book *The Biology of Belief,* science writer Joseph Giovannoli asserts: "If we see ourselves as defined by our beliefs, then our beliefs become 'self,' and to challenge belief is to challenge self."[28] He also quotes an observation attributed to the venerable Oliver Wendell Homes Jr., associate justice of the US Supreme Court: "The Mind of the bigot is like the pupil of the eye: the more light you pour upon it, the more it will contract."

How often have we seen a fanatical minister, politician, academician, or other authority figure spew out beliefs on television or at gatherings that seem to us to be specious or downright illogical? Yet they appear to be in rapture, as the words flow from their mouths, believing that they are revealing to us ultimate truths. Worse, if they have the right mix of charisma, power, and energy, as Marshall Applewhite of the Heaven's Gate cult obviously did, they can more easily bring people into their fold, giving their followers an apparent boost in status; after all, they *know* something that everyone else doesn't.

John Bowlby, in his landmark book *Attachment*, observes that when we attach ourselves to people we perceive as more powerful than we are, we frequently adopt their system of beliefs as well. He observes:

> A school or college, a work group, a religious group, or a political group can come to constitute for many people a subordinate attachment "figure." In such cases, it seems probable, the development of attachment to a group is mediated, at least initially, by attachment to a person holding a prominent position within that group. Thus, for many a citizen, attachment to his state is a derivative of and initially dependent on his attachment to its sovereign or president.[29]

This might help explain why millions of followers became attached to Adolf Hitler's lunatic beliefs about the superiority of Aryan blood. Think of yourself transformed in time, back to

1939, when Hitler was at the height of his power. You certainly couldn't address a group of Nazis back then, dangling a six-foot length of thread, and tell them: "Look, let me try to explain things to you. We all came out of this same genetic thread and the differences between one race of humans and another are infinitesimal and insignificant. So if you are going to hate Jews, gypsies, Negroes, homosexuals, and all Slavs east of Germany's borders (as the closest followers of Hitler did), you should probably hate yourselves as well."

Those Nazis would have stared at you as if you were the one with lunatic beliefs. They were not only presumably attached to their beliefs but also nurtured them as if they were their pet dogs. After the defeat of Germany in World War I, and the ensuing economic instability, those hateful beliefs gave them a status boost. They *knew* something that the rest of the world didn't.

It is apparent that we can become emotionally "hijacked," as Daniel Goleman explains, by the beliefs we absorb, both spiritual and nonspiritual, regardless of how irrational and warped they are.[30] The beliefs that boost our status thus become part of our individual virtual realities, which, as described, are extremely difficult to penetrate.

This process may be harmless, if our basic belief systems are harmless and if they are based on altruism and not warped rationalizations. Unfortunately, much of the misery of the world over the centuries has emanated from rationalizations of cruel and inhumane behavior. Southerners prior to the US Civil War solemnly believed that slavery was a positive institution that was intended to help Negroes advance themselves in life. Well after the war in 1881, Jefferson Davis, the deposed president of the Confederacy, described how "this benign institution had transformed 'unprofitable savages' into millions of efficient Christian laborers and trained them in the gentle arts of peace and order and civilization."[31] He never believed otherwise. Many of the great wars fought in recent centuries were rationalized as the necessary medicine to raise the subhuman qualities of the enemy to the standards of the invaders or to reclaim land that the adversaries thought belonged to them.

Germany's initial invasions during World War II were rationalized by the need to take back areas that were given to other countries during the 1919 peace conference. In Israel there are settlers willing to fight to the death to defend their land because they believe it is "a sacred heritage," a "legacy of God," which makes their attachment to the land not subject to compromise. Try reasoning against a spiritual argument. And there are Palestinians who believe their right to return to the lands they left after the 1948 Arab-Israeli war are based on the rationale that Israel doesn't have the right to exist. Therefore the lands that they occupied for centuries, but vacated during and following the war, despite Israeli assurances that they could safely stay, still belong to them. All over the world, disputes over land, such as the conflict over Kashmir between Indians and Pakistanis, are based on beliefs of one form or another of sacred heritage. In this particular instance, the nations of East and West Pakistan (now Bangladesh) were created in the first place because Muslims and Hindus battled incessantly and irrationally—both religions thinking the other subhuman in its practices, following India's independence from the British empire in 1949. To solve the problem, Pakistan was created for Muslims. Thus vast migrations amid bloody battles ensued as Muslims traveled north and Hindus who were in the north traveled south. Examples of blood baths created between and among nations by irrational beliefs could fill volumes.

Robert Ardrey's quote in his book the *Territorial Imperative* that "the territorial imperative is as blind as a cave fish, as consuming as a furnace, and it commands beyond logic, opposes all reason, suborns all moralities" is obviously right on target. And this dominates an Earth that is lost in the universe, that has existed for more than 5 billion years, whose borders are human-made, and whose territories were undoubtedly occupied by a myriad of tribes, shortly after the human migration out of Africa about 1.7 million years ago.

The same stubbornness of outlook that pervades fanaticism is similar in its impenetrability to a phobia, or an irrational anxiety, or any one of the personality disorders described earlier. You can't just talk people out of them through reason. You couldn't have talked Ronald Reagan into flying during the years immediately following his harrowing flight to Catalina Island. Nor could you have talked singer Karen Carpenter into eating properly after she was told she looked thirty pounds overweight and believed it. Nor could you have talked Hollywood magnate Howard Hughes into coming out of his hotel suite after he became a phobic recluse. Intelligent as these people were, their phobias and anxieties created warpéd outlooks that became deeply buried in the neural circuitry that formed their virtual realities. They thus became impervious to reason. As Sigmund Freud says in his book *Future of an Illusion*, people like these become victims of "an ego that has been overwhelmed."[32]

Think about this statement the next time you see two pundits with opposing views on a television talk show, each absolutely certain of his or her diametrically opposed viewpoints. Maybe we should just call in and request that they act less certain in a world filled with uncertainty.

The status imperative may not be all bad. We live today in a highly competitive world, and there appears to be nothing we can do about it. Some of us might look longingly at the Amish communities where greed and competitiveness are repressed, horse carriages are used for transportation, and life in general is slowed to a pace that was common before the industrial revolution. In the real world, however, and in the business world, in particular, changes are taking place at warp speed, and unless we are motivated to keep up with them, particularly in communication, logistics, and the latest technologies covering our fields of work, we can soon be left behind.

The theory of emotional intelligence was originally developed by psychology professors John Mayer and Peter Salovey, and published in a 1990 article "Emotional Intelligence, Imagination, Cognition and Personality."[33] Daniel Goleman then borrowed the name for his 1995 book *Emotional Intelligence*, which popularized the concept. It has since been amplified by other researchers and authors. It basically describes the need to maintain a sense of balance of our emotions so that we remain, overall, in control of ourselves. We can then learn to harness those emotions that may be impelling us to take irrational action and channel them instead into motivating us to attack the challenges before us in a productive way and, at the same time, be empathetic to and accepting of others.

If we are in a lawsuit, most of us don't want an Amish farmer who may have read a few law books to defend us. We want the best man or woman that we can find, who in court can transform easily into a power mode (as Cecil B. DeMille did on movie sets) and defend us with passion, energy, and honesty. But we also want him or her to later communicate with us calmly and logically on what he or she perceives are the next steps. Goleman writes the following in concluding his book *Emotional Intelligence*:

> The bedrock of character is self-discipline; the virtuous life, as philosophers since Aristotle have observed, is based on self-control. A related keystone of character is being able to motivate and guide oneself, whether in doing homework, finishing a job, or getting up in the morning. And, as we have seen, the ability to defer gratification and to channel one's urges to act is a basic emotional skill, one that in a former day was called will. "We need to be in control

of ourselves—our appetites, our passions—to do right by others," notes Thomas Lickona, writing about character education. It takes will to keep emotion under the control of reason. . . . Being able to put aside one's self-centered focus and impulses has social benefits: it opens the way to empathy, to real listening, to taking another person's perspective.[34]

Many of us have learned the ability to exert our rational will over our irrational, emotional impulses. We can control and sublimate our need to satisfy the expectations of our status imperative, including the urge to demean others in one or more of hundreds of ways.

Too many of us haven't.

Finally, in an odd twist of nature, the things we do and the experiences we have that can boost our status may have nothing to do with our self-esteem. In the book *Self-Esteem, Paradoxes and Innovations in Clinical Theory and Practice*, Richard L. Bednar notes:

> The [following] is a statement from a 70-year-old man, reflecting on his lifetime effort to better the world he lived in:
>
> "My whole life has been a succession of disappointments. I can scarcely recollect a single instance of success in anything that I ever undertook."
>
> The origins of this statement are not to be found in a life dominated by failure, nor was this person an object of pity and scorn to his contemporaries— nothing could be further from the truth. The writer was John Quincy Adams, who served with distinction as the sixth president of the United States, a senator, a congressman, a minister to major European countries, and a vital participant in many of the early and

crucial events influencing the development of the nation.[35]

The actress Judy Garland, despite her many obvious successes, was known to have low self-esteem throughout her life. I have known many highly successful people who had low opinions of themselves and suffered from feelings of inferiority. On the other hand, most of us have known people of low accomplishment and talent who thought that they were really fantastic—that they were God's gift to the earth. The Chicago Bears football team several years ago had a rookie quarterback who obviously had very high self-esteem but was a complete failure in the game. When he was taken out, he begged to get back in the game, where he simply repeated his failures. He had no clue—the failures never humbled him.

Psychologist Nathaniel Branden, an expert on self-esteem, contends that it is highly difficult to define "self esteem":

> [T]he assumption that we all know what it means is mistaken. If we were to ask anyone what self-esteem means, we might receive an answer such as, "I feel competent, sure of myself," or "I like myself," or "Thinking I'm superior to other people." The first two statements would not be wrong, but would be incomplete; the third would simply be false. . . . A person who does not feel competent in the performance of some particular task, such as flying an airplane, designing a computer program, or operating a business, does not necessarily suffer from poor self-esteem. . . . But a physically healthy person who feels fundamentally inadequate to the normal challenges of life, such as earning a living, certainly does. [36]

In other words, self-esteem is compartmentalized. It might be described as what our opinion is of ourselves in specific situations. Someone who is riding on a Harley motorcycle with leather jacket and other accoutrements might be feeling on top of the world. But if he were forced into a contemporary art museum by a significant other on her birthday, he might quickly form a low opinion of himself, feel ignorant, and become depressed. Back on the Harley, he is high as a kite again.

I have known CEOs who in their work and social lives have a very high opinion of themselves. They are confident and competent. But if they happen to be physically uncoordinated and lousy golfers, and they need to play with an important customer or client, their opinion of themselves may quickly nose dive, their self-esteem and confidence may sink, and they'll likely be relieved when they can slink off into the woods to find a ball.

The brain's amygdala, that almond-sized structure (amygdala is Greek for almond), appears not only to create fear to help us get through and survive a threatening situation, but it also appears to use fear and anxiety to protect our self-esteem. It is basically warning the hacker CEO not to go out on the golf course in the first place. "I'm going to make you feel bad," it basically tells him.

On the other hand, I have known CEOs with generally high self-esteem who don't care how they perform on a golf course. If they are hackers, they hack their way through, trying their very best until the end, and garner in the process the astonished admiration of others.

We all know people who refrain from an activity in which they might do poorly, even though they might end up finding it fun or useful. They may feel that their general self-esteem is basically at risk, and so they stick only to what they know and do relatively well.

How many older adults won't use a computer because they don't want to look inferior while they are learning it? They'll even make up specious excuses for themselves. "I understand that e-mail is 90 percent spam anyway." "I don't need the Internet, I read newspapers and watch television." "I'm doing fine without a computer."

Persons with higher levels of general self-esteem dig right in. They are less vulnerable to what others think as they tackle something new.

Further, victories and defeats in our day-to-day lives don't appear to have lingering effects on the levels of our self-esteem. If we are a lawyer with a lower level of self-esteem and we win a great case, our self-esteem rises. It may stay high for a day, or a week, or a month, but then it will fall to our baseline of self-esteem after a time. Conversely, we may suffer defeats in our lives, such as losing a lawsuit for our client. Our self-esteem may fall hard, but, over time, it will likely rise to its baseline.

On the other hand, a series of truly significant defeats may push down our baseline of self-esteem, and we may relatively quickly lose confidence in ourselves. As Rosabeth Moss Kanter asserts in her book *Confidence: How Winning Streaks and Losing Streaks Begin and End*, "Destroying confidence can take minutes, while restoring confidence can take millennia."[37]

It would appear that the rate at which our self-esteem may slip after a series of significant defeats depends on our individual vulnerabilities, similar to our levels of resistance to mental dysfunction. Some of us are more vulnerable to significant defeats than others. Others of us use the defeats as motivation to do better the next time.

The upshot of all this appears to be that the little status boosts we give ourselves (as described earlier in this chapter) may have little or no effect on a relatively low self-esteem baseline. The new car or house may raise our self-esteem, but only temporarily. Shortly we'll be looking for other boosts, a room addition, another child, more tattoos, another degree in martial arts.

One of the keys to raising self-esteem, according to

Nathaniel Branden and other experts, is the use of self-assertiveness, to strike against the fears that inhibit us. We should engage in areas in which we think our self-esteem may be at risk. Easier said than done, of course.

Perhaps the essence of this subject is seen in the animal kingdom. As noted earlier, some chimps, among other animals, after a series of defeats, will just give up trying, accepting their lowly position in the social hierarchy of their groups. Did their self-esteem drop after these defeats? Is self-esteem a biological device that helps mediate our fight for status? Other chimps continue to challenge the next chimps up their hierarchies, creating what Charles Snowdon calls "status tension."[38] Even though they have been continually defeated, they still keep trying.

It would appear that, in some odd way, our drive for status and our baseline level of self-esteem seem to work together, but as Richard L. Bednar points out, in a manner that is "intriguingly paradoxical." Sometimes a series of victories and defeats will work to raise or lower our baseline of self-esteem over long periods of time. At other times, the result is temporary.

If our brains didn't all emerge from the womb different from all other brains on the planet, but instead came out of an IBM factory, this would all be easier to explain, as well as to fix.

In the meantime, we need to work with the brains we have. Many of us are fortunate to have a cerebral cortex capable of observing the irrational drives and reactive emotions served up by our limbic brain components. We can contain the treacherous status imperative by repressing or controlling its impulses when they are inappropriate and ultimately damaging to us and others around us. Only by acknowledging their existence, however, can we begin to transcend them, as well as our virtual realities, which harbor them.

13.

THERE ARE MORE THAN 10,000 DISTINCT RELIGIONS IN THE WORLD, EACH WITH ITS FANATIC BELIEVERS: WE OBVIOUSLY KNOW NOTHING FOR CERTAIN

> On the one hand our lives seems so important—with all those cherished highly personal memories—and yet we know that in the cosmic scheme of things, our brief existence amounts to nothing at all. So how do people make sense of this dilemma? For many the answer is straightforward. They seek solace in religion.
> **V. S. Ramachandran[1]**

> I envy people of faith. I'm incapable of believing in anything supernatural. So far, at least. Not that I wouldn't like to. I mean, I want to believe. I do pray. I pray to something . . . up there. I have a God sense. It's not religious so much as superstitious. It's part of being human, I guess.
> **Jack Nicholson[2]**

It was almost as difficult to find out the number of religions in the world as it was to learn the number of sperm produced per hour by the average healthy male.

One day I saw an obscure reference to the *World Christian Encyclopedia: A Comparative Survey of Churches and Religions in the Modern World*, a two-volume set published by the Oxford University Press, which I purchased. It reports that there are "at least 10,000 distinct and different religions across the world,"[3] of which 270 have more than 500,000 adherents.[4]

For example, the Yanamamos of Venezuela, 15,000 strong, live in 125 villages and believe in the "powers of medicine men or shamans (*shabori*), spirits (*Yai*), and a divinity called Wada-wadariwa (Son of Thunder)."[5]

Another religion, Shamanism, is still practiced widely in North Korea and other countries, and its adherents believe in "the existence of good and evil spirits residing in material objects such as rocks and trees, which may be controlled by priests (*mundang*). The belief system also includes some concepts of Confucianism, which focuses on how we should behave."[6]

In South Africa, 8 percent of the population continue to practice religions traditional to the country, including those worshiping the supreme being Lovedu, which includes a role played by a "divine queen who must be without physical weakness and who eventually commits ritual suicide by poison before the young male initiates emerge from her reign's fourth circumcision school."[7]

This makes perfect sense to me.

In the Ukraine, there are more than 32 distinct religions, plus 13 separate denominations of the Catholic Church, and 30 denominations of the Ukrainian Orthodox Church.

Then there are traditional South American animist cults such as candomble, macumba, and umbanda, which have similar roots to those of Caribbean voodoo and Santeria. The *New York Times* reports that these cults "are practiced by millions of Brazilians who also consider themselves Catholics."[8]

Among the 270 religions worldwide with at least 500,000 adherents are the Geddatsukai, Hossoshu, Qadiritya, Saktist, Tendai, Soto, and Zaydis religions. And, of course, Christianity, Islam, Judaism, Hinduism, Buddhism, Confucianism, Sikhism, Taoism, and Shinto.

In addition, according to Barrett, there were 33,820 Christian denominations worldwide as of the year 2000, up from 26,350 in 1970. Each has some variation from the others.[9]

I asked a friend of mine how there could possibly be 33,820 Christian denominations. His reply was, "Have you ever been to Arkansas?"

"No, why?"

"Because I worked in that state for five years, and it seemed to me that on almost every corner of every city or town there was a church, and they all appeared to have a different name. I think this same situation runs through the entire Bible Belt."

The point is that when you see such diversity of belief, 270 religions with large numbers of adherents—disregarding the thousands of smaller ones, and with believers who are fanatic in each of them—what does this tell a thinking person? It must tell him that *when it comes to religion and spiritual beliefs, nobody knows anything for certain.*

This should be obvious to the intellectually curious, even if we narrow down the conflicting beliefs to simply Christians, Muslims, Jews, Hindus, and Buddhists, whose altercations and animosity toward each other are the basis of much of our daily news. The problem of maintaining an open view on religion is that our individual beliefs apparently become part of our own virtual realities and thus cannot be penetrated by reason. We cannot walk up to a militant, fanatic Hindu in India, who has recently killed a Muslim for no reason other than prejudice, and say, "It seems absurd that your religion forbids you to kill monkeys and cows and such, which are littering your cities with excrement, but you feel you have the right to kill a Muslim."

The Hindu may answer you with quotations or references from Hindu scripture, just as the Christian may justify irrational answers through references to the Bible, the Muslim to the Koran, or the Jew to the Talmud. For example, in the September 13, 2004, issue of *Time* magazine, Hassan Butt, a twenty-four-year-old British Pakistani, who is a self-described radical, says, "There is no way to interpret the Koran other than literally . . . and therefore no room for moderation. If in the Koran . . . Allah says fight, then you fight. How can anyone take a moderate view of this?"[10]

Strict espousers of the Bible and other religious scriptures would take much the same view on a whole host of issues, and therefore you can't argue with them.

On the other hand, it would appear that most religionists simply expound on the beliefs that they were taught by their families. If you were born into a Catholic household and you are a practicing Catholic today, the overwhelming odds are that this is the result of that upbringing.

Moreover, try to imagine yourself as the winning sperm that happened to travel up your mother's vaginal tract in a religious Jewish household. If you remain religious today, the overwhelming odds are that you would not be a practicing Catholic, Protestant, or Muslim, but a practicing Jew, perhaps even an Orthodox Jew with a long beard and distinctive dress. Your religious beliefs, just as your language and culture, *are primarily an accident of your birth.*

As noted earlier, John Bowlby, an authority on attachment, states that we first become attached to an authority figure, and then to his or her beliefs. As children, our fathers and mothers are our primary authority figures, who in religious households decree that we believe in the tenets and symbols of their religions. These teachings are then reinforced by our places of worship, where we are asked to read from prayer books, follow rituals by rote, and attend religious classes. Pulpits in many religious denominations are raised high above the congregants to reflect power and authority in places of worship, whose ceilings often soar high to further raise the status of the ministers who represent the dominion of god. This all serves to diminish the status of the congregants. The perception of authority among the clergy may be enhanced even further if the denomination calls for him to wear flowing gowns or other vestments. The upshot is that at a young age we may see these ministers, priests, rabbis, and so on, as greater spiritual authority figures than even our parents and other adherents within our families.

And so those of us who carry the same beliefs from childhood to adulthood continue to perpetuate the separateness of the 270 religions with 500,000 or more adherents. Although as thinking and independent adults, we have the right to choose any religion at all. While there is shifting from one denomination to another among Christians, Jews, and others, the number of people who convert from one major religion to another in any given year in the United States is less than 2 percent.[11] More of us, however, may become more secular, while holding onto only vestiges of our basic faith.

I was born into a Jewish household. There were ten of us who lived in an apartment on Chicago's south side: my mother, father, grandmother, grandfather, aunt, uncle, two single uncles, sister, and me. It was the 1930s, the era of the Great Depression, and many families lived together to save expenses. My grandfather was orthodox and attended an orthodox synagogue. My mother and father were more moderate, and we attended a conservative temple, where I also attended Hebrew school for eight years and became a bar mitzvah at age thirteen. I remained a temple goer until I was in my early forties, when it began to dawn on me that I was spouting prayers and beliefs that for me had little basis in rationality. I became an apostate, an agnostic who feels a sense of spirituality but follows no ritual. Today, I seek out answers to all the mysteries that shroud our lives.

One result of this outlook is that I stare long and hard at people who lecture me on their faith. If you consider the fact that we are so diverse in our religious beliefs, how can they all be so convinced? I have read books by religious intellectuals who attempt to apply reason to their beliefs, even though most admit that as thinking adults we have to at some point take a "leap of faith" to believe. I have heard critics of religion describe the term "religious intellectual" as an oxymoron, under the supposition that no one can be an intellectual of any kind who is not totally open to newly discovered facts as they are uncovered for us.

New York Times columnist David Brooks, in describing why people can be as enduringly passionate about being a Democrat or a Republican as some are about the Yankees and Red Sox, asks: "Why does everything in America change except politics?"[12] He should have said politics and religion, because most religionists are practicing the doctrines that have been handed down over centuries or even millennia, doctrines that were contrived during eras when life was even more of a mystery than it is today. And they continue to practice them despite every scientific fact that has shed light on our existence and should have made them at least moderately skeptical. But like a serious phobia or an extreme anxiety, religious belief devoid of doubt persists.

On the other hand, in an existence surrounded in mystery, who can really criticize the religious families in a small Iowa town who try to do good; who don't bully or demean others in any way; who are accepting of others regardless of their religion or race; who are sympathetic and empathetic; who work hard to harness their baser emotions and drives whether at home, in the workplace, or the community; and who go to a church, synagogue, or mosque because it reinforces their spirituality and they find comfort in it?

Unfortunately, too many religionists appear to practice their faith along the lines described by Russell Shorto in an article in the *New York Times Magazine*, where he describes a recent infusion of Christian faith in the workplace. Although many Christians lamented that they felt a moral vacuum in the workplace, Shorto notes that "all the marketplace Christians I encountered were firmly of the belief that Christian truth is the only truth and that part of their duty as Christians is to save the unsaved."[13]

In other words, they believe of the thousands of other distinct religions in the world Christianity is the only true one. This renders everyone else godless heathens. And doubtless, extremists in the other 10,000 religions would spout the same line, except for the duty to "save the unsaved," which is not an objective among religions that are not missionary, such as Buddhism, Hinduism, and Judaism.

My only argument with religion is that too many of the people I've come across over the years, who proclaimed themselves devout Christians, Jews, Muslims, Hindus, or other faiths, would travel to their places of worship on the appointed days and times of prayer, and follow all the ritual and prayers. But once back in the real world, they would become the true assholes they always were. In the workplace, they would revert to their jealousies and envies, tormenting others, and playing power games behind their backs. At home, they would revert to screaming at their spouses, sniping at their neighbors, and lording it over their children, finding it hard to forgive any transgression. Even before they got home from a church or temple, everything they supposedly learned was lost. Have you ever watched the cars bolting out of the church's or temple's parking lot? It is almost a miracle that no one is killed. I recall watching a documentary about Francisco Franco, who ruled over Spain through World War II and beyond and who was a devout Catholic. Yet, I recall him saying, "I go to Mass every morning, but I can forgive nobody." What's with that? If you can't forgive, then don't make the pretension that you are devout. Save your time going to places of worship. Take in a movie. Or read about Albert Schweitzer who exemplified Christian teachings.

I also recall watching motion picture producer and director

Mel Gibson being interviewed about his movie *The Passion of the Christ*. He talked about how this movie needed to be seen by everyone because it displayed the truth of how Jesus was brutally tortured and then died for our sins. He continued that through Jesus we could have redemption, and our sins would be forgiven. In the interview, Gibson was asked about his own behavior, and, scrunching his face, he said that he was "vile." By this, I presume he meant that in his world of entertainment you need to do things that border on the unethical. Or perhaps he was referring to past conduct.

If religion actually worked, if people lived their lives post–religious services in accordance with the Beatitudes of Jesus, for example, or worked hard to do good, as per the Iowa families described, then what a marvelous institution religion would be.

One of my favorite books is *The Complete Idiot's Guide to the Life of Christ*, written by William R. Grimbol, a graduate of the Princeton Theological Seminary, minister of Shelter Island Presbyterian Church, in New York, and director of Shelter Island Community Youth Center. The book filters out the confusion of liturgy and ritual to describe what Jesus the man was all about. Grimbol quotes the Beatitudes, from the Sermon on the Mount, in a fashion that diminishes the Ten Commandments, which comedian George Carlin in one of his routines reduced to just two: Thou shalt not kill, and thou shalt not steal. Here are the Beatitudes with my comments in the brackets:

> Jesus . . . assigned blessings and happiness to those who . . .
>
> - Are aware of their deep need for God. [Or perhaps a deep need for spirituality in general, presumably to become more caring and sensitive.]
> - Are compassionate and genuinely merciful. [How many follow this one as they talk behind the backs of, or in other ways hurt, others?]

- Know the brutal pain of loss. [And so can empathize with the pain of others.]
- Are willing to claim their grief. [They show the pain they feel, they display humanness.]
- Value justice. [And will speak up against injustice.]
- Strive to defeat or harm nobody. [Even extreme religionists appear to forget this one, particularly during elections.]
- Respect all of God's children. [Respect everybody, treat everyone as equal, no matter their station in life.]
- Have a heart that desires only the best for all people.
- Are peacemakers, not troublemakers.
- Are creators of community and celebrators of diversity. [Celebrators of diversity? Hello? Where has this one been for the past two thousand years?]
- Are unwilling to sit in judgment.
- Are unwilling to see faith as a means of superiority. [Another big one that has gotten lost in translation.][14]

The Beatitudes should form the basis for any religion. But that's not the way it has worked out.

In his 2004 book *The End of Faith: Religion, Terror and the Future of Reason*, neuroscientist Sam Harris describes the extreme religionists who, instead of focusing on the peace and harmony that religion should promote, are inciting the preponderance of wars and terrorism that plague the world today. He says:

> The recent conflicts in Palestine (Jews v. Muslims), the Balkans (Orthodox Serbians v. Catholic Croations; Orthodox Serbians v. Bosnian and Albanian Muslims), Northern Ireland (Protestants v. Catholics), Kashmir (Muslims v. Hindus), Sudan (Muslims v. Christians and animists), Nigeria (Muslims v. Christians), Sri Lanka (Sinhalese Buddhists v. Tamil Hindus),

Indonesia (Muslims v. Timorese Christians), and the Caucasus (Orthodox Russians v. Chechen Muslims; Muslim Azerbaijanis v. Catholic and Orthodox Armenians) are merely a few cases in point. In these places religion has been the explicit cause of literally millions of deaths in the last ten years. These events should strike us like psychological experiments run amok, for that is what they are. Give people divergent, irreconcilable, and untestable notions about what happens after death, and then oblige them to live together with limited resources. The result is just what we see: An unending cycle of murder and cease-fire.[15]

He then cites a report on how: "Mothers were skewered on swords as their children watched, young women stripped and raped in broad daylight, then set on fire, a pregnant woman's belly slit open, her fetus raised skyward on the tip of a sword, then tossed into a fire." This is not an account of the aftermath of a successful rout of a walled Ancient or Medieval city, but a chronicle of the violence that erupted between Hindus and Muslims in India in the winter of 2002.[16]

One would think that a look at the history of the conflicts among religions and an assessment of the misery and killings that have resulted from them would be enough to sober the leaders of today's extremist religious factions. In just one night, on August 4, 1572, in France, as part of a battle between Catholics and Huguenots for control of the French monarchy, more than fifty thousand Huguenots were slaughtered in what has been called the St. Bartholomew's Day Massacre.[17] History is replete with such incidents, including full-scale battles and wars that took place over differences of a few words in the liturgy. *The World Christian Encyclopedia* lists 69,420,000 "martyrs" created by varying religions between 33 and 2000 CE.[18]

All in all, religion doesn't have a great track record, although religious conflicts have been dwarfed in general by geopolitical disputes over land and economic power—that is, World War I and World War II.

Nonetheless, the Beatitudes and similar messages in other religions were lost somewhere among the wars and battles over liturgy and religious culture.

One of the basic problems that religion creates is its close-mindedness—its submersion within the walls of our virtual realities—so that it prohibits any rational discourse.

I recently received an e-mail that said:

> Before it's too late make peace with GOD, and make sure the ones you love do also. You need to pick between an eternity of joy or one of torment:
>
> • Accept him.
> • Repent.
> • Get baptized
> • And have a nice eternity.

I showed this note to a friend of mine, who is a quiet, highly observant Eastern Orthodox Catholic, and asked, "Surely it can't be as simple as all that."

"It is, if you truly believe."

"And so you are assuming that everyone in the world is a sinner. He or she is born with sin, as part of genetics, and this can all be swept away by being baptized, repenting, and accepting Jesus."

"It is that simple, yes."

"Now I assume that the eternity referred to in the e-mail means heaven, and that torment means hell."

"That's correct."

"But we don't know where heaven is."

"Yet we know it exists in a spiritual sense, which is well beyond the material world in which we live. Heaven is a transcendent, spiritual place."

"That's not much of an answer. If we talk about heaven as if it were a place, then it should exist somewhere. Is it at the far ranges of our own solar system, beyond Pluto? If it is, and our spirits travel at the speed of light, we can get there in about seven hours. Is it somewhere in the middle of our galaxy, the Milky Way? If so, it might take us 50,000 years or so to get there? And then what about the 140 billion other galaxies, each with some 200 billion stars? At close to the speed of light, our spirits might take billions of years to get to some centrally located heaven within the universe. And then what language would we speak? Is there some common language that would transcend all the galaxies, including our own Milky Way? Would we be able to understand each other? Just on the Earth, we have something like twelve thousand languages. Communication in heaven could be an enormous problem."

"You don't understand, these calculations mean nothing in the spiritual realm. Time can be instant. You could travel to the edges of the universe, or even above it, instantly. Communication would be universal."

"Okay, so we can get there soon and we can communicate. But what age are we when we get there? And what are the ages of our parents and grandparents and great-grandparents who might be there before us? At my age today, I am older than my mother and even my grandfather when they died. How will we adjust that?"

"All of this will be answered."

"And how do we live? Artists have pictured the angels living on clouds with a blue sky behind them? That doesn't seem likely, since outer space itself is pitch black. Do we have homes? And if we do, how many of our ancestors are living in them? If we go back only seven hundred years or so, we have more than 1,000,000 parents of parents of parents we have descended from. Do we live with them all? That kind of overcrowding seems more like hell than heaven. Doesn't this all get a little confusing?"

"Everything will be sorted out by God."

"Then what about pets? There are many people who, if they died, would rather be with their pets, who have passed away, than with parents who might have been physically abusive to them. Do we get to see our old pets in heaven? Will I get a chance to be with my old dog, Suzette?"

"That may be possible."

"But if that's possible, then it means that all the higher animals with brains that are very close to ours may get to go to heaven. Do they wander around the way we do, or are there zoos up there with cages for those that are still wild? Or does heaven make the wild ones all tame? And where is the line drawn? Are all the dead rats who tried to do their best in life in heaven? Their emotional structures are very similar to ours."

"All this will be answered."

"And what about divorces? Will we need, if all is forgiven, to associate with our ex-spouses, and how is that all sorted out, like if we have to be with them, do we also have to be with their parents, who we might not have considered great company? And how will our current wife feel about all of that? In other words, do we get a choice as to whom we are with?"

"When you die, you will know."

"But will I? According to Christianity, unless I am baptized, repent, and accept Jesus, I don't even get to go to heaven. This is a marvelous concept for attracting converts, but rational people who are religious should know that a fair God would extend his blessings to everyone. How could he be so narrowminded to doom avid followers of other religions into which they were born? And even those of all religions, including Christians, who may have committed some form of evil, are they all doomed for eternity?"

"Well, if they're evil, they will go directly to hell or be placed in purgatory, where they'll have a chance to cleanse their sins."

"So you mean our spirits carry our brain's limbic system with them?"

"What do you mean?"

"I mean totally evil people are apparently either psychopathic or have strong psychopathic tendencies. The neural circuitry in their brains prevents them from feeling guilt, shame, remorse, empathy—they feel uninhibited in whatever they do—and if they have a strong drive for power and status, they wreak havoc. Presumably, our spirits which leave our bodies, if they do, are cleansed of these disorders, because it appears impossible that a spirit can carry a human brain. So why would we need a purgatory or a hell? We'd all be cleansed and good."

"It is possible that these tendencies remain in the spirit realm."

"I don't know, that wouldn't make much sense, would it?"

"It must make sense if there is a heaven, hell, and purgatory."

"But how do we really know that? Nobody has come back from the grave, after six months of being dead, and told us what it's all about. We haven't the vaguest idea of what happens to us after we die. It's all guesswork. Even the white light, we supposedly see at the end, is thought to be a biological process of the brain. There is nothing about the after-death experience that we can prove."

"As I told you before, you have to believe, you need to have faith."

"Okay, but then in your belief system, how do you address the idea of reincarnation, embraced by Hindus and others? They believe we keep coming back to new lives until we get it right. This may take endless generations. How do we know which bodies we'll come back in when we are reincarnated. How do you answer that?"

"I don't believe in reincarnation."

"But millions do. Are they all wrong?"

"I believe they are."

"Then let's get back to hell. We are led to believe that

heaven is up and hell is down. But in the universe, going down from Earth is practically the same as going up. Or is it meant that hell is just far away from heaven."

"It is in the opposite direction."

"Okay, I looked this up, it's estimated that there have been approximately 106 billion people born since 50,000 BCE.[19] That sounds like a long time ago, but it appears there have been people who have lived to at least one hundred years for most of recorded history. Cicero divorced his wife during the era of the Roman republic, and she lived to 103. So assuming a one-hundred-year generation, it would only take five hundred people to stretch back fifty thousand years. Let's guess that 15 percent, I think a conservative estimate, were condemned to hell, roughly accounting for those who in their lifetimes were predominantly psychopathic, or sadistic, or narcissistic, or just plain nasty and mean. That would mean that there are about 15.9 billion people already dwelling in hell, not accounting for the Christian contention, since it was expressed that people who don't give themselves to Christ, including many wonderful non-Christian mothers and fathers, also go to hell, which means many billions of additional people more. Does this all sound right to you?"

"I am unaware of those figures."

"Okay, but assuming the figure of 15.9 billion people is close, are they all still suffering down there, with terribly high outdoor temperatures, devil assistants whipping them, and bad food? Does it go on forever, this kind of suffering? And then assuming the conservative figure about the number of people in hell is correct, this means there are some 90 billion people in heaven. That is about fifteen times the existing population of Earth. How are they organized? Do they have elections?"

"Again, all this will be answered after you die."

"Then let's switch to Muslims. Among other things, the males believe that if they are martyred, if they die in the cause of advancing Islam, they can go to heaven with seventy dark-eyed virgins. Do you believe that is possible? Do they live in the same house, or on the same cloud, or in the same neighborhood?"

"I don't believe it is possible, only people who give themselves to Jesus, who are saved, can go to heaven."

"Look," I said, "if believing all this makes you feel better, more secure and comfortable, then believe it."

"Thank you for your permission."

"I mean you're not out there killing people if they don't believe as you do, and you're not even knocking on doors like the Jehovah's Witnesses, invading people's privacy to sell them on their religious concepts. Further, your beliefs may be true, since there is no proof that they aren't. We basically know nothing on this Earth, and so any belief about an afterlife can't necessarily be disproved."

"Well, there you are, then."

This is the kind of discussion one might have with a strong religionist while attempting to use reason to elicit answers. If my discussion was with someone who had memorized the Bible, then most of the answers would have involved his quoting scripture. In the world of faith, as we've noted, there is little place for reason in discourse. Further, there appears to be some fear among the more doctrinal religionists that science's explorations might uncover facts that will directly prove their religious beliefs to be wrong. As described earlier, a pastor being interviewed about the radio telescope project seeking messages from other planets was worried that if we were ultimately able to communicate with intelligent humans on another planet, they might not know about Jesus. His conjecture seemed to be that this might cause enough controversy and doubt to undermine the religion.

This elicits the thought that if there are 10,000 distinct religions on Earth and there is life on planets surrounding just one one-thousandth of the stars in only our galaxy alone, that would be 20,000 stars. If each of them had 10,000 religions, there might be the potential for 200,000,000 distinct religions in our galaxy, and Jesus, or Moses, or Mohammed, or Gautama may not be known by any of them.

Then there is the biology of religion.

There is growing evidence that ritual and spirituality have a biological basis. For starters, all cultures studied all over the Earth by anthropologists and others have had some form of ritual, even the most isolated. They all prayed or appealed in some way to a higher, spiritual force or forces.

In the book *Phantoms of the Brain*, neurologist V. S. Ramachandran and science writer Sandra Blakeslee describe the use of a "transcranial magnetic stimulator," which when applied to the scalp, shoots a powerful magnetic field "onto a patch of brain tissue, thereby activating it and providing hints about its function."[20] They describe how, if applied to certain parts of our motor cortex, our fingers or shoulder might twitch. They also discuss an account from a popular Canadian magazine about a man who was able to stimulate his temporal lobe and experience religion. Ramachandran wonders if the stimulation would have the same effect on an atheist, but obviously has never tried it. He and Blakeslee continue:

> If religious beliefs are merely the combined result of wishful thinking and a longing for immortality, how do you explain the flights of intense religious ecstacy experienced by patients with temporal lobe seizures or their claim that God speaks directly to them? Many a patient has told me of a "divine light that illuminates all things, or of an ultimate truth that lies completely beyond the reach of ordinary minds. . . ." Of course, they might simply be suffering from hallucinations and delusions of the kind that a schizophrenic might experience, but if that's the case, why do such hallucinations occur mainly when the tem-

poral lobes are involved? Even more puzzling, why do they take this particular form? Why don't these patients hallucinate pigs or donkeys?[21]

The authors also describe how seizures in the limbic system and temporal lobes of the brain might elicit deep spiritual experiences

including a divine presence and the sense that they are in direct communication with God. I find it ironic that this sense of enlightenment, this absolute conviction that Truth is revealed at last, should derive from limbic structures concerned with emotions, rather than from the thinking, rational parts of the brain that take so much pride in their ability to discern truth and falsehood.[22]

Could this be the explanation for the fierce unbending nature of religious belief—that it attaches to the neural circuitry of the limbic system, much like an unyielding phobia, paranoia, or narcissism? As noted earlier, Pastor Joel Oesteen found (although later regretting it) that he stubbornly turned left, after his wife insisted that he turn right, and then later returned and did go right. However, if a Muslim presented Oesteen with incontrovertible proof that the beliefs of Islam were truer than the beliefs of Christianity, would Oesteen continue to cling to his views? Most likely, yes.

In this sense, our religious beliefs may become part of our neural circuitry that drives the status imperative. Religion not only appeals to our limbic drive for security and safety, but it gives us status as well. As a believer of a specific faith, we now *know* something that the nonbelievers do not. We can look down at the nonbelievers and unconsciously feel our serotonin rise. It can raise us up on the dominance hierarchy, no matter what our station in life is. Consider what would happen if all of a sudden there was a voice from the sky, spoken in a language that everyone on Earth could somehow understand, who introduced himself as the god Nammun and said he thought it was time everyone understood that there was only one creator, and he was it.

You can imagine the look on the faces of all the clergy in the world, hundreds of thousands of them, who have based their status primarily on their position of instructing their congregants in their faith but who now learned that they were wrong all along. Their faces would drop, and they would be despondent and lost, as would be many of their congregants. They, as well as atheists, who harbor their own belief system, would show all the characteristics of a status loss (as described in the last chapter).

In this sense, neuroscientist Rhawn Joseph theorizes that humans have evolved the capacity to experience god primarily through the limbic system's amygdala, which, as was described earlier, mediates our emotions of fear. In a correlation with the limbic system's hippocampus and hypothalamus, the tissues become "highly activated when we dream, when we pray or when we take drugs such as LSD, enabling us to experience . . . the reality of God, the spirit, the soul, and life after death. . . . Spiritual experience is not based on superstition but is instead real, biological and part or our primitive biological drives."[23]

He also states in his book *The Transmitter to God, the Limbic System, the Soul and Spirituality* that

> hyperactivation of the amygdala, hippocampus and overly temporal lobe gives a person the sense that they're floating or flying above their surroundings. . . . It can trigger memories, hallucinations, create brilliant lights, and at the same time secrete neurotransmitters that induce feelings of euphoria, peace and harmony.[24]

Radiologist Andrew Newberg, coauthor of the book *Why God Won't Go Away: Brain Science and the Biology of Belief*, like Joseph, believes in the physiological basis for religion. Working three days a week at the hospital of the University of Pennsylvania, he "photographs" kidneys, lungs, and hearts, looking for signs of disease. Two days a week, when he has willing subjects, he takes pictures of the brains of deeply religious people, looking for signs of god. Among those he has examined as they meditate and pray have been Tibetian Buddhists and Franciscan nuns. Among other things, Newberg found increased blood flow in the frontal lobes, just above the temporal lobes (right behind the temple, see p. 14), where higher thinking takes place, as well as within the limbic system. However, he also found decreased blood flow in the back of the brain in its parietal lobes, where the ability for spatial organization is housed.[25] These lobes apparently help the brain determine where the body ends and the rest of the world begins. An injury to this area may cripple your ability to maneuver in physical space so that you cannot figure the distance and angles to navigate the route to a chair across the room. When these lobes are less active, the boundaries of the self appear to melt away, and there is a proclivity to feel at one with the universe.[26]

Research by these neurobiologists, neuropsychologists, and others have created the rapidly growing field of *neurotheology*, the study of the neurobiology of religion and spirituality.

In an article in *Newsweek* titled "Religion and the Brain," Michael J. Baime, a colleague of Newberg at the University of Pennsylvania, describes how he felt when he practiced Tibetan Buddhist meditation:

> There was a relaxing of the dualistic mind, and an intense feeling of love. I felt a profound letting go of the boundaries around me, and a connection with some kind of energy and state of being that had a

quality of clarity, transparency and joy. I felt a deep connection to everything, recognizing that there never was a true separation at all.[27]

Change a few words, and this might describe how people in a variety of religions feel when they are in a state of deep prayer. There is also some evidence that epilepsy in the temporal lobe, as Ramachandran points out, can create spiritual experiences.

However, it is hard to take anything for granted when it comes to tracing the exact biologies of emotions and feelings. Richie Davidson of the University of Wisconsin holds professorships both in the medical school and in the psychology department and is a cofounder of the HealthEmotions Research Institute. He writes as a contributor to the book *Destructive Emotions* by Daniel Goleman that

> one of the most important things that we've learned in neuroscience is that any kind of complex behavior, such as emotion, is not based in a single area of the brain. Rather, many parts of the brain work together to produce complex behavior. There is no one center for emotion, just as there is none for playing tennis— nor for anything complicated. It involves interactions across different brain areas.[28]

Richie's favorite answer, when I've asked him at symposiums where the brain centers for violence, fanaticism, or religion are located, is that "they are broadly distributed."

So while there appears to be a biological basis for religion in the brain, just as all thought is ultimately biological, more work needs to be done to determine exactly how and where it is processed. However, as Michael Persinger, professor of behavioral neuroscience at Laurentian University in Sudbury, Ontario, bluntly put it, "God is an artifact of the brain."[29]

*   *   *

There also appears to be evidence that there is a genetic predisposition that creates the biology for religious thought, as part of a general spiritual inclination. Molecular biologist Dean Hamer is chief of gene structure at the National Cancer Institute. In his book *The God Gene: How Faith Is Hardwired into Our Genes*, he asserts that he has located one of the genes that is responsible for human spirituality. The book has been controversial, of course. Hamer points out that there is skepticism of his research even among some of his colleagues. "'The God Gene,' one said. 'Do you mean there's just one?' What I meant to say, of course, was 'a' God gene, not 'the' God gene. It wouldn't make sense that a single gene was responsible for such a complex trait."[30]

Interestingly enough, Hamer began his research with a test that measures for what he calls *self-transcendence*, which consists of three basic traits: self-forgetfulness, or the ability to get entirely lost in an experience, such as playing or listening to music, playing a game, or becoming lost within an extremely loving relationship; transpersonal identification, or a feeling of connectedness to a larger universe and mysticism; and an openness to things not literally provable.[31]

We can all understand that there may be a genetic predisposition toward sensitivity and nurturance, which may be hardened or reinforced by the environment in which we're raised. Further, sensitivity may be compartmentalized into numerous categories, such as sensitivity to the feelings of others, a proclivity for the arts—for literature, poetry—and an affinity for a whole host of categories, which some of us may be more sensitive to than others.

A close friend of mine told me about going to his first opera, *La Boheme*, at the age of fifteen, with his father and older sister. In the middle of the first act, he watched them as their eyes teared up, while he, in the meantime, was wondering how he could sneak out. He felt nothing. More than fifty years later, despite a great effort in listening to great music and attending different operas, he still feels nothing. Yet thousands of people around the world each year attend their first opera and are profoundly moved. Similarly, there are millions of people in Spain and other countries who are sensitive to the artistry of bull fighting. They don't come to the arenas to see bulls killed. They could go to a slaughterhouse for that. They come to appreciate the artistry of the matadors and the events as a whole, just as fans of the ballet are sensitive to the overall artistry of their productions.

And so it appears to be with spirituality. Some of us are more inclined to it than others. And if we are so inclined, we may take the religion of the household we are born into and nurture it through our entire lives. Or at some point in our adulthood, we'll look for other forms of spirituality that we find more comforting. The less spiritual among us will avoid places of worship, except for major holidays, or avoid them altogether. If we go regularly, we'll do so more for our religious spouse, mother, or friend, or from force of habit, and simply go through the motions, sometimes hoping that we'll get the feeling that others around us seem to have absorbed.

The less sensitive of us to religion may also scoff at those who practice meditation or other methods of feeling spiritual inclinations.

In his book, Hamer describes results from the University of Minnesota's ongoing study of identical twins reared apart, as noted earlier. Identical twins share the exact same DNA, versus fraternal twins. He compared the findings of the inheritability of mental characteristics in general, as well as self-transcendence, and found that the correlation was high. "Regardless of race or culture, if one member of a pair scored particularly high or low for self-transcendence, his or her sibling did too."

Hamer continues:

> These results don't mean that siblings are always the same. There are plenty of exceptions, which is to be expected, since although siblings share 50 percent of their DNA variations, the other 50 percent are different. And even though siblings grow up in the same shared environment, their unique environment is just that—unique. [32]

Finally, in Hamer's research work, he found that "there was a clear association between the VMAT2 [a name for a gene], polymorphism and self-transcendence."[33] Coincidentally, this gene also codes for dopamine, which can give us feelings of reward, even euphoria, and has some correlation with serotonin, which, as described ealier, may mediate our feelings of confidence.

However, as Hamer pointed out, merely having a predisposition to feel self-transcendence "did not mean those people would take the next step and translate their transcendence into a belief in—or even a quest for—God. But they seemed likelier to do so than those who never got the feeling at all."[34]

So what does this all mean?

It would appear that there is a biological basis to spirituality, just as there is for our intelligence, creativity, emotions, impulses, and feelings. The possibility exists that we were given this genetic propensity for spirituality—that could devolve into thousands of distinct religious beliefs—because it would work to provide purpose and meaning for us in an otherwise cold, hard world. The same possibility exists with regard to our virtual realities. Do we have a genetic propensity for them? Were we given this "gift" of a virtual reality so that we could go about our everyday lives without a second thought about why we exist and what is the meaning of it all? And so we could ignore or circumvent in relative bliss what we are discovering about such unsettling things as the gargantuan and brutal nature of the universe?

If so, is nature being devious or kind to us?

In the end, however, the only answer we need is that our virtual realities don't have to be our destinies. If they are creating needless conflicts in our lives, hurting others, generating self-defeating behavior, and causing other damage, we need to know that they are physical—that they are embedded in the neural circuitry of our brains. And so we may be capable of doing the hard work that will change them. After all, given the world situation of wars and hatred, and mental trauma, the peril of our very existence, including our ability to continue passing our genes into the future, will depend on our ability to change, literally to come to our senses.

The question is—what would it take, short of bludgeoning, for the people who require this the most to do so?

AFTERWORD

In this book I have only skimmed the realities of life, which, as they are uncovered for us, should put us in a constant state of awe, wonderment, and curiosity. The circumstances of our life, as it turns out, are indeed miraculous. But for most of us, as we've seen, these realities don't register, or we simply don't want to think about them, because they might upset the applecart of beliefs and ideologies that we've carefully constructed for ourselves, and which have become part of our individual virtual realities, to carry us through the day.

More to the point, our status imperative keeps most of us from being humbled, from feeling insignificant in the face of the vast, new evidence that is discovered. But this shouldn't surprise us. Priests, ministers, rabbis, gurus, and clergymen in general have been telling us to be humble before an almighty deity and his works for centuries, and yet, they have had no significant success. While we may kneel, bow, or prostrate ourselves in places of worship, to reflect that we indeed feel humbled before his force, for far too many of us it is acting. When the play is over, we rush off the set and crash out of the parking lot to resume our real characters of know-it-alls. We then return to challenging, demeaning, and hurting others to give ourselves daily boosts of status—an addiction that has done far more harm to us over the years, through wars, terrorism, and sheer mental trauma, than all the recreational drugs combined. And yet this addiction is not a criminal offense.

How can we not feel humbled by the discovery of the DNA molecule, which is so tiny that it is invisible to all but our strongest microscopes, thousands of times smaller than this dot (.). Yet, we learn it contains the coding for our entire bodies, including our brain, the most complex object in the known universe, and replicates itself almost perfectly with the aid of enzymes that check for accuracy. And it is the basis for every other form of life, from chimps to turtles, to roses and trees, with the only basic difference being in how the coding along the DNA filament is arranged. And, that we are, as humans, all basically accidents, caused by the mixing and matching of the DNA's genetic units in our fathers' testes, making every sperm cell unique. Who we are is basically the result of a horse race of some 300,000,000 of these cells up the vaginal canals of our mothers to be the first accepted by her waiting egg at the finish line.

Or what about the discoveries that time is imaginary, or that the universe is so vast, it would take 7,000 years traveling at 400,000 miles per hour to reach the star closest to us, and that traveling close to the speed of light, nearly 670 million miles an hour, it would take us 2,000,000 years to reach the galaxy closest to us? And that beyond the Milky Way there are 140 billion galaxies at last count? Or what about the fact that we have discovered that our minds are biological, the result of neural circuitry that when disordered, as neurologist Oliver Sacks tells us, may cause us to look at our wife and think she is a hat?

Shouldn't these facts alone humble us? Shouldn't they make even the most extreme egomaniacs among us realize that we haven't as yet figured out ourselves and think twice about it? Maybe come down a few pegs? Shouldn't facts such as these work to open our minds and make us curious to learn more?

Ah, but nature apparently doesn't want all of us humbled and open minded. It gave us the status imperative, which made sense in primitive times to provide strong and fearless leaders. But today it unfortunately helps create our virtual realities that protect our status by clinging to reassuring answers, whether based on fact or not. This contributes to all forms of egoism. Rarely will we hear the phrase "I don't know." Many of us will always give answers, right or wrong, believing that if we don't our status will be deflated. Worse, any questioning of our beliefs may be interpreted as an attack on ourselves, our families, our religion, even our world. We have what my friend Ron Rattner calls "Chronic Belief Syndrome." What we need instead is chronic curiosity.

The truly humble among us—regardless of station, whether from spiritual beliefs, ethical agnosticism, or atheism; or an upbringing that fostered humility; or a genetic propensity for humility; or the ability to comprehend the realities of our lives as expressed in this book and elsewhere; or a combination of these factors—are the real winners, if we are also capable of maintaining an open mind.

Those who have achieved this combination of temperament and outlook have won the hardest of battles, the one against our own biological nature.

NOTES

CHAPTER 1

1. http://www.quotationspage.com/search.php3?homesearch =Mind (accessed February 10, 2004).

2. Susan A. Greenfield, *The Human Brain* (New York: Basic Books, 1997), p. 4.

3. Carl Zimmer, *Soul Made Flesh: The Discovery of the Brain—and How It Changed the World* (New York: Free Press, 2004), p. 5.

4. Ibid., p. 37.

5. Eric R. Kandel, James H. Schwartz, and Thomas M. Jessell, *Principles of Neural Science* (New York: McGraw Hill, 2000), p. 1317.

6. Zimmer, *Soul Made Flesh*, p. 223.

7. Ibid., pp. 196–97.

8. Rabbi Elie Kaplan Spitz, *Does the Soul Survive: A Jewish Journey to Belief in Afterlife, Past Lives and Living with Purpose* (Woodstock, VT: Jewish Lights Publishing, 2000), p. 23.

9. Daniel G. Amen, *Healing the Hardware of the Soul* (New York: Free Press, 2002), p. 5.

10. Ibid., p. 5.

11. Carol Ritberger, *Your Personality, Your Health: Connecting Personality with the Human Energy System, Chakris and Wellness* (Carlsbad, CA: Hay House, 1998), pp. 30–31.

12. "Concepts of Hinduism," http://hinduwebsite.com/hinduism/atma.htm (accessed April 4, 2004).

13. James Redfield, *The Celestine Prophecy* (New York: Warner Books, 1993).

14. Richard Bach, *Illusions: The Adventures of a Reluctant Messiah* (New York: Dell, 1989).

15. David R. Hawkins, *Power vs. Force: The Hidden Determinants of Human Behavior* (Carlsbad, CA: Hay House, 2002), pp. 70, 73, 94.

16. Ibid., p. 149.

17. Michael Talbot, *Holographic Universe* (New York: Perennial, 1992), p. 1.

18. Sandra Blakeslee, "How Does the Brain Work?" *New York Times*, November 11, 2003, p. D4.

19. Vernon B. Mountcastle, "Brain Science at the Century's Ebb," in *The Brain*, ed. Gerald M. Edelman and Jean-Pierre Changeux (New Brunswick, NJ: Transaction Publishers, 2001), p. 1.

CHAPTER 2

1. http://www.quotationreference.com/quotefinder.php?strt=1&subj=Bertrand+Arthur+William+Russell&byax=1&lr=R (accessed May 27, 2004).

2. Tony Whalen, http://www.physlink.com/Education/Ask Experts/ae430.cfm (accessed May 29, 2004).

3. Larry W. Swanson, *Brain Architecture: Understanding the Basic Plan* (Oxford: Oxford University Press, 2003), p. 169.

4. Ibid., p. 2.

5. Steven Pinker, *How the Mind Works* (New York: Norton, 2004).

6. Gerald M. Edelman, *Wider Than the Sky* (New Haven, CT: Yale University Press, 2004).

7. Jerry Fodor, *The Mind Doesn't Work That Way* (Cambridge, MA: MIT Press, 2001).

8. Jack Fincher, *The Brain: Mastery of Matter and Mind* (Washington, DC: US News Books, 1981), p. 33.

9. Susan A. Greenfield, *The Human Brain* (New York: Basic Books, 1997), p. 27.

10. Ibid.

11. Eric R. Kandel, James H. Schwartz, and Thomas M. Jessell, *Principles of Neural Science* (New York: McGraw Hill, 2000), p. 294.

12. Joseph LeDoux, *Synaptic Self: How Our Brains Become Who We Are* (New York: Penguin Books, 2002), p. 18.

13. Ibid., p. 49.

14. Kandel, Schwartz, and Jessell, *Principles of Neural Science*, p. 25.

15. Frank Oellien, http://www.2.ccc.uni-erlangen.de/projects/ChemVis/motm/ (accessed May 5, 2004).

16. Steven Johnson, *Mind Wide Open: Your Brain and the Neuroscience of Everyday Life* (New York: Scribner, 2004), p. 13.

17. Steven Levy, "Dr. Edelman's Brain," *New Yorker*, May 2, 1994, pp. 66–68.

18. Gerald M. Edelman, "Building a Picture of the Brain," in *The Brain*, ed. Gerald M. Edelman and Jean-Pierre Changeux (New Brunswick, NJ: Transaction Publishers, 2001), p. 39.

CHAPTER 3

1. http://www.quotationspage.com/search.php3?homesearch=Mind&page+2.

2. Eric R. Kandel, James H. Schwartz, and Thomas M. Jessell, *Principles of Neural Science* (New York: McGraw Hill, 2000), p. 318.

3. http://www.iseek.org/sv/13000.jsp?id=100425, updated May 2004 (accessed June 15, 2004).

4. Emilo Bizzi and Ferdinando A. Mussa-Ivaldi, "The Acquistion of Motor Behavior," in *The Brain*, ed. Gerald M. Edelman and Jean-Pierre Changeux (New Brunswick, NJ: Transaction Publishers, 2001), p. 217.

CHAPTER 4

1. Daniel C. Dennett, *Consciousness Explained* (Boston: Back Bay Books, 1991), p. 227.

2. Ibid., p. 107.

3. Antonio Damasio, *Feeling of What Happens: Body and Emotion in the Making of Conscousness* (New York: Harcourt Brace, 1999), p. 11.

4. Steven Pinker, *How the Mind Works* (New York: Norton, 2004), p. 60.

5. Dennett, *Consciousness Explained*, pp. 21–22.

6. Mark F. Bear and Leon N. Cooper, "From Molecules to Mental States," in *The Brain*, ed. Gerald M. Edelman and Jean-Pierre Changeux (New Brunswick, NJ: Transaction Publishers, 2001), p. 141.

7. Gerhard Roth, "The Quest to Find Consciousness," *Scientific American Mind* 14, no. 1 (2004): 34.

8. Oliver Sacks, *The Man Who Mistook His Wife for a Hat: And Other Clinical Tales* (New York: Touchstone, 1985), p. 21.

9. Joseph LeDoux, *Synaptic Self: How Our Brains Become Who We Are* (New York: Penguin Books, 2002), p. 14.

10. Steven Johnson, *Mind Wide Open: Your Brain and the Neuroscience of Everyday Life* (New York: Scribner, 2004), p. 6.

CHAPTER 5

1. http://www.bartleby.com//66/64/64464.html (accessed June 19, 2004).

2. Francis H. C. Crick, *The Astonishing Hypothesis: The Scientific Search for the Soul* (New York: Macmillan, 1994), p. 21.

3. Information e-mailed to author by Dr. Snowdon, January 2005.

4. J. Krishnamurti, *The Collected Works of J. Krishnamurti, 1945–1948: The Observer Is the Observed* (Dubuque, IA: Kendall Hunt, 1991).

5. This is the premise of his book—Richard Dawkins, *The Selfish Gene* (Oxford: Oxford University Press, 1989).

6. Snowdon, e-mail to author, January 2005.

7. Bandura, quoted in Michael Eysenck, *Psychology: An Integrated Approach* (Essex, England: Longman, 1998), p. 457.

8. One of the best compendiums on the subject is *Pleasure beyond the Pleasure Principle: The Role of Affect in Motivation Development and*

Adaptation, ed. Robert A. Glick and Stanley Bone (New Haven, CT: Yale University Press, 1990).

9. Sharon L. Johnson, *Therapist's Guide to Clinical Intervention: The 1-2-3's of Treatment Planning* (San Diego: Academic Press, 1997), p. 183.

10. Gerald M. Edelman, "Building a Picture of the Brain," in *The Brain*, ed. Gerald M. Edelman and Jean-Pierre Changeux (New Brunswick, NJ: Transaction Publishers, 2001), p. 39.

11. Antonio Damasio, *Looking for Spinoza: Joy, Sorrow, and the Feeling Brain* (New York: Harcourt, 2003), p. 67.

12. Ibid., p. 68.

13. Ibid., p. 68.

14. Ibid., p. 75.

15. Steven Johnson, *Mind Wide Open: Your Brain and the Neuroscience of Everyday Life* (New York: Scribner, 2004), p. 3.

16. Joseph F. LeDoux, *The Emotional Brain: The Mysterious Underpinnings of Emotional Life* (New York: Simon & Schuster, 1996), p. 101.

17. Ibid., 186–89.

18. Richard L. Gregory, ed., *The Oxford Companion to the Mind* (Oxford: Oxford University Press, 1987), p. 549.

19. These descriptions combine data from the following: Gregory, *The Oxford Companion to the Mind*; Aaron T. Beck and Gary Emery, *Anxiety Disorders and Phobias: A Cognitive Perspective* (New York: Basic Books, 1985); Otto Fenichel, *The Psychoanalytic Theory of Neurosis* (New York: Norton, 1972); Ian Osborn, *Tormenting Thoughts and Secret Rituals: The Hidden Epidemic of Obsessive Compulsive Disorder* (New York: Pantheon Books, 1998); and *Diagnostic and Statistical Manual of Mental Disorders: DSM-IV* (Washington, DC: American Psychiatric Association, 1994).

20. Ronald M. Doctor and Ada P. Kahn, *The Encyclopedia of Phobias, Fears and Anxieties* (New York: Facts on File, 1989).

21. These descriptions combine data from the following: *Diagnostic and Statistical Manual of Mental Disorders: DSM-IV*; V. Mark Durand and David H. Barlow, *Abnormal Psychology: An Introduction* (Belmont, CA: Brooks/Cole, 1997); Aaron T. Beck and Arthur Freeman & Associates, *Cognitive Therapy of Personality Disorders* (New York:

Guilford, 1990); and W. John Livesley, ed., *Handbook of Personality Disorders: Theory, Research, and Treatment* (New York: Guilford, 2001).

22. Durand and Barlow, *Abnormal Psychology*, p. 375.

23. These descriptions combine data from the following: *Diagnostic and Statistical Manual of Mental Disorders: DSM-IV*; Durand and Barlow, *Abnormal Psychology*; Allen E. Bergin and Sol L. Garfield, *Handbook of Psychotherapy and Behavior Change* (New York: Wiley, 1994); Maria Ramirez Basco and Augustus John Rush, *Cognitive Behavioral Therapy for Bi-Polar Disorder* (New York: Guilford, 1996); and David G. Kingdon and Douglas Turkington, *Cognitive-Behavioral Therapy of Schizophrenia* (New York: Guilford, 1994).

24. http://www.drugabuse.gov/about/AboutNIDA.html (accessed June 12, 2004).

25. Otto F. Kernberg, "Hatred as Pleasure," in Glick and Bone, *Pleasure beyond the Pleasure Principle*, pp. 179–80.

26. This information comes from Ann Snowdon and was sent to me in an e-mail from Dr. Snowdon, January 2005.

27. Norman Doidge, "Appetitive Pleasure States: A Biopsychoanalytic Model of the Pleasure Threshold, Mental Representation and Defense," in Glick and Bone, *Pleasure beyond the Pleasure Principle*, p. 155.

28. Martin E. P. Seligman, *Authentic Happiness: Using the New Positive Psychology to Realize Your Potential for Lasting Fulfillment* (New York: Free Press, 2002), p. 8.

29. Claudia Willis, "The New Science of Happiness," *Time*, January 17, 2005, p. A9.

30. Michael R. Lemonick, "The Biology of Joy," *Time*, January 17, 2005, p. A12.

CHAPTER 6

1. Roy Baumeister, *Evil: Inside Human Violence and Cruelty* (New York: W. H. Freeman, 1997), p. 75.

2. Digital History Resource, University of Houston, http://www.hfac.uh.edu/mintz/evilsyl.htm (acessed July 8, 2004).

3. Stephen J. Whitfield, JewishVirtual Library, http://www .jewishvirtuallibrary.org/jsource/biography/arendt.html (accessed July 10, 2004).

4. http://www.bbc.co.uk/religion/re/4ashorthistoryof_res1.pdf (accessed July 11, 2004).

5. Harvey Cleckley, *The Mask of Sanity* (Augusta, GA: Emily S. Cleckley, 1988), p. viii.

6. Robert D. Hare, *Without Conscience: The Disturbing World of the Psychopaths among Us* (New York: Guilford, 1999), p. 24.

7. These characteristics were taken from Cleckley, *The Mask of Sanity*, and Hare, *Without Conscience*. Cleckley was recognized in the early 1940s as the world's leading expert on psychopathy. Hare has that recognition, today.

8. Cleckley, *The Mask of Sanity*, pp. 192, 195.

9. Included in reports by Paul Frick, "Cognitive Function in Early Development of Physical Aggression and Hyperactivity: The Preschool Years," and by Don Lynam, "The Development of Psychopathy from Childhood to Young Adulthood." The reports were delivered on Saturday, July 19, 2003, at the University of Wisconsin, during a conference on "Developmental and Neuroscience Perspectives on Psychopathy." I attended and helped sponsor this conference.

10. Robert D. Hare, David J. Cooke, and Stephen D. Hart, "Psychopathy and Sadistic Personality Disorder," in *Oxford Textbook of Psychopathology*, ed. Theodore Millon, Paul H. Blaney, and Roger D. Davis (Oxford: Oxford University Press, 1999), pp. 572–73.

11. Sadistic Personality Disorder was included in *DSM III*, but deleted from *DSM-IV*, the primary reason being that it might provide legal status to the disorder, which could lead to its misuse in forensic settings.

12. Karen Caplovitz Barrett, "A Functionalist Approach to Shame and Guilt," in *Self-Conscious Emotions: The Psychology of Shame, Guilt, Embarrassment and Pride*, ed. June Price Tangney and Kurt W. Fisher (New York: Guilford, 1995), pp. 25–26.

13. Jane Price Tangney et al., "Shamed into Anger? The Relation of Shame and Guilt to Anger and Self-Reported Aggression," in *Emo-*

tions in Social Psychology: Key Readings, ed. W. Gerrod Parrott (New York: Taylor & Francis Group, 2001), p. 295.

14. Roy F. Baumeister et al., "Interpersonal Aspects of Guilt: Evidence from Narrative Studies," in Parrott, *Emotions in Social Psychology*, p. 286.

15. Jeffrey M. Masson, *Dogs Never Lie about Love: Reflections on the Emotional World of Dogs* (New York: Crown, 1997), p. 105.

16. Jaak Panksepp, *Affective Neuroscience: The Foundations of Human and Animal Emotions* (Oxford: Oxford University Press, 1998), p. 341.

17. http://www.medicinenet.com/scipt/main/art.asp?articleky =32700 (accessed July 19, 2004).

18. Ibid.

19. David L. Weiner, *Power Freaks: Dealing with Them in the Workplace or Anyplace* (Amherst, NY: Prometheus Books, 2002), pp. 83, 84.

20. Iris Chang, *The Rape of Nanking: The Forgotten Holocaust of World War II* (New York: Basic Books, 1997), p. 59.

21. Ibid., p. 58.

22. Hideo Kojima, "Becoming Nurturant in Japan: Past and Present," in *Origins of Nurturance*, ed. Alan Fogel and Gail F. Melson (Hillsdale, NJ: Lawrence Erlbaum Associates, 1986), pp. 135–36.

23. These figures were reported during opening remarks at a symposium on psychopathy held at the University of Wisconsin, Madison, in July 2003—Developmental and Neuroscience Perspectives on Psychopathy. As one result of this symposium, the Society for the Scientific Study of Psychopathy has been formed.

CHAPTER 7

1. http://www.bartleby.com/66/60/17660.html (accesssed June 4, 2004).

2. Carl Zimmer's *Washington Post* review of Diane Ackerman's *The Alchemy of Mind: The Marvel and Mystery of the Brain* (New York: Scribner, 2004) is on the Amazon Web site and contains Zimmer's comments about brain metaphors.

3. Jaak Panksepp, *Affective Neuroscience: The Foundations of Human and Animal Emotions* (Oxford: Oxford University Press, 1998), p. 321.

4. Ibid., p. 301.

5. Stanislas Dehaene, review of *The Mathematical Brain* by Brian Butterworth, www.mathematicalbrain.com/revs.02.html (accessed July 10, 2004).

6. Amy C. Brualdi, "Multiple Intelligences: Gardner's Theory, ERIC Digest," www.ericfacility.net/ericdigests/ed410226.html (accessed July 24, 2004).

7. V. S. Ramachandran and Sandra Blakeslee, *Phantoms in the Brain: Probing the Mysteries of the Human Mind* (New York: Quill, 1998), p. 192.

8. www.ecs.soton.ac.ku/-harnad/Papers/Py104/searle.comp.html (accessed July 21, 2004).

9. David L. Weiner with Gilbert M. Hefter, *Battling the Inner Dummy: The Craziness of Apparently Normal People* (Amherst, NY: Prometheus Books, 1999), p. 65.

10. As described in the general description of this interview. I watched it on Charlie Rose's PBS program, on July 28, 2004.

CHAPTER 8

1. Heiman, quoted in David L. Weiner, *Brain Tricks: Coping with Your Defective Brain* (Amherst, NY: Prometheus Books, 1995), p. 174.

2. I recall an astronomer discussing this method a couple of years ago on a television documentary about the universe. I didn't make a note of the program, but this description stuck in my mind. It makes sense. We can't count to 140 billion in one lifetime.

3. John Van Der Kiste, *Kaiser Wilhelm II: Germany's Last Emperor* (Gloucestershire, UK: Sutton, 1999), p. 74.

4. Jonathon Fenby, *Chiang Kai-Shek: China's Generalissimo and the Nation He Lost* (New York: Carroll & Graf, 2003), p. 502.

5. Brian Greene, *The Elegant Universe: Superstrings, Hidden Dimensions, and the Quest for the Ultimate Theory* (New York: Vintage Books, 2003), p. 4.

6. Bill Bryson, *A Short History of Everything* (New York: Broadway Books, 2003), p. 14.

7. Alan Guth, *The Inflationary Universe: The Quest for a New Theory of Cosmic Origins* (Cambridge: Perseus Books, 1997), p. 254.

8. Stephen Hawking, *Black Holes and Baby Universes and Other Essays* (New York: Bantam Doubleday Dell Audio Publishing, 1993).

9. "Theorists Ponder What, If Anything, There Was before the Big Bang," *New York Times*, May, 22, 2001, p. D4.

10. This program aired on CNN, at 7:00 PM, on August 8, 2004. I made a note of the discussion, but didn't catch the name of the scientist.

CHAPTER 9

1. Brian Greene, *The Elegant Universe: Superstrings, Hidden Dimensions, and the Quest for the Ultimate Theory* (New York: Vintage Books, 2003), p. 34.

2. http://www.quotationspage.com/quotes/National_Lampoon/ (accessed August 10, 2004).

3. Greene, *Elegant Universe*, p. 51.

4. Stephen Hawking, *A Brief History of Time: The Updated and Expanded Tenth Anniversary Edition* (New York: Bantam, 1996).

5. Bill Bryson, *A Short History of Nearly Everything* (New York: Broadway Books, 2003), p. 125. I reviewed Russell's book as cited by Bryson—Bertrand Russell, *ABC of Relativity* (New York: Routledge, 1957)—and couldn't find the story exactly as written, but it appeared to be a compilation of facts that Russell put forth.

6. Barry Parker, *Einstein's Brainchild: Relativity Made Relatively Easy!* (Amherst, NY: Prometheus Books, 2000), p. 133.

7. Stephen Hawking, *Black Holes and Baby Universes and Other Essays* (New York: Bantam Doubleday Dell Audio Publishing, 1993).

8. Bryson, *A Short History of Nearly Everything*, p. 125.

9. Ronald W. Clark, *Einstein: The Life and Times* (New York: Avon, 1984), p. 124.

10. Ibid., p. 136.

CHAPTER 10

1. Matt Ridley, *Genome: The Autobiography of a Species in 23 Chapters* (New York: HarperCollins, 1999), p. 21.

2. I met this man at a cocktail party in 1998. He was a friend of the host, who is a good friend of mine. After we talked for a bit, I told him I was writing a book called *Battling the Inner Dummy: The Craziness of Apparently Normal People* and would like to use my discussion with him as a change of pace in the book. He agreed as along as I didn't use his name. We began talking, and I took copious notes. About two weeks after that party, I visited him at a location near Argonne National Laboratories, about twenty-five miles southwest of Chicago, where he was doing some research work at the time. He reviewed the manuscript of the interview. He made a few changes and that was it. When I began this chapter for *Reality Check*, I thought the interview with him was very pertinent, so I called him, and he updated the material, since our initial interview took place before the Human Genome Project was completed. The updated material is included in the context of our talk at the cocktail party.

3. Janet Yagoda Shagam, "Genetics, Genomics and Molecular Medicine," *Radiologic Technology* 74, no. 3 (January 1, 2003).

4. Andy Coghlan, "The Enemy within That Targets Genes," *New Scientist*, September 18, 2004, p. 11.

5. Matt Ridley, *Nature via Nurture* (New York: HarperCollins, 2003), p. 160.

6. Ibid.

7. Ibid., p. 238.

8. Sent to me in an e-mail note in January 2005.

9. Oppenheimer, quoted in Tom Abate, "Oracle Helps to Fund Protein Map," *San Francisco Chronicle*, April 5, 2001, p. D1.

10. Andrew Pollack, "New Way to Turn Off Bad Genes Is Set for Testing on Human Eyes," *New York Times*, September 14, 2004, p. 1.

11. Lisa Stubbs, "How Closely Related Are Mice and Humans? How Many Genes Are the Same?" http://www.ornl.gov/sci/techresources/Human_Genome/faq/compgen.shtml (accessed September 3, 2004).

CHAPTER 11

1. David L. Weiner, *Brain Tricks: Coping with Your Defective Brain* (Amherst, NY: Prometheus Books, 1995), p. 34.

2. V. S. Ramachandran and Sandra Blakeslee, *Phantoms in the Brain: Probing the Mysteries of the Human Mind* (New York: Quill, 1998), p. 176.

3. Chuck Snowdon sent this information in an e-mail in January 2005.

4. Information supplied by database research firm, FIND/SVP, under document titled Dominant and Recessive Traits.doc.

5. Robert S. Boyd, "Genes Influence Behavior but Don't Control It, Most Experts Agree," *Knight-Ridder Tribune Business News*: Knight Ridder Washington, DC, Bureau, May 8, 2003.

6. Richard Dawkins, *The Selfish Gene* (Oxford: Oxford University Press, 1989), pp. 27–28.

7. Janet Shibley Hyde and John D. DeLamater, *Understanding Human Sexuality*, 7th ed. (New York: McGraw Hill, 2000), p. 145.

8. PBS Nova Series, *The Miracle of Life* (New York: Crown Video, 1986).

9. R. Robin Baker and Mark A. Bellis, *Human Sperm Competition: Copulation, Masturbation and Infidelity* (London: Chapman & Hall, 1995), p. 208.

10. This information was requested by an acquaintance who knows Sijo Parekattil and was sent to me via e-mail.

11. Bill Bryson, *A Short History of Nearly Everything* (New York: Broadway Books, 2003), pp. 397–98.

12. Ibid., p. 398.

13. Baker and Bellis, *Human Sperm Competition*, pp. 23–24.

14. Robert Plomin, *Nature and Nurture: An Introduction to Behavioral Genetics* (Belmont, CA: Brooks/Cole, 1990), p. 7.

15. Dawkins, *The Selfish Gene*, pp. 35–36.

16. Sherwin B. Nuland, *How We Live* (New York: Vintage, 1998), p. 108.

CHAPTER 12

1. David McCullough, *John Adams* (New York: Simon & Schuster, 2001), p. 170.

2. Robert Ardrey, *The Territorial Imperative: A Personal Inquiry into the Animal Origins of Property and Nations* (New York: Kodansha International, 1996), p. 236.

3. Ibid., p. 350.

4. "Chicago Tonight," WTTW, a PBS Station, Tuesday, October 28, 2004.

5. CNN Sports Illustrated, http://cnnsi.com, Tuesday, September 12, 2000, (accessed September 8, 2004).

6. Religion & Ethics Newsweekly, http://www.pbs.org/wnet/religionandethics/week419/cover.html (accessed September 8, 2004).

7. Dan Rozek, "Hockey Dad Guilty of Giving Kid a 'Swirly,'" *Chicago Sun-Times*, October 8, 2004, p. 12.

8. Jane Golden, http://seattletimes.com, November 22, 1998, pp. 1–2.

9. Robert Pedone and Rosaria Conte, "Dynamics of Status Symbols and Social Complexity," National Research Council, Institute of Psychology, http://www.iss.uw.edu.pl/osrodki/obuz/simsoc5/contrib/PedoneConte.pdf (accessed September 12, 2004).

10. Candace Pert, *Molecules of Emotion* (New York: Scribner, 1997).

11. Doris Kearns Goodwin, *No Ordinary Time: Franklin and Eleanor Roosevelt: The Home Front in World War II* (New York: Simon & Schuster, 1994), p. 209.

12. Phil Jackson, *The Last Season: A Team in Search of Its Soul* (New York: Penguin, 2004), p. 140.

13. Jim Sidanius and Felicia Pratto, *Social Dominance: An Intergroup Theory of Social Hierarchy and Oppression* (Cambridge: Cambridge University Press, 1999), p. 37.

14. Boye De Mente, *Japanese Etiquette and Ethics in Business* (Chicago: Passport Books, 1987), p. 26.

15. Matt Ridley, *Genome: The Autobiography of a Species in 23 Chapters* (New York: HarperCollins, 1999), p. 171.

16. Marler named Bernhardt et al.'s study (published in *Physiological Behavior* 65 [1998]: 59–62) regarding testosterone among sports fans.

17. This information was sent to me by Charles Snowdon, a primatologist, and chair of the University of Wisconsin Psychology Department, in January 2005.

18. Jerome H. Barkow, "Beneath New Culture Is Old Psychology: Gossip and Social Stratification," in *The Adapted Mind: Evolutionary Psychology and the Generation of Culture*, ed. Jerome H. Barkown, Leda Cosmides, and John Tooby (Oxford: Oxford Press University, 1992), pp. 633–34, and as reported in my book *Power Freaks*.

19. This information was sent to me by Charles Snowdon in January 2005.

20. Carl Sagan and Ann Druyan, *Shadows of Forgotten Ancestors: A Search for Who We Are* (New York: Ballantine Books, 1992), pp. 210–11, and as reported in my book *Power Freaks*.

21. David M. Buss, *Evolutionary Psychology* (Needham Heights, MA: Allyn & Bacon, 1999), p. 346.

22. Ibid., p. 347.

23. Dr. Akil made her presentation at a symposium on the biology of emotions sponsored in April 2001 by the HealthEmotions Research Institute of the University of Wisconsin.

24. Jackson, *The Last Season*, p. 223.

25. Frans De Waal, *The Ape and the Sushi Master: Cultural Reflections of a Primatologist* (New York: Basic Books, 2001), p. 304.

26. Jane Goodall, *In The Shadow of Man* (Boston: Houghton Mifflin, 1971), pp. 116–17.

27. Ibid., p. 115.

28. Joseph Giovannoli, *The Biology of Belief: How Our Biology Biases Our Beliefs and Perceptions* (Oxford: Rosetta Press, 2000), pp. 53–54.

29. John Bowlby, *Attachment*, 2nd ed. (New York: Basic Books, 1982), p. 207.

30. Daniel Goleman, *Emotional Intelligence* (New York: Bantam, 1995), pp. 13–14.

31. Jefferson Davis, *The Rise and Fall of the Confederate Government* (New York: DeCapo Press, 1990), p. iii.

32. Sigmund Freud, excerpt from *The Future of an Illusion*, in *The Freud Reader*, ed. Peter Gay (New York: Norton, 1989), p. 699.

33. John (Jack) Mayer and Peter Salovey, "Emotional Intelligence, Imagination, Cognition, and Personality," *Intelligence* 9 (1990): 185–211.

34. Goleman, *Emotional Intelligence*, p. 295.

35. Richard L. Bednar and Scott R. Peterson, *Self-Esteem: Paradoxes and Innovations in Clinical Theory and Practice*, 2nd ed. (Washington, DC: American Psychological Association, 1995), p. 5.

36. Nathaniel Branden, *Honoring the Self: Self-Esteem and Personal Transformation* (New York: Bantam Books, 1983), p. 3.

37. Rosabeth Moss Kanter, *Confidence: How Winning Streaks and Losing Streaks Begin and End* (New York: Crown Business, 2004), p. 177.

38. Charles Snowdon told me about this during a discussion about the dominance hierarchy.

CHAPTER 13

1. V. S. Ramachandran and Sandra Blakeslee, *Phantoms in the Brain: Probing the Mysteries of the Human Mind* (New York: Quill, 1998), p. 176.

2. Mike Sager, "Jack Nicholson, 66," *Esquire*, January 2004, p. 71.

3. David B. Barrett, George T. Kurian, and Todd M. Johnson, *The World by Segments: Religions, Peoples, Languages, Cities, Topics*, 2nd ed., vol. 2 of *World Christian Encyclopedia: A Comparative Survey of Churches and Religions in the Modern World* (Oxford: Oxford University Press, 2001), p. 3.

4. Ibid., p. 5.

5. David B. Barrett, George T. Kurian, and Todd M. Johnson, *The World by Countries: Religionists, Churches, Ministeries*, 2nd ed., vol. 1 of *World Christian Encyclopedia: A Comparative Survey of Churches and Religions in the Modern World* (Oxford: Oxford University Press, 2001), p. 799.

6. Ibid., p. 559.

7. Ibid., p. 677.

8. Somini Sengupta and Larry Rohter, *New York Times*, October 14, 2004, p. A10.

9. Barrett, Kurian, and Johnson, *The World by Countries*, p. 10.

10. Bill Powell, "Struggle for the Soul of Islam," *Time*, September 13, 2004, p. 56.

11. FIND/SVP Report, December 28, 2004.

12. David Brooks, "The More Things Change . . . ," *New York Times*, October 23, 2004, p. A31.

13. Russell Shorto, "With God at Our Desks," *New York Times Magazine*, October 31, 2004, p. 42.

14. William R. Grimbol, *The Complete Idiot's Guide to the Life of Christ* (Indianapolis: Alpha Books, 2001), p. 97.

15. Sam Harris, *The End of Faith: Religion, Terror, and the Future of Reason* (New York: Norton, 2004), p. 26.

16. Ibid., p. 27.

17. http://www.beyond.fr/history/religion.html (accessed November 3, 2004).

18. Barrett, Kurian, and Johnson, *The World by Countries*, p. 11.

19. "World Overpopulation Awareness" site, http://www.overpopulation.org/faq.html (accessed November 10, 2004).

20. Ramachandran and Blakeslee, *Phantoms in the Brain*, p. 174.

21. Ibid., pp. 176–77.

22. Ibid., p. 179.

23. "Is the Brain a Modem for God," http://www.souldtravel.nu/3003/030918-human-brain/index.asp (accessed November 5, 2004).

24. Ibid., the same Internet report contains this quote from Rhawn Joseph's book.

25. Andrew Newberg, Eugene D'Aquill, and Vince Rause, *Why God Won't Go Away: Brain Science and the Biology of Belief* (New York: Ballantine, 2001), p. 189.

26. Sharon Begley, "Religion and the Brain" *Newsweek*, May 7, 2001, http://www.passig.com/pic/Religion&The Brain.htm (accessed November 16, 2004).

27. Ibid.

28. Daniel Goleman et al., *Destructive Emotions: How Can We*

Overcome Them? A Scientific Dialogue with the Dalai Lama (New York: Bantam, 2003), p. 185.

29. Jeff Chu et al., "Is God in Our Genes?" *Time*, October 25, 2004, p. 68.

30. Dean Hamer, *The God Gene: How Faith Is Hardwired into Our Genes* (New York: Doubleday, 2004), p. 76.

31. Ibid., p. 18.

32. Ibid., p. 53.

33. Ibid., p. 73.

34. Ibid.

BIBLIOGRAPHY

Abate, Tom. "Oracle Helps to Fund Protein Map." *San Francisco Chronicle*, April 5, 2001, p. D1.

Ackerman, Diane. *The Alchemy of Mind: The Marvel and Mystery of the Brain*. New York: Scribner, 2004.

Aggleton, John P. *The Amygdala: A Functional Analysis*. Oxford: Oxford University Press, 2000.

Amen, Daniel G. *Healing the Hardware of the Soul*. New York: Free Press, 2002.

Ardrey, Robert. *The Territorial Imperative: A Personal Inquiry into the Animal Origins of Property and Nations*. New York: Kodansha International, 1996.

Bach, Richard. *Illusions: The Adventures of a Reluctant Messiah*. New York: Dell, 1989.

Baker, Robin R., and Mark A. Bellis. *Human Sperm Competition: Copulation, Masturbation and Infidelity*. London: Chapman & Hall, 1995.

Barchas, Patricia R., and M. Hamit Fisek. "Hierarchal Differentiation in Newly Formed Groups of Rhesu and Humans." In *Social Hierarchies: Essays Toward a Sociophysiological Perspective*, edited by Patricia R. Barchas. Westport, CT: Greenwood, 1984.

Barkow, Jerome H. "Beneath New Culture Is Old Psychology: Gossip and Social Stratification." In *The Adapted Mind: Evolutionary Psychology and the Generation of Culture*, edited by Jerome H. Barkown, Leda Cosmides, and John Tooby. Oxford: Oxford Press University, 1992.

Barrett, Karen Caplovitz. "A Functionalist Approach to Shame and Guilt." In *Self-Conscious Emotions: The Psychology of Shame, Guilt, Embarrassment and Pride*, edited by June Price Tangney and Kurt W. Fischer. New York: Guilford, 1995.

Basco, Maria Ramirez, and John A. Rush. *Cognitive Behavioral Therapy for Bi-Polar Disorder*. New York: Guilford, 1996.

Baumeister, Roy. *Evil: Inside Human Cruelty and Violence*. New York: W. H. Freeman, 1997.

Bear, Mark F., and Leon N. Cooper. "From Molecules to Mental States." In *The Brain*, edited by Gerald M. Edelman and Jean-Pierre Changeux, p. 141. New Brunswick, NJ: Transaction Publishers, 2001.

Beck, Aaron T., and Gary Emery, with Ruth L. Greenberg. *Anxiety Disorders and Phobias: A Cognitive Perspective*. New York: Basic Books, 1985.

Beck, Aaron T., and Arthur Freeman & Associates. *Cognitive Therapy of Personality Disorders*. New York: Guilford, 1990.

Bednar, Richard L., and Scott R. Peterson. *Self-Esteem: Paradoxes and Innovations in Clinical Theory and Practice*. 2nd ed. Washington, DC: American Psychological Association, 1995.

Bergin, Allen E., and Sol L. Garfield. 4th ed. *Handbook of Psychotherapy and Behavior Change*. New York: Wiley, 1994.

Birkhead, T. R., and A. P. Moller, eds. *Sperm Competition and Sexual Selection*. London: Academic Press, 1998.

Bizzi, Emilo, and Ferdinando A. Mussa-Ivaldi. "The Acquistion of Motor Behavior." In *The Brain*, edited by Gerald M. Edelman and Jean-Pierre Changeux, p. 217. New Brunswick, NJ: Transaction Publishers, 2001.

Blakeslee, Sandra. "How Does the Brain Work?" *New York Times*, November 11, 2003, p. D4.

———. "Scientists Examine How 'Social Rewards' Can Hijack the Brain's Circuits." *New York Times*, February 19, 2002, pp. D1, D5.

Bowlby, John. *Attachment*. 2nd ed. New York: Basic Books, 1982.

Boyd, Robert S. "Genes Influence Behavior but Don't Control It, Most Experts Agree." *Knight-Ridder Tribune Business News*: Knight Ridder Washington, DC, Bureau, May 8, 2003.

Branden, Nathaniel. *Honoring the Self: Self-Esteem and Personal Transformation.* New York: Bantam Books, 1983.

Brualdi, Amy C. "Multiple Intelligences: Gardner's Theory, ERIC Digest." http://www.ericfacility.net/ericdigests/ed410226.html (accessed July 24, 2004).

Bryson, Bill. *A Short History of Nearly Everything.* New York: Broadway Books, 2003.

Buss, David M. *Evolutionary Psychology.* Needham Heights, MA: Allyn & Bacon, 1999.

Cadoret, Remi J. "Epidemiology of Antisocial Personality." In *Unmasking the Psychopath,* edited by William H. Reid, Darwin Door, John I. Walker, and Jack W. Bonner III. New York: Norton, 1986.

Carter, Rita. *Exploring Consciousness.* Berkeley: University of California Press, 2002.

———. *Mapping the Mind.* Berkeley: University of California Press, 1998.

Cartwright, John. *Evolution and Human Behavior.* Cambridge, MA: MIT Press, 2000.

Chang, Iris. *The Rape of Nanking: The Forgotten Holocaust of World War II.* New York: Basic Books, 1997.

Changeux, Jean-Pierre. *Neuronal Man: The Biology of Mind.* New York: Pantheon, 1995.

Churchland, Patricia Smith. *Brain-Wise: Studies in Neurophilosophy.* Cambridge: MIT Press, 2002.

Clark, Ronald W. *Einstein: The Life and Times.* New York: Avon, 1984.

Cleckley, Harvey. *The Mask of Sanity.* Augusta, GA: Emily S. Cleckley, 1988.

Crick, Francis H. C. *The Astonishing Hypothesis: The Scientific Search for the Soul.* New York: Macmillan, 1994.

Damasio, Antonio. *Feeling of What Happens: Body and Emotion in the Making of Conscousness.* New York: Harcourt Brace, 1999.

———. *Looking for Spinoza: Joy, Sorrow, and the Feeling Brain.* New York: Harcourt, 2003.

Davis, Jefferson. *The Rise and Fall of the Confederate Government.* New York: DeCapo Press, 1990.

Davis, Joel. *Mapping the Mind: The Secrets of the Human Brain and How It Works.* Secaucus, NJ: Carol, 1997.

Dawkins, Richard. *The Selfish Gene.* Oxford: Oxford University Press, 1989.

Dehaene, Stanislas. "Reviewing the *Mathematical Brain*" by Brian Butterworth. http://www.mathematicalbrain.com/revs.02.html.

De Mente, Boye. *Japanese Etiquette and Ethics in Business.* Chicago: Passport Books, 1987.

Dennett, Daniel C. *Consciousness Explained.* Boston: Back Bay Books, 1991.

De Waal, Frans. *The Ape and the Sushi Master: Cultural Reflections of a Primatologist.* New York: Basic Books, 2001.

Diagnostic and Statistical Manual of Mental Disorders: DSM-IV. Washington, DC: American Psychiatric Association, 1994.

Digital History Resource, University of Houston. www.hfac.uh.edu/mintz/evilsyl.htm. (Acessed July 8, 2004).

Doctor, Ronald M., and Ada P. Kahn. *The Encyclopedia of Phobias, Fears and Anxieties.* New York: Facts of File, 1989.

Doidge, Norman. "Appetitive Pleasure States: A Biopsychoanalytic Model of the Pleasure Threshold, Mental Representation and Defense." In *Pleasure beyond the Pleasure Principle,* edited by Robert A. Glick and Stanley Bone. New Haven, CT: Yale University Press, 1990.

Durand, V. Mark, and David H. Barlow. *Abnormal Psychology: An Introduction.* Belmont, CA: Brooks/Cole, 1997.

Edelman, Gerald M. "Building a Picture of the Brain." In *The Brain,* edited by Gerald M. Edelman and Jean-Pierre Changeux. New Brunswick, NJ: Transaction Publishers, 2001.

———. *Wider Than the Sky.* New Haven, CT: Yale University Press, 2004.

Edelman, Gerald M., and Guilio Tonomi. *A Universe of Consciousness: How Matter Becomes Imagination.* New York: Basic Books, 2000.

Eysenck, Michael. *Psychology: An Integrated Approach.* Essex, England: Longman, 1998.

Fenby, Jonathon. *Chiang Kai-Shek: China's Generalissimo and the Nation He Lost.* New York: Carroll & Graf, 2003.

Fenichel, Otto. *The Psychoanalytic Theory of Neurosis*. New York: Norton, 1972.

Fincher, Jack. *The Brain: Mystery of Matter and Mind*. Washington, DC: US News Books, 1981.

Fodor, Jerry. *The Mind Doesn't Work That Way*. Cambridge, MA: MIT Press, 2001.

Fossey, Dian. *Gorillas in the Mist*. Boston: Houghton Mifflin, 1983.

Freud, Sigmund. *The Ego and the Id*. New York: Norton, 1960.

———. Excerpt from *The Future of an Illusion*. In *The Freud Reader*, edited by Peter Gay. New York: Norton, 1989.

Giovannoli, Joseph. *The Biology of Belief: How Our Biology Biases Our Beliefs and Perceptions*. Oxford: Rosetta Press, 2000.

Goleman, Daniel. *Emotional Intelligence*. New York: Bantam, 1995.

Goodall, Jane. *In the Shadow of Man*. Boston: Houghton Mifflin, 1971.

Goodwin, Doris Kearns. *No Ordinary Time: Franklin and Eleanor Roosevelt: The Home Front in World War II*. New York: Simon & Schuster, 1994.

Greene, Brian. *The Elegant Universe: Superstrings, Hidden Dimensions, and the Quest for the Ultimate Theory*. New York: Vintage Books, 2003.

———. *The Fabric of the Cosmos: Space, Time, and the Texture of Reality*. New York: Knopf, 2004.

Greenfield, Susan A, ed. *The Human Mind Explained*. New York: Holt, 1996.

———. *The Human Brain*. New York: Basic Books, 1997.

Gregory, Richard L., ed. *The Oxford Companion to the Mind*. Oxford: Oxford University Press, 1987.

Guth, Alan. *The Inflationary Universe: The Quest for a New Theory of Cosmic Origins*. Cambridge: Perseus Books, 1997.

Hare, Robert D. *Without Conscience: The Disturbing World of the Psychopaths among Us*. New York: Guilford, 1999.

Hare, Robert D., David J. Cooke, and Stephen D. Hart. "Psychopathy and Sadistic Personality Disorder." In *Oxford Textbook of Psychopathology*, edited by Theodore Millon, Paul H. Blaney, and Roger D. Davis. Oxford: Oxford University Press, 1999.

Hare, Robert D., and Stephen D. Hart. "Association between Psychopathy and Narcissism." In *Disorders of Narcissism: Diagnostic, Clinical, and Empirical Implications*, edited by Elsa F. Ronningstam. Washington, DC: American Psychiatric Press, 1998.

Harris, Judith R. *The Nurture Assumption: Why Children Turn Out the Way They Do.* New York: Simon & Schuster, 1998.

Hathaway, Nancy. *The Friendly Guide to the Universe.* New York: Viking, 1994.

Hawking, Stephen. *Black Holes and Baby Universes and Other Essays.* New York: Bantam Doubleday Dell Audio Publishing, 1993.

———. *A Brief History of Times: The Updated and Expanded Tenth Anniversary Edition.* New York: Bantam, 1996.

———. *The Nature of Space and Time.* Princeton, NJ: Princeton University Press, 1996.

Hawkins, David R. *Power vs. Force: The Hidden Determinants of Human Behavior.* Carlsbad, CA: Hay House, 2002.

Hawkins, Jeff, with Sandra Blakeslee. *On Intelligence.* New York: Times Books, 2004.

Hazan, Cindy, and Phillip Shaver. "Romantic Love Conceptualized as an Attachment Process." *Journal of Personality and Social Psychology* 52, no. 3 (1987): 511–24.

Hyde, Janet Shibley, and John D. DeLamater. *Understanding Human Sexuality.* 7th ed. New York: McGraw Hill, 2000.

Janov, Arthur. *The Biology of Love.* Amherst, NY: Prometheus Books, 2000.

Johnson, Sharon L. *Therapist's Guide to Clinical Intervention: The 1-2-3's of Treatment Planning.* San Diego: Academic Press, 1997.

Johnson, Steven. *Mind Wide Open: Your Brain and the Neuroscience of Everyday Life.* New York: Scribner, 2004.

Joseph, Rhawn. *Neuropsychology, Neuropsychiatry and Behavioral Neurology.* New York: Plenum, 1990.

Kandel, Eric R., James H. Schwartz, and Thomas M. Jessell. *Principles of Neural Science.* New York: McGraw Hill, 2000.

Kanter, Rosabeth Moss. *Confidence: How Winning Streaks and Losing Streaks Begin and End.* New York: Crown Business, 2004.

Kernberg, Otto F. "Hatred as Pleasure." In *Pleasure beyond the Pleasure Principle: The Role of Affect in Motivation, Development and Adapta-*

tion, edited by Robert A. Glick and Stanley Bone. New Haven, CT: Yale University Press, 1990.

Kingdon, David G., and Douglas Turkington. *Cognitive-Behavioral Therapy of Schizophrenia*. New York: Guilford, 1994.

Kircher, Tito, and David Anthony, eds. *The Self in Neuroscience and Psychiatry*. Cambridge: Cambridge University Press, 2003.

Krishnamurti, J. *The Collected Works of J. Krishnamurti, 1945–1948: The Observer Is the Observed*. Dubuque, IA, Kendall Hunt, 1991.

Kurtz, Paul, ed. *Skeptical Odysseys*. Amherst, NY: Prometheus Books, 2001.

———. *Skepticism and Humanism: The New Paradigm*. New Brunswick, NJ: Transaction Publishers, 2001.

Lederman, Leon, with Dick Teresi. *The God Particle: If the Universe Is the Answer, What Is the Question?* New York: Delta, 1993.

LeDoux, Joseph. *The Emotional Brain: The Mysterious Underpinnings of Emotional Life*. New York: Simon & Schuster, 1996.

———. *Synaptic Self: How Our Brains Become Who We Are*. New York: Penguin Books, 2002.

Lemonick, Michael R. "The Biology of Joy." *Time*, January 17, 2005, p. A12.

Levy, Steven. "Dr. Edelman's Brain," *New Yorker*, May 2, 1994, pp. 66–68.

Livesley, W. John, ed. *Handbook of Personality Disorders: Theory, Research, and Treatment*. New York: Guilford, 2001.

Masson, Jeffrey M. *Dogs Never Lie about Love: Reflections on the Emotional*. New York: Random House, 1997.

McClelland, David C. *Human Motivation*. Cambridge: Cambridge University Press, 1987.

McCullough, David. *John Adams*. New York: Simon & Schuster, 2001.

Montgomery, Sy. *Walking with the Great Apes: Jane Goodall, Dian Fossey, Birute Galdikas*. Boston: Houghton Mifflin, 1991.

Mountcastle, Vernon B. "Brain Science at the Century's Ebb." In *The Brain*, edited by Gerald M. Edelman and Jean-Pierre Changeux, p. 1. New Brunswick, NJ: Transaction Publishers, 2001.

Nakken, Craig. *The Addictive Personality*. Center City, MN: Hazelden, 1988.

Northoff, George. *Philosophy of the Brain*. Philadelphia: John Benjamins, 2004.

Nuland, Sherwin B. *How We Live*. New York: Vintage, 1998.

Oellien, Frank. www.2.ccc.uni-erlangen.de/projects/ChemVis/motm/ (accessed May 5, 2004).

Osborn, Ian. *Tormenting Thoughts and Secret Rituals: The Hidden Epidemic of Obsessive Compulsive Disorder*. New York: Pantheon Books, 1998.

Panksepp, Jaak. *Affective Neuroscience: The Foundations of Human and Animal Emotions*. Oxford: Oxford University Press, 1998.

Parrott, W. Gerrod. *Emotions in Social Psychology: Key Readings*. New York: Taylor & Francis Group, 2001.

PBS Nova Series. *The Miracle of Life*. New York: Crown Video, 1986.

Pedone, Robert, and Rosaria Conte. "Dynamics of Status Symbols and Social Complexity." National Research Council, Institute of Psychology. *Social Science Computer Review* 19, no. 3 (2001): 249–62.

Pert, Candace. *Molecules of Emotion*. New York: Scribner, 1997.

Pinker, Steven. *How the Mind Works*. New York: Norton, 2004.

Plomin, Robert. *Nature and Nurture: An Introduction to Behavioral Genetics*. Belmont, CA: Brooks/Cole, 1996.

Plomin, Robert, John C. DeFries, Gerald E. McClearn, and Michael Rutter. *Behavioral Genetics*. 3rd ed. New York: Freeman, 1997.

Pollack, Andrew. "New Way to Turn Off Bad Genes Is Set for Testing on Human Eyes." *New York Times*, September 14, 2004, p. 1.

Ramachandran, V. S., and Sandra Blakeslee. *Phantoms in the Brain: Probing the Mysteries of the Human Mind*. New York: Quill, 1998.

Redfield, James. *The Celestine Prophecy*. New York: Warner Books, 1993.

Religion & Ethics Newsweekly. http://www.pbs.org/wnet/religionand ethics/week419/cover.html (accessed September 8, 2004).

Ridley, Matt. *Genome: The Autobiography of a Species in 23 Chapters*. New York: HarperCollins, 1999.

———. *Nature via Nurture*. New York: HarperCollins, 2003.

Ritberger, Carol. *Your Personality, Your Health: Connecting Personality with the Human Energy System, Chakris and Wellness*. Carlsbad, CA: Hay House, 1998.

Roth, Gerhard. "The Quest to Find Consciousness." *Scientific American Mind* 14, no. 1 (2004): 34.

Rozek, Dan. "Hockey Dad Guilty of Giving Kid a 'Swirly.'" *Chicago Sun-Times*, October 8, 2004, p. 12.

Russell, Bertrand. *ABC of Relativity*. New York: Routledge, 1957.

Sacks, Oliver. *The Man Who Mistook His Wife for a Hat: And Other Clinical Tales*. New York: Touchstone, 1985.

Sagan, Carl, and Ann Druyan. *Shadows of Forgotten Ancestors: A Search for Who We Are*. New York: Ballantine Books, 1992.

Seligman, Martin E. P. *Authentic Happiness: Using the New Positive Psychology to Realize Your Potential for Lasting Fulfillment*. New York: Free Press, 2002.

Shagam, Janet Yagoda. "Genetics, Genomics and Molecular Medicine." *Radiologic Technology* 74, no. 3 (January 1, 2003).

Sherman, Carl. "Treatment for Psychopaths Is Likely to Make Them Worse." *Clinical Psychiatry News* 28, no. 5 (2000): 38.

Sidanius, Jim, and Felicia Pratto. *Social Dominance: An Intergroup Theory of Social Hierarchy and Oppression*. Cambridge: Cambridge University Press, 1999.

Simmel, Georg. *On Individuality and Social Forms*. Chicago: University of Chicago Press, 1971.

Smolin, Lee. *The Life of the Cosmos*. New York: Oxford University Press, 1997.

Spitz, Rabbi Elie Kaplan. *Does the Soul Survive: A Jewish Journey to Belief in Afterlife, Past Lives and Living with Purpose*. Woodstock, VT: Jewish Lights Publishing, 2000.

Stapp, Henry P. *Mind, Matter and Quantum Mechanics*. 2nd ed. Berlin, Germany: Springer, 2004.

Steen, R. Grant. *DNA and Destiny: Nature and Nurture in Human Behavior*. New York: Plenum, 1996.

Strobel, Lee. *The Case for a Creator: A Journalist Investigates Scientific Evidence That Points toward God*. Grand Rapids, MI: Zondervan, 2004.

Stubbs, Lisa. "How Closely Related Are Mice and Humans? How Many Genes Are the Same? http://www.ornl.gov/sci/techresources/Human _Genome/faq/compgen.shtml (accessed September 3, 2004).

Swanson, Larry W. *Brain Architecture: Understanding the Basic Plan.* Oxford: Oxford University Press, 2003.

Talbot, Michael. *Holographic Universe.* New York: Perennial, 1992.

Temple, Christine. *The Brain: An Introduction to the Psychology of the Human Brain and Behaviour.* New York: Penguin, 1993.

Van Der Kiste, John. *Kaiser Wilhelm II: Germany's Last Emperor.* Gloucestershire, UK: Sutton Publishing, 2001.

Wallis, Claudia. "The New Science of Happiness," *Time,* January 17, 2005, p. A9.

Weiner, David L., with Gilbert M. Hefter. *Battling the Inner Dummy: The Craziness of Apparently Normal People.* Amherst, NY: Prometheus Books, 1999.

———. *Brain Tricks: Coping with Your Defective Brain.* Amherst, NY: Prometheus Books, 1995.

———. *Power Freaks: Dealing with Them in the Workplace or Anyplace.* Amherst NY: Prometheus Books, 2002.

Whalen, Tony. http://www.physlink.com/Education/AskExperts/ae430.cfm (accessed May 29, 2004).

White, Ron. *How Computers Work.* Indianapolis: Que, 2004.

Wilson, Edward O. *Concilience: The Unity of Knowledge.* New York: Knopf, 1998.

Winter, David G. *The Power Motive.* London: Free Press, 1973.

World of Dogs. New York: Crown Publishers, 1997.

Wright, Lawrence. *Twins: And What They Tell Us about Who We Are.* New York: Wiley, 1997.

Wright, William. *Born That Way: Genes Behavior Personality.* New York: Knopf, 1998.

Zimmer, Carl. *Soul Made Flesh: The Discovery of the Brain—and How It Changed the World.* New York: Free Press, 2004.

INDEX

David L. Weiner (Chicago, IL) is the author of three previous popular psychology books, including two psychology bestsellers, *Battling the Inner Dummy: The Craziness of Apparently Normal People* (also published in Chinese, Spanish, and Braille) and *Power Freaks: Dealing with Them in the Workplace or Anyplace*. He is also the author of *Brain Tricks: Coping with Your Defective Brain*. Weiner serves on the external board of advisors for the HealthEmotions Research Institute of the University of Wisconsin, Madison. The institute seeks to use state-of-the-art scientific methods developed for the study of illness to study the relationship between positive emotions and health. Weiner was also instrumental in the founding of the Scientific Society for the Study of Psychopathy, which held its first symposium and conference in 2005, featuring the top academics worldwide in the field. On the business side of his career, he is the founder and CEO of Marketing Support, Inc., with 130 employees.

Robert B. Hare, PhD, is professor emeritus of psychology at the University of British Columbia and, among other achievements, is considered one of the world's foremost experts in the area of psychopathy. He is the author of the best-seller *Without Conscience*, two other books, and numerous articles.